Brainstorms

Brainstorms

Understanding and Treating the Emotional Storms of Attention Deficit Hyperactivity Disorder from Childhood through Adulthood

H. Joseph Horacek, M.D.

ILLUSTRATIONS BY
David Earl Edwards, Jr.

JASON ARONSON INC.
Northvale, New Jersey
London

This book is not intended to replace appropriate diagnosis and/or treatment, when indicated, by a qualified physician. Do not alter any medication treatment program without the explicit approval and direction of the treating physician.

Director of Editorial Production: Robert D. Hack

This book was set in 11½ pt. Perpetua by Alpha Graphics of Pittsfield, NH and printed and bound by Book-mart Press, Inc. of North Bergen, NJ.

Library of Congress Cataloging-in-Publication Data

Horacek, H. Joseph.
     Brainstorms : understanding and treating the emotional storms of attention deficit hyperactivity disorder from childhood through adulthood / H. Joseph Horacek.
          p.   cm.
     Includes bibliographical references and index.
     ISBN 0-7657-0080-8
     1. Attention-deficit disorder in adults.   2. Attention-deficit hyperactivity disorder.   3. Minimal brain dysfunction.   4. Minimal brain dysfunction in children.   5. Dysautonomia.   I. Title.
     RC394.A85H67   1997
     616.85'89—dc21   97-9832

Printed in the United States of America on acid-free paper. For information and catalog write to Jason Aronson Inc., 230 Livingston Street, Northvale, New Jersey 07647-1726. Or visit our website: http://www.aronson.com

This book is dedicated to Debbie,
for her love,
patience,
wisdom,
faith,
and stamina.

Contents

Preface

Children cannot be corrected with effect when their whole body is vibrating with anger and the motor impulses are necessarily too strong for resistance. That intensity of feeling must be given time to spend itself, and a normal functioning resumed if reason and kindliness are to be substituted as motives.

> *The Normal Child and Primary Education*
> Gesell, A.L. and Gesell, B.C., 1912

This turn-of-the-century advice of Gesell and Gesell remains fresh and salient today, as if we were hearing it spoken for the first time this morning. Instead, we find this age-old wisdom in a book written at the turn of the century. Gesell and Gesell recognized then that such emotional episodes were to be found normally in children. The same insight can be applied to the children of today, and to adolescents and adults for that matter. Everyone has experienced emotional "storms" at times. Sometimes, stormy emotions can reach very high intensity. When their intensity, frequency, and duration become excessive, they may then be part of a cluster of symptoms that frequently occur together (a syndrome) and reflect an underlying neurobiological abnormality.

In 1902 British pediatrician George Still published an account in *The Lancet* of twenty children in his practice who were "passionate, defiant, spiteful and lacking inhibitory volition" (p. 1077), a syndrome he referred to as the "defective moral control." Of these characteristics, "an extreme degree of passionateness was the most constant feature" (p. 1080). Dr. Still made the then radical suggestion that bad parenting was not to blame; instead, he suspected a subtle brain injury, "the result of congenital limitation of the capacity of its development by some morbid condition of the brain dating from antenatal life, but also that it may be due to arrest or delay of its development by physical disease occurring in infancy and, further, that after there has already been considerable progress in its development it may be lost to a greater or less degree as the result of physical disease, particularly lesions of the brain and certain febrile conditions" (p. 1079). In the 1970s Virginia Douglas noted a central feature of a group of children she was studying to be "a problem in regulating one's level of arousal" (pp. 149–168).

The mood lability, hyperarousal and hyperreactivity symptoms are a familiar aspect of many neurobiological disorders. Yet Still's passion and Douglas's arousal dysregulation are still not currently recognized as core features of such disorders. Diagnoses often associated with such dysregulated, or "stormy," passion and arousal include:

Attention deficit hyperactivity disorder (ADHD)[1]
Impulse disorder
Chemical dependency (alcohol, caffeine, marijuana, stimulants, cocaine)
Conduct disorder
Bipolar disorder
Anxiety, panic disorders, phobias, and selective mutism
Dysthymia and depressive episodes
Learning disorders
Personality disorder
Oppositional defiant disorder
Post-traumatic stress disorder (PTSD)
Obsessive compulsive disorder (OCD)
Motor tics
Tourette's syndrome
Autism and pervasive developmental disorders
Psychosis
Narcolepsy
Asthma and allergies
Coronary artery disease and hypertension
Irritable bowel syndrome (chronic diarrhea)
Asthma and allergies
Sleep apnea and insomnia
Vaso vagal syncope (fainting spells)

The word sydrome is defined in *Dorland's Illustrated Medical Dictionary 27th Edition* (1985, p. 1629) as: Syndrome [Gr. *syndrome* concurrence] a set of symptoms which occur together. Syndromes may cross diagnostic lines and span many diagnostic categories. We will examine, in this book, a syndrome that I have hypothesized accounts for many core aspects of a wide spectrum of disorders.

---

1. We will use the terms ADD and ADHD synonymously in keeping with current and popular usage.

   This book has a clinical focus. I have tried to offer what I hope are useful and practical guidelines on how to understand and weather these storms. I hope that not only will patients, physicians, and therapists find strategies here, but also that parents and teachers will learn from what was taught to me by hundreds who were in their shoes. I have tried to pass along what I have gleaned from my vantage point of working day to day in my office practice.

   This book is aimed toward all who care for those with the stormy brains. It is also aimed toward those adolescent and adult brainstormers who, though they find reading difficult, are willing to try to weather reading this text. I especially hope that their efforts are rewarded.

   Finally, *Brainstorms* is written for the spouses, family members, co-workers and friends who struggle to better understand the emotional storms that "blow" through the brains and souls of the people they love. They are the ones who can most clearly see the treasures submerged and hidden beneath the noise.

H. Joseph Horacek, M.D.
Charlotte, North Carolina
January 1988

1
What are Brainstorms?

Brainstorm: n. a sudden attack of uncontrolled emotion or confusion (a sudden good idea).

The New World Lexicon Webster's Dictionary
of The English Language, 1990

JOHNNY AND THE CASE OF LITTLE AL: "OPPOSITIONAL" OR "ADDLED"?

"How have things been going in school lately," I asked my little second grade patient.

"I got in trouble again this week. My teacher says I don't get to go on the field trip to the science museum on Friday. I have to stay behind."

"What was the 'crime' for which you got the 'time'?" I asked.

Johnny shrugged. "Same as always, drawing in class."

"What's wrong with drawing?" I wondered.

"The teacher says I'm supposed to be listening in class and that I can't listen if I draw."

I was Johnny's doctor. Johnny had previously been given the diagnosis of attention deficit hyperactivity disorder (ADHD). In particular, he had much difficulty paying attention to spoken language. This was referred to as a central auditory processing disorder involving auditory attention. Johnny was referred to me when it was determined that, in addition, he showed increasing oppositional and defiant behavior and episodes of emotional outbursts. When frustrated, Johnny could burst into a fury as sudden and intense as a thunderstorm. After this emotional "storm" ran its course, Johnny would become just as suddenly calm, like the calm that suddenly appears after a storm. What Johnny did not remember, or was unwilling to discuss, was the emotional storm that was the real reason he was held back from the class field trip.

Johnny had a combination of intellectual gifts and disabilities that I had come to see quite frequently. He was extremely bright, with IQ scores in the "Very Superior" range. In spite of his high IQ, he had severe problems paying the kind of attention required to function well in the classroom. He was brilliant in his ability to come up with original ideas, or to "figure things out" when allowed to do it his way. He had taught himself to read, for example, from the back of breakfast cereal boxes long before starting kindergarten. Johnny had, however, severe difficulty listening to verbal instructions. He even missed whole lessons while he sat and "daydreamed" during class. Johnny had great difficulty with handwriting (dysgraphia), but he loved to draw and was quite good at it.

Over the years in my medical practice I have worked with many patients, young and old alike, with similar problems. Many school-age children, like Johnny, were labled "Gifted and Talented, Learning Disabled" and "Behaviorally and Emotionally Handicapped." Such students experience certain problems with regularity. I suspected Johnny's "defiance of the rules" might be better understood if related to a common difficulty I have come across in many patients like Johnny. I put the question to him directly:

"Johnny, do you have trouble listening because you draw, or do you draw because you have trouble listening?"

"What?" Johnny responded, apparently already no longer listening to me.

I repeated my question in as short and direct a sentence as I could.

"Can you listen better when you draw?"

Johnny paused. His eyes looked up into the air and a little to the side. He looked as if he were trying to replay the scene on television in his mind. "Yes," he finally said decisively.

"Well, did you ever tell anyone about that?"

"No."

"Why not?"

"I never knew it before."

I sat back in my chair. "Johnny, I feel a story coming on." Johnny immediately acquired a glazed expression at the prospect of listening. "Let me tell you about a kid who was also in the second grade," I went on, "and who was a lot like you. He got in trouble for drawing in class. He also liked to look around and watch what everyone around him was doing. He was always full of questions, wanting to know 'why?' When the teacher asked him a question, however, he did not answer. This was seen as oppositional and defiant behavior. In those days such 'defiance' met with the hickory stick. Little Al's teachers could not understand why no amount of thrashing seemed to make Little Al 'willing' to answer. Finally they concluded that he was just 'addled,' which meant 'foolish,' or 'mentally retarded' in those days. Johnny, do you know what the real reason was that Little Al did not answer the teacher's questions?" I asked, trying to see if he was still with me.

"Why?" he asked back.

"I'm asking you," I insisted, passing the question back to him.

"Asking me what?" Johnny repeated, now beginning to fiddle around with a pencil and a sheet of paper on the desk.

"Why do you think Little Al didn't answer the teacher when she would ask him questions?"

"I guess he didn't hear what the question was."

"Well, why didn't he just ask what the question was?"

"He was probably scared he would get in trouble."

I went back to my story.

"Little Al's brain was so busy asking its own questions that it would get too crowded in his thoughts for the teacher's questions to get in. Little Al probably did not even know he was not paying attention to the teacher."

With unexpected quickness Johnny suddenly became animated. "When the teacher called on him he probably said, 'Uh-oh, I'm in trouble now!'"

Johnny re-created the little turn-of-the-century schoolhouse drama. He pretended to stare off in a daze. He then suddenly woke up with a start and leapt out of his chair to attention, almost knocking the chair over.

"Yes, Johnny, I guess it probably happened about like that." (I agreed, thinking to myself, "This brilliant little brainstormer is probably better at playing the part of Edison as a second grader than he realizes!")

"One day," I continued, "a policeman visited Little Al's classroom. Little Al overheard the teacher talking to the policeman. 'That boy is addled,' reported the teacher, 'He is not worth keeping in school any longer.'"

"I will not ever step my foot in a school again as long as I live," declared young Al when he returned home and told his mother. "The teacher says that I am addled."

"His mother was incensed. 'I have been a schoolteacher myself and that is no way to treat a boy.' She took Little Al by the hand, walked him back to the school and faced the teacher."

"'You don't know what you are talking about,' Al's mother said. 'He has more brains than you, and that is what the trouble is. I will take him home and teach him myself, and show what can be done with him.' They marched home—Little Al and his mother—and the education of Thomas Alva Edison began."

As I finished the story I realized Johnny had started drawing. "Have you been listening to me?" I asked.

Without looking up, he answered, "What?"

"I was telling you the story about Little Al" I explained. "He got in trouble for drawing in class and for not listening, just like you."

Johnny was trying to listen but his mind appeared to be taking brief field trips of its own into the world of his thoughts. Perhaps a thought of some fantastic invention was tugging at his sleeves. Suddenly he asked with a burst of interest, "Did he used to be one of your patients like me?"

"No, Johnny, when Edison died in 1931, I wasn't born yet."

"How did you meet him then?" he asked.

I thought to myself, "This young brainstormer has an auditory attention span with holes in it like Swiss cheese!"

"I read about him in a book," I explained.

"Oh," he said, looking a little disappointed, as if I'd lied to him, or worse, tricked him into a school lesson.

"This is a true story!" I objected. "It happened many years ago."

"What happened to Little Al when he grew up? If he didn't get good grades, he couldn't get a good job so he could buy a car and have a nice family and pay taxes and stuff." (Johnny now seemed genuinely worried about his little colleague from a distant time.)

"Well, Little Al was Thomas Alva Edison, one of the most brilliant and productive inventors in our history," I announced, dropping my punch line (and feeling quite satisfied with my precision). "When Edison died in 1931, he had patented over 1,300 inventions!" Johnny didn't seem impressed by my revelation. "Johnny," I quizzed, "do you know who Thomas Alva Edison was?"

"No," he said, apologetically.

"Well, I'll give you a hint. He invented something really important, something that uses electricity. It's something you see and use every day, something that emanates light!"

Johnny thought hard. His eyebrows knitted together. "Sega Genesis?" he offered, perhaps hoping for a lucky guess.

"No, Johnny, the light bulb! Edison was the one who invented the light bulb!"

"He did? How did he invent it?"

"Well, he tried over 10,000 different light bulbs until he made one that finally worked. Someone once asked him if it upset him to fail 10,000 times.

Edison said he never thought of it that way. He just thought he'd discovered 10,000 ways how not to make a light bulb!" Edison was the one who said, 'Invention is one percent inspiration and 99 percent perspiration.' He also invented the alkaline storage battery and the record player, and he and Alexander Graham Bell invented the telephone. Edison was the one who invented the word 'Hello!' He thought it was a great word for demonstrating the telephone at the World's Fair. It caught on and became the word we still answer the phone with."

"I invent things, too. I like to take things apart and use the parts to make new things. My mom got mad at me because I took her alarm clock apart. I was going to put it back together, but I got in trouble too fast."

"Edison got in trouble once for taking an alarm clock apart."

"Did his mother get mad at him?"

"No, he was grown up by then. It was his alarm clock. He was working for the railroad as a signal person."

"What does a signal person do?"

"He's kind of like an air traffic controller," I explained, "except he uses lights to warn the trains so they won't collide on the same track. Anyway, Edison had to 'punch the clock' exactly at the top of each hour. He did this by tapping out his security code number on a hand telegraph key."

"Did he use the Morse code? I'll bet he did! I know some Morse code! Listen: dot-dot-dot, dash-dash-dash, dot-dot-dot! Do you know what I said?"

"What did you say, Johnny?" I asked, (trying to tolerate the digression from my fantastic story).

"That's Morse code for Emergency! It's S-O-S! That's like 911! They used to talk like that in the cowboy days and it would go over the telegraph wires. The outlaws used to cut the telegraph wires when they robbed the trains and stuff so nobody could call the sheriff."

"You're right, Johnny. In fact, when Edison was a boy not much older than you, he used the Morse code to save a whole train from crashing. A bridge washed away in a storm and there was no way to warn the train. Little Al had a brainstorm that saved the day. He convinced a train engineer to take him out to the river on another train so he could toot out a warning using the train whistle and the Morse code. The only one on the train that knew the Morse code was Little Al's sister who was returning from a trip. She and Little Al used to play Morse code and send secret messages to each other by tapping on things, like a glass at the dinner table. Little Al's sister heard the train toots and understood her brother's message. She convinced the conductor to stop the train. The 'addle brained Edison boy' suddenly became the town's hero! But that's another story. So where was I? Oh, yes! Edison had to key in his security code with the telegraph key every hour to prove to the railroad boss that he was on the job, on time, and was awake and paying attention."

"Is that really a true story?" Johnny was still back on the train.

"Yes, Johnny, it is completely true," I answered. Now let me tell you . . ."

"Did he get the job for saving the train?" Johnny interrupted.

"I don't know, Johnny. If I'm going to finish this story you're going to have to pay attention and not interrupt."

"You sound like my teacher," Johnny sighed.

"Sorry," I apologized.

"That's OK. Tell me the rest of the story."

"OK. Where was I?"

"Al was sending his security code to prove he was awake on the job."

"Oh, you were listening! Anyway, all of his life Edison had trouble being on time. He had trouble sensing whether a little or a lot of time had passed. Edison had been fired from all his previous jobs for being late and not paying attention to details. He was afraid he would forget to key in his security code on time. He didn't want to get in trouble again. One day, while Edison was worrying about losing his job, suddenly he had a brainstorm. He brought an alarm clock from home, took it apart, and rigged it up to the telegraph key. He had it carefully set up so that when the alarm clock went off on the hour his little device would make the telegraph key tap his code automatically for him all by itself." (Johnny was paying keen attention now. Maybe he could relate to this brilliant inventor who was always getting "in trouble again!")

"Little Al wouldn't get in trouble for taking the clock apart, because it was his alarm clock!" he said, reassuring me.

"That's right, Johnny, but he did get in trouble when they found this little invention one day."

"What happened?"

"He was fired."

Johnny looked sad. "I guess that's worse than me not getting to go on the field trip."

"I don't know," I wondered out loud. "I'm not sure which is worse."

"I'll bet he felt dumb after he got in trouble." (Johnny, now on familiar ground, was the expert.) Then, scolding Little Al, he chided, "He should learn to take responsibility! What if a train came along and he was not paying attention?"

"I guess that's what the train people were worried about too, and why they fired him." Some good did come out of Edison's failure in the end, though. Edison's little brainstorm turned out to be the first time in history anyone had made an automatic telegraph device. He kept working on it and improving it. He had many other brainstorms that started from that one idea. He developed his idea into the first stock ticker machine. He was paid $40,000 for the patent rights for it. The stock ticker is still in widespread use today in the stock market."

"Is that where the ticker tape comes from like in the old movies my dad watches when you're a hero and you get to ride down the street in a big convertible and they throw junk down on you from way up in these buildings?"

"Yes, I guess it was. Hey, who's the expert here, anyway?"

"What did Little Al do with the money?"

"He used the money to start an inventions laboratory. He worked for himself, inventing things for the rest of his life. He never got fired again. He never did get the hang of being on time, though. He seemed to follow no schedule at all. He would often work all night and just be leaving for home when his employees arrived at work in the morning. He also had difficulty remembering whether something had happened a few days or a few months before. His inventions lab was very messy. He would work on as many as forty projects at once, and kept inventing new things before halfway completing his original idea. Fortunately he was able to use the money from his patented inventions to hire a staff to help him see things through and stay organized."

"I would like to be an inventor like Little Al when I grow up. Do people get jobs like that now?"

"Yes, many people earn a living off their curiosity and their love of making new and useful things. Some of these people had problems paying attention in class when they were kids like you and Little Al."

"My dad says that necessity is the mother of invention."

"Then maybe brainstorm is the father of invention," I mused out loud. "What do you think, Johnny?"

Johnny didn't answer. He was drawing again, lost deep in this thoughts. I wondered what he was thinking. He had a far-off but excited look in his eyes, like he was setting out on an adventure with a new invention, a brainstorm of his own. I knew if I asked him what he was thinking he would have no idea. I had the feeling I would find out if I watched him draw for a while.

* * *

What was happening with this little second grader with such brightness and creative energy that could suddenly turn so "dark" and "stormy"? From where or what did these emotional "squalls" spring as suddenly as a summer thunderstorm, only to evaporate as quickly into thin air?

Such paradoxes are alluded to in *The New Lexicon Webster's Dictionary* definition of the word brainstorm. In the first part of the definition, there is an
"attack" of sudden loss of control of our emotions and cognition. We are swept
up into confusion. Yet in the second, and seemingly contradictory, part of the
definition, a brainstorm is characterized as "a sudden good idea."

Webster's Ninth New Collegiate Dictionary lists a similar definition for the word
brainstorm but with a more pathological flavor: BRAINSTORM *n*. (ca. 1894) 1: a
violent transient fit of insanity 2 A: a sudden bright idea B: a harebrained idea.

It seems as if our language cannot make up its mind whether brainstorms
are of madness or genius. Are they normal? Are they symptoms of an underlying dysfunction of the brain, even of insanity? What is the difference between a
"bright idea" and a "harebrained" one? For that matter, what is the difference
between ideas and emotions? If we continue to explore these words in the
dictionary we learn that *harebrained* refers to: *flighty*, or *foolish. Flighty* means:
swift, lacking stability or steadiness, easily upset, volatile (as in a *volatile temper*), *easily
excited, irresponsible, silly. Bright*, on the other hand, means *radiating or reflecting
light, shining, sparkling, sunny, radiant with happiness, illustrious, glorious, beautiful,
lively, cheerful, intelligent, clever, auspicious, promising.*

The paradoxical nature of this word *brainstorm* is inescapable. Both lists of
adjectives seem to describe Johnny well, however. Johnny seems to be full of
paradoxes. The word brainstorm, however, cannot be found in any diagnostic
medical book. Is there a diagnosis that fits Johnny, one that can reconcile and
unify such a broad, seemingly diverse, and even contradictory or paradoxical
list of characteristics? We already know that Johnny has been given the diagnosis of ADHD. Johnny actually did not have the minimum eight out of fourteen
criteria then required for ADHD, though he did have problems with attention.
He was not particularly impulsive or hyperactive, however, as defined in the
diagnostic manuals. The main concern when I first saw him was directed to an
emotional "explosiveness" and increasing oppositionalism and defiance. These
are not listed as diagnostic criteria for ADHD. Johnny had a fine motor coordination problem that resulted in an expressive writing disorder, or "dysgraphia."
These are also not listed as diagnostic criteria for ADHD. Johnny was also a bit
obsessive, but his symptoms came short of meeting the criteria for obsessive
compulsive disorder (OCD). Johnny was not troubled by specific intrusive repetitive thoughts or ritualistic behaviors. Instead, Johnny was meticulous, a
"perfectionist." He also exhibited traits of mild but chronic anxiety and a tendency toward brief depressive episodes that were too mild and effervescent to
meet any diagnostic criteria for an official depressive illness.

Let's look at a list of Johnny's symptoms and characteristics:

Short attention span
Distractible
Oppositional and defiant
Temper outbursts
Meticulousness
Emotional sensitivity, intensity, and reactivity
Unusual creative abilities
Dysgraphia
High intelligence
Speech problems
Mild chronic anxiety and worry
Mild chronic depression
Sleep problems
Poor frustration tolerance

Is there one diagnosis that can capture the full range of Johnny's difficulties? Shall we diagnose a dozen or so "comorbid" (two or more independent disorders occurring together in the same person) conditions? What would we choose from the diagnostic manuals? Would Johnny meet the diagnostic criteria for a specific "mental illness"? Perhaps a thyroid abnormality or one of various developmental disorders or learning disabilities? What about ADD? Should we conclude that Johnny's problems are really a myth?

In his book, *The Myth of the A.D.D. Child*, Armstrong (1995) asserts that "A.D.D. appears to exist largely because of a unique coming together of the interests of frustrated parents, a highly developed psychopharmacological technology, a new cognitive research paradigm, a growth industry in new educational products and a group of professionals (teachers, doctors, and psychologists) eager to introduce them to each other (p. 10)." Dr. Armstrong concludes that A.D.D. is a myth and that with close inspection, "We discover that, as with the disappearing Cheshire cat in Lewis Carroll's classic children's tale, all we're really left with in the end is the smile, if that (p. 11)."

Rosemond (1995), a newspaper columnist, applauded Armstrong's assertion: "The fact is, A.D.D. lacks scientific status as a disease; there is no conclusive proof of genetic origin. . . . Thanks to Thomas Armstrong and others who are willing to challenge the orthodoxy of the A.D.D. establishment, we may soon see the Cheshire cat of A.D.D. begin fading from view."

I did not believe Johnny's problems were mythological. Still, I could find no single medical diagnosis that fully captured the full range and paradoxical nature of Johnny's assets and difficulties. The diagnosis of ADD seemed incomplete. Perhaps the term I needed could not be found in any existing medical diagnostic manual. What about this word brainstorm? It seems a pretty pedestrian term, a simple bit of common slang.

Over the past fifteen years of treating thousands of children, adolescents, and adults like Johnny, I have come to appreciate how his symptoms, traits, and aspects of temperament form a loose unity, a cluster, or group of symptoms, in other words, a "syndrome." There was no name I could attach to this syndrome. I referred to it in various ways and at various times as "central autonomic hyperreactivity and hyperarousal" cognitive and/or emotional lability, dysregulation, and so on. In my private thoughts I gave it a nickname, "brainstorm."

I could find no other completely satisfactory term for what seemed to me to be a syndrome. There was no-scientific sounding multisyllabic Latin or Greek term that entirely captured the essence of the paradoxical characteristics that the many patients I worked with, like Johnny, exhibited. Naturally, there were many diagnoses that described a particular feature here and another there. There was no single word, however, that could coherently unify all of the pieces that made up what was unique and yet similar in all of these "brainstormers."

My attempts to diagnose patients like Johnny had previously resulted in a list of a dozen or so diagnoses or no diagnosis at all. Johnny, for example, had been previously diagnosed using the term attention deficit hyperactivity disorder. He did exhibit the inattention criteria of this diagnosis, but the label ADHD did not address his much broader spectrum of symptoms. Most of all there was no diagnostic concept that could capture the paradoxical character of such brainstormers, whose greatest disabilities often seemed to spring from the same well as their greatest talents.

So, with apologies to Mr. Webster, I borrowed the word brainstorm, promising to return it in good condition if a better one came along. I never spoke the term out loud, or referred to it in any public or official context until the writing of this book. "Brainstorm" was just the private nickname I gave to something that had no name.

What do we mean when we use the word *brainstorm*? Is this just a word we use when we wish to exaggerate a bit, to sound a little dramatic, put a little spice of metaphor in the word soup? When we use the word are we hinting at some fundamental quality of our human brain, of human experience?

We all know brainstormers. These are people who are always in "hot pursuit" of their latest brainstorms. We know these people with the stormy brains to be easily excited. They are quick to become inspired, even exuberant, possessing an almost rampant enthusiasm that is, unfortunately, often spent before much gets accomplished. They are often great "out of the gate," rushing head-long into their latest inspiration, but have enormous difficulty sustaining their efforts. Their greatest dreams are seldom actualized: they simply accumulate more half-finished projects to add to their collection. Their "bright" ideas then turn out to be "harebrained" ideas when their intense inspiration fades to boredom, and soon they are pulled off course by the next brainstorm that blows by. They cannot resist the shiny new idea that captures their imagination and attention. We see them darting about, then disappearing over the hill, following the Pied Piper of their insatiable curiosity.

Brainstormers are often thin-skinned, that is to say, easily upset, overly sensitive to the slightest signs of criticism or rejection. When they feel rebuffed or frustrated, they often display a volatile, firecracker temper. Their temper blows up in a second, but then as quickly cools off. After an emotional outburst they may react as though nothing happened at all. At other times they seem to suffer great remorse. Tolerant friends and family might affectionately refer to the brainstormer as the "mad scientist" or the temperamental poet, artist, or entrepreneur.

By now the reader might be thinking, "This sounds like me sometimes, and I'm certainly not insane! Aren't brainstorms just a part of everyday normal life? Doesn't everyone have a brainstorm now and then?"

We can all remember times when such storms swept across our brains and souls. We have all experienced brief, intense moments of confusion that then burst into a sudden lucid insight, the "ah-hah!" experience, the "great idea." We have all exclaimed many times, "Boy, did I have a brainstorm!" We recognized the flash of Edison's light bulb, striking like a lightning bolt from the clouded and murky darkness of our thoughts and emotions. Then there are those moments of unexpected and sudden bursts of highly charged emotions, of exuberance, of glee, of being swept up in a rush of passion.

We must also admit to those regretted times when our brains "stormed" out of our control, turning minor frustrations to outbursts of inappropriate and misdirected rage. These were the moments when we panicked, the times that uncontrollable actions took flight, blown from their tether by the gust of the irresistible impulse.

We also hope for and welcome those rare and fleeting moments of lucid, inspired, creative, and joyful gifts of grace bestowed upon us when we least expect them. These are the memorable moments, the ones we most cherish.

Such mysterious storms have commanded our respect and awe, much as the sailor for the sea, when we perceive a storm beginning to stir within our brains and souls. We realize with hope and dread that we cannot always control the direction in which these winds may point us any more than the sailor can always command the wind that fills the sail.

Brainstorms, as we usually think of them, are, of course, a part of normal, everyday life. When too frequent, intense, or disabling, they may reflect symptoms of an underlying neurobiological abnormality. I have come to refer to such a syndrome as the "brainstorm syndrome" to set it apart from its more benign little cousin, the brainstorm.

In recent years scientific and medical research has pointed to unstable regulation of certain neural "circuits" or "systems" in the brain. Such brain dysfunctions may be very subtle and have a variety of contributing causes. Genes that control production and regulate the brain's many chemical messengers (neurotransmitters) are just now being mapped out. It appears likely that variants of these genes may play a major role in the aberrant neurotransmitter functioning of some brain dysfunctions. In other cases, neuronal dysfunctions are acquired after birth, later in life, as a result of a wide variety of brain insults.

One example of an important brain neurotransmitter or chemical messenger is noradrenaline (NA).[1] This is the brain's adrenaline. Noradrenaline plays a significant role in controlling and regulating the nervous system's levels of arousal (sleep, wakefulness, alertness, and so forth) as well as the intensity of cognitive, emotional, and motoric activity and reactivity. NA clicks on the switch of the well-known fight or flight reaction to danger that activates and enables a quick and fearful retreat or, if necessary, the aggression necessary to prevail in combat. Neurotransmitters like noradrenaline, serotonin, and dopamine play a fundamental role in the adaptive regulation of normal, or the maladaptive dysregulation of abnormal, brain processes. Could the brainstorm syndrome be a manifestation of a neurotransmitter (or group of neurotransmitters) dysfunction?

I first began to think about brainstorms and the brainstorm syndrome while treating hundreds of patients who, like Johnny were diagnosed ADHD. Their symptoms didn't fit well the "classic triad" of inattention, impulsivity, and motoric hyperactivity that defined the diagnosis of ADHD.

In my early days of treating ADHD a good number of straightforward cases were referred to me that often, if not usually, responded miraculously

---

1. In this book, "noradrenaline" will be used rather than "norepinephrine," which is a synonymous term.

to treatment with a psychostimulant such as Ritalin, Dexedrine, or Cylert. These were the "plain vanilla" cases that easily met the diagnostic criteria for ADHD and for which the diagnosis of ADHD appeared to capture the most salient clinical features.

As time went on, efforts of grass roots advocacy groups such as Children and Adults with Attention Deficit Disorder (CHADD) succeeded in educating the primary-care medical community about ADHD. Referrals of "pure vanilla" ADHD became fewer. In their place were the more complex cases like Johnny's, for which a sprinkle of Ritalin and some brief supportive therapy alone were clearly not going to do the trick. These were the cases with so called "comorbid" disorders: oppositional defiant disorder, anxiety and phobic disorders, depression, eating disorders, substance abuse, and so forth. These patients tended to meet some criteria for a long list of diagnoses but not enough criteria to fit any specific diagnosis well. They had a range of symptoms or "traits," such as a tendency to be meticulous, dysthymic, anxious, and emotionally hyperactive and hyperreactive.

As the patients referred to me came with increasingly more complex symptoms, ADHD became a less adequate idea to define the pathology that disabled my patients and to guide the treatment that would most help them. As the range of symptoms broadened beyond purely behavioral ones to include clearly neurologically based disorders of arousal, sleep, emotional regulation, fine motor control, and so forth, the diagnosis of ADHD became less conceptually and clinically meaningful. Soon I was seeing cases complicated by general medical conditions such as constant pain, spastic colon, hypertension, diabetes, allergies, and asthma. Rather than representing comorbid disorders, these groups of symptoms somehow seemed to fit together, to be part of a spectrum of symptoms that all had in common: high and variable arousal, inhibitory control, and ability to sustain. The mental illness conceptual and diagnostic system became increasingly restrictive and decreasingly valid to me.

Should we have an "official" diagnosis for the brainstormers like Johnny other than ADHD? What would we call it? How would it fit into the current diagnostic nomenclature?

These are some of the topics we explore in later chapters of this volume. For those readers who would like a quick start, the Brainstorm Self-Assessment Questionnaire (BSAQ) is provided at the end of this chapter. This is an informal instrument that may help the reader to get a general feeling for the material we will examine in this book.

Perhaps the best way to get an in-depth feel for brainstorms and the brainstorm syndrome is the way I did. In successive chapters we will watch how this idea unfolded in the context of individual patients' lives. We will see how the brainstorm syndrome helped to define common threads that connect their lives, and their responses to treatment. I will begin to lay the foundation in the next chapter with four clinical case examples from my practice.

Because I am a specialist, the patients who came to me for help often considered me to be "the last stop." The patient and family were often discouraged. They would report that they were "at the end of their rope," having been diagnosed and treated many times before with only partial or no success. Feeling that they had tried everything, they were usually willing to try something new. This allowed for a rich experience of exploring innovative approaches.

The rapid progress I saw in so many patients caused me to rethink much of what I had previously been taught or had assumed about the interfaces between neurobiology and psychology. I was repeatedly surprised to find that what appeared at first to be the fire was often only the smoke. What was thought to be pathology turned out to represent health and strength. What was seen as "the problem" turned out to be the best coping mechanisms that could be mustered to deal with a subtle but very real underlying disorder of neurobiology. To address such neurobiological underpinnings was to intervene at a prepsychological level more akin to temperament than personality. Medical treatment often resulted in spontaneous resolution of many psychological problems that had previously been considered ingrained and intractable.

I realized repeatedly that my patients' stormy nervous systems, while accounting for their greatest disabilities, often also accounted for their greatest talents. This paradox kept directing me back to the dictionary, to the dual and seemingly contradictory definitions of the word *brainstorm*.

This book is about *brainstorms*, *brainstormers*, and *the brainstorm syndrome*. It is about understanding the regulation of normal cognitive, emotional, and motoric arousal and reactivity, and how to diagnose when symptoms of excessive autonomic hyperarousal and hyperreactivity point to a neurobiological disorder or syndrome.

Brainstorms is about how to manage these stormy brains medically and psychologically. It is largely based on my clinical experiences. This book is written from my point of view. It does not represent any single school of thought. I bear responsibility for its contents. I apologize for any unintentional errors or oversights I may have made. This book includes what I've been able to glean from scientific literature, my colleagues, and most of all, my patients. Most of all, *Brainstorms* is about the gifts and creative talents that stormy temperaments often bestow. The trick is to discover better ways to exploit these gifts—to capture, harness and channel the wind before the windmill blows down.

THE BRAINSTORM SELF-ASSESSMENT QUESTIONNAIRE (BSAQ)

The following set of questions reflects those an experienced diagnostician will ask. While this questionnaire cannot confirm the diagnosis, it can help the reader to get a feel for what I will be referring to as brainstorms and the brainstorm syndrome. It can also provide a rough screening assessment as to whether professional help should be sought for a more formal diagnostic evaluation.

The more questions that are answered yes, the more likely it is that the subject may be "a brainstormer." There are no established norms for the BSAQ. For this reason, it should only be used as an informal guide to help facilitate a more formal diagnostic interview.

Please answer Yes (Y) or no (N) whether a particular characteristic is present more often than not and/or more intensely than in most people you know. Give your immediate, "off the cuff" responses.

1) _____ Do you have a low frustration tolerance (get frustrated easily)?

2) _____ Are you "touchy," or easily annoyed by others, or by minor irritations?

3) _____ Are you unusually intuitive?

4) _____ Are you highly sensitive to criticism?

5) _____ Are you unusually creative?

6) _____ Do you have a low stress tolerance?

7) _____ Are you highly perceptive of things others don't notice?

8) _____ Do you lose your temper?

9) _____ Are you generous "to a fault"?

10) _____ Do you tend to react out of proportion to the situation?

11) _____ Do you have a "short fuse"?

12) _____ Does your anger result in being verbally or physically aggressive toward others?

13) _____ Do you give up too easily at times while at other times show unusual persistence?

14) _____ When you are verbally or physically aggressive, does it tend to be an unexpected reaction rather than planned on your part?

15) _____ Are you easily upset ("tenderhearted")?

16) _____ Are you highly energetic at times and very lethargic at others?

17) _____ Do you often feel very restless and fidgety when you have to remain seated?

18) _____ Do you have a hard time relaxing unless you are "on the move"?

19) _____ Are you known for your spontaneity?

20) _____ Are you apprehensive, cautious?

21) _____ Are you too easily excited?

22) _____ Are you impulsive (often act before thinking, or have trouble restraining impulses)?

23) _____ Are you charming, charismatic? Good at persuading others?

24) _____ Do you interrupt others in conversation?

25) _____ Are you impatient waiting for your turn in a line?

26) _____ Are you "honest to a fault" (lacking tact)?

27) _____ Do you tend to be an impulsive spender?

28) _____ Are you moody (frequent mood swings)?

29) _____ Do you have a "firecracker temperament" (quick to heat up, quick to cool down)?

30) _____ Do others comment that you are irresponsible or unreliable?

31) _____ Are you sensitive to rejection?

32) _____ Do you have a family history of depression and/or alcoholism?

33) _____ Do you exaggerate when you get excited?

34) _____ Would others describe you as "demanding"?

35) _____ Do others complain that you are stubborn, bossy?

36) _____ Are you overly sensitive to conflict?

37) _____ Do you become overly distracted when you are excited, finding it hard to concentrate?

38) _____ Are you "great out of the starting gate" but then lose your initial enthusiasm for a project?

39) _____ Have you had anxiety or panic attacks?

40) _____ Are you an "idea person" with many original ideas or inventions that need other people to carry them out?

41) _____ Do you work best in short spurts of intense involvement?

42) _____ Do you withdraw, pout, or go off to be alone when you feel slighted?

43) _____ Are you a "worrier"?

44) _____ Do you get demoralized, feeling that everything is "just no use"?

45) _____ Do you have a low sense of self-worth (self-esteem)?

46) _____ Do you often feel rejected by your peers?

47) _____ Does your emotional intensity put people off?

48) _____ Do you feel isolated and lonely?

49) _____ Would this phrase describe you: "When you're hot you're hot, and when you're not, you're not"?

50) _____ Do you or have you used alcohol, caffeine, or nicotine regularly to calm you down, improve your mood, or help you sleep?

51) _____ Have you had sleep problems most of your life (trouble getting to sleep, staying asleep, waking up)?

52) _____ Are you shy?

53) _____ Do you have a heightened awareness of the emotional needs of others?

54) _____ Are you compassionate, warmhearted?

55) _____ Do you find that you become too witty or playful in situations where this is not appreciated?

56) _____ Do you have an "off the wall" sense of humor?

57) _____ Are you unusually curious?

58) _____ Can you easily generate a "contagious enthusiasm"?

59) _____ Do you have a high sense of adventure? Always eager to try something new? Like to be on a "quest"?

60) _____ Do you find it easy to "forgive because you tend to forget"?

61) _____ Do you tend to be meticulous, a "perfectionist"?

62) _____ Are you highly sensitive to loss?

63) _____ Do you feel like an outsider?

64) _____ Do you have musical or other artistic abilities?

65) _____ Do you quickly shift from feeling lively and carefree to melancholy with little or no apparent reason?

66) _____ Are you much harder on yourself than others are?

67) _____ Were you the child that brought the lost dog or cat home and wanted to keep it?

2
Four Brainstormers

This chapter introduces, a child, a preschooler, an adolescent, and an adult from my clinical practice. Later, in Chapter 16, I will follow up with how these cases were treated and how they turned out. Each case is a composite of a number of cases. Names and circumstances have been changed to respect the privacy of the patients, while still retaining the integrity of the clinical issues illustrated.

EMILY: THE CHILD WHO WOULD NOT PLAY

It was midnight and Emily's parents sat in the living room, exhausted. Her father sat in his recliner, rubbing his eyes, and her mother was on the couch going through the mail. Emily was finally quiet after the customary three-hour ordeal to get her to go to sleep.

"She's always had problems getting to sleep, even since she was a baby, but its gotten much worse since she's been on the Ritalin," said Dad, still rubbing his tired eyes. "I guess this is the price we have to pay for her doing well in school. She's made a lot of progress this year since she's been on the medication."

Mom had waited until Emily was asleep to show Dad the letter from the school. "Here, read this." She handed him the handwritten note from Ms. Jones, Emily's second grade teacher.

Dear Mr. and Mrs. Smith,

I am writing because I am concerned about Emily. Academically she is doing quite well this year, and does not have a discipline problem in my class. The medication also has not been a problem. Emily accepts taking medication. She says that its just something she needs to do to get her body to do what her brain tells it to.

My concern is that she has no friends and seems to be isolating herself from her classmates. She says she doesn't like to run around and get hot and her class-mates play games that she doesn't enjoy.

Emily appears to lack the ability to form close friends. She is a sweet child who is quiet and shy, although she is constantly fidgeting. She appears mortified by any criticism and responds by pouting and withdrawing or becoming hostile and rude. At times she seems to be in a trance, and focuses on one thing and you can't seem to get her mind off it.

Emily is a very sensitive child, with very "thin skin." She is easily provoked by peers who tease her and seems to have unusually intense feelings. Emily is industrious and tries very hard to please. She has so many scintillating ideas! She's one of the most creative students I've had. In fact, she is making all A's and B's. She is so extremely imaginative and inventive! In spite of this, she appears in-creasingly anxious to the point of confusion, and seems to fear the slightest sign of rejection.

Emily often gives up at the first mistake, refusing to try further. If you try to put any pressure on her she becomes upset and rapidly escalates to ex-tremes of her temper. She can't seem to "chill out," or "get a grip" as her class-mates would say. She can rapidly become irritable and irrational and anything anyone says to her just makes it worse. Then she withdraws and pouts or makes rude remarks. If everyone leaves her alone, her "stormy" mood quickly passes and her sunny disposition returns. She then acts as though it never happened and doesn't want to talk about it.

I think the medication is helping her, but I feel she needs something more. Are there any additional ways that I can help Emily?

Sincerely,
Ms. Jones

"Something's still not quite right," Emily's father said decidedly. "Some-times I wonder if Ms. Jones just expects too much from Emily. Sure she's bright, artistic, and creative. Does that mean she has to be a social butterfly too? I think I was just like Emily when I was her age."

"Yes, and you still are in a lot of ways," Mom said, only half teasing. "Your anxiety medicine seemed to have helped you a lot. Maybe that's what Emily needs."

"Maybe she's just a very shy, anxious kid." Dad frowned. "I wasn't too happy about putting her on one medicine. I hate to think of adding another. Are we going to make her into some kind of junkie? There are so many problems with alcohol and drugs on my side of the family. I swore when I stopped drinking eight years ago I would never even take an aspirin. Now I've gotten myself and my child on drugs! Are we just teaching her to depend on drugs?"

Dad was on a roll now. Emily's Mom had learned not to interrupt or disagree with him at times like this. He just needed to let off steam and she knew that this storm would quickly pass if she did not argue with him.

"We can't even get the experts to agree with each other!" he continued. "The psychiatrist says she's on the right amount of medicine, but her pediatrician says its too much. Every day after school when her medication begins wearing off, the backlash hits with the regularity of a train schedule. At 3:46 P.M. suddenly she's moody, and at constant war with her little sister! At night it's like pulling teeth to get her to do her homework. I don't know how she gets such good grades! Certainly not based on her homework! We've taken her all over the place. She's been evaluated, diagnosed, and is taking her medication as prescribed. I don't know what else we can do."

"Well, I agree with you," Mom said. "There's an obvious benefit from the Ritalin. Her grades came way up this year. Something *is* still wrong with this picture. Something could be better. Something is missing. . . ."

Mom was testing the waters, waiting to see if her timing was right. She decided that now was as good a time as any to talk. "I visited the school today," she began. "I observed Emily in her class. She was so focused on some baseball cards that she was fidgeting with in her lap that she didn't even notice I was there. She seemed too quiet, subdued, and kind of 'flattened out.' She didn't have that mischievous 'Emily the menace' sparkle in her eye. I didn't like the way she looked. I've made an appointment for another opinion. Do you think you can get off work and come?"

JULIE: THE EXPLOSIVE PRESCHOOLER

Julie was a beautiful little 2½-year-old who looked like Shirley Temple. She had an angelic face and a head full of curly brown hair, bright blue eyes that lit up when she smiled, and dimples in both cheeks. She looked like any second she could spring into a rendition of "The Good Ship Lollipop."

When I first met her, she would not say a word to me. She smiled coyly and hid in her mother's skirt. Julie talked only to members of her immediate family. At her preschool, she was shy and reserved, clinging to her teacher, Ms. Samborski, who reported that Julie just whined and cried for the entire three hours the first month of school. After she eventually settled down, she still would not speak to anyone and kept to herself. She was quiet and appeared very shy.

At home she was stormy. When she was with her family, she would quickly escalate into fits of temper that would rage on like a Carolina thunderstorm for half an hour or more. She became aggressive. She would begin biting and hitting others and throwing objects. No one could console her. Her grandmother, who watched her and her cousins during the day, had raised four children of her own and had never seen anything like it. She tried all the usual behavior modification methods: time out, spanking, and so forth. Nothing worked. When Julie escalated into one of her furies, there was nothing anyone could do but ride out the storm. Afterwards, exhausted from her fury, Julie appeared perplexed and genuinely remorseful. "I know it's hard on her too," her mother observed. Julie was as perplexed as anyone. She had no idea why she felt and acted the way she did.

Julie's mother described the temper tantrums: "Julie's fits of rage last for thirty minutes or more. She can destroy a room in no time. She slams the doors and pulls things off the walls, kicking and screaming the whole time. Her whole facial structure seems to change. She looks as if she could pierce holes through you with that look she gets. The more we try to reason with her, the worse off we are. Everything we say to her just makes her escalate. We've learned it's just better to leave her alone and let her calm down on her own."

Julie's parents were searching for answers to explain her unusual behavior. How could their otherwise sweet and loving daughter fly into such rages in a split second?

At larger family gatherings, which occurred every few weeks, Julie would remain shy, coy, and angelic. On occasion she would speak a little to a favorite uncle or aunt whom she knew well, but not a word to the others, whom she watched with keen interest. When addressed, she would smile her cute smile and run to her mother or father, appearing paralyzed by a cat-got-your-tongue shyness. It was not fear that silenced her. She seemed as if paralyzed with delight. She was highly engaging, drawing you in but hiding from you at the same time. She would approach, then become flooded with excitement and withdraw. It was as if she could not handle her excitement except by withdrawing to modulate the flood of social stimulation to a level she could process. When, and if, she was ready, she would gradually approach again.

Her mother wondered if it was her fault. At first, Julie's tantrums occurred mostly in her mother's and father's presence. "Maybe I am not a good mother" she thought. Why did she escalate only with the two people she loved most? As Grandma began to see the temper outbursts too, it became more apparent that this was more than a parent–child issue. When she started biting her little cousins, her aunts and uncles also began to see this other side of her. The entire family was constantly walking on eggshells, afraid that the slightest frustration would provoke Julie to burst into one of her rages.

Julie's parents were young but knowledgeable. They read every book on parenting they could find. Soon it became apparent that Julie's outbursts of temper were more extreme than normal temper tantrums. They discussed this with her pediatrician. He encouraged them to be hard on Julie, suggesting that they lock her in her room during her fits, and spank her with a wooden spoon on her calf. While this is sound advice for managing some children, Julie's parents knew it would not work with Julie. Neither punishment nor rewards ever seemed to affect her in the least. Julie's parents decided to bring her in for another opinion.

JESSE: THE JUVENILE DELINQUENT IN SEARCH OF SELF

Jesse was a handsome teenager with blond hair, blue eyes, and a Prince Charming smile. He was failing in school and was increasingly truant, running off with his friends to smoke pot, drink beer, and "hang out." Jesse was a 14-year-old "juvenile delinquent," on probation for vandalism.

From birth Jesse had been a "difficult" baby. His mother described him as "hyperactive with temper tantrums, difficult to get to sleep, and difficult to wake up in the morning." In elementary school his teachers complained that he would "clown around, act silly, and would not follow rules." He had always been accident prone, and had sustained numerous minor lacerations necessitating trips to the emergency room. He was touchy, irritable, and oppositional. He displayed facial blinking and sniffling that had been attributed to allergies. He often got in fights and was suspended from school. When he was caught smoking on the school grounds for the third time, school officials considered expulsion and enrollment in an alternative school.

Jesse's future seemed doomed until one looked closer. He was a talented artist and often liked to draw instead of doing his work. He had won several art contests. It was not as if Jesse was a loser. He always got very high grades in elementary school. He scored well on tests and was an excellent soccer player. He had a loving family. Why was he "screwing up" his life?

Jesse was first prescribed the cortical stimulant Ritalin by his pediatrician. The teachers immediately noticed that he was more focused in class, completed his work, was more organized, understood verbal instructions and carried them out, and was less irritable. His outbursts of anger were less frequent, but when they occurred they were more intense. These outbursts or brainstorms were often at about 4 P.M. as he was riding home on the bus. When he engaged in fighting, he was excluded from the bus for the rest of the year. His parents reported that he was more irritable at home and refused to do his homework. When an additional dose of Ritalin was added after school to help with homework, he would refuse to take it. He was physically aggressive with his younger sister, which was of great concern to his parents, who feared he would seriously harm her.

On days that he missed taking the Ritalin, the school would inevitably call his parents at work and they would have to pick him up as his behavior was out of control. He would be stubborn, disrespectful, and hostile. In the morning he would refuse to get up until his parents practically dragged him out of bed, with him cursing and swinging. Once his morning dose of Ritalin "kicked in," he was Prince Charming again. He continued having difficulties with impulsivity, and his quick mouth caused him ongoing problems with his teachers, and, especially with his father, who also had a "short fuse."

Jesse was big for his age and looked older. He wanted to hang out with kids who were 16 and had their driver's licenses. His parents did not approve of these friends as they were aware that these kids had been in trouble in the past, smoked cigarettes, and were poor students.

If he was this hard to handle at 14, how were his parents going to manage him at 16? "If he gets any bigger, even his father won't be able to handle him," said his mother. Jesse had one foot in jail and one foot on a banana peel.

BEN: BEAM ME UP, SCOTTIE!

Ben was a very successful surgeon. He had no trouble going through college, medical school, and his residency training in surgery. He was highly intelligent and a good reader. After three of his children were given the diagnosis of ADHD and successfully treated, he asked to talk with me about his wife, Joyce.

Ben, by his own report, was doing well. At work he was happy and things always went smoothly. He enjoyed the quiet environment of the operating room and working with his hands. He liked the fact that no one had to talk much and he could focus on his work and do a good job. He was highly regarded for his work. His problems began when he walked through the front door of his home. His wife was always at the end of her rope, exhausted from being the "ringmaster of a four-ring circus," featuring their four young children. She would hold on for Ben to come home and give her some relief.

Ben couldn't help her much. Within a few minutes he would feel that if he didn't leave the house he would "go nuts." He would find an excuse to have to go back to work. Over time he avoided coming home as much as possible. Ben had a temper that was rarely seen and that he took care to keep under control, fearing that he would lose it and become abusive to his family when he became overcome by the "racket." He took up flying and in record time passed all the requirements for a pilot's license and even instrument rating. In the sky he found the solitude he needed.

I talked with his wife Joyce. She was lonely and tired, and felt she had failed as a wife and mother. Her own family had been even larger, but her parents had a wonderful relationship and the house always looked like a model home. In school she had been an A student and successful at everything she ever did. Now she was ashamed to have anyone come to her house because it was always so messy. When Ben suggested they get a maid, Joyce adamantly refused. "I would never let a maid see my house so messy. I'd have to clean it up first before I would let a maid come in!"

Joyce and Ben moved far away from her family after they married. There was no help available from an extended family and she had been unable to find anyone who would baby-sit her four active children. As her resentment of her husband's lack of commitment to the family and his failure to help her grew, so did her loneliness for the man with whom she had fallen in love. He used to cook her gourmet meals and even do the dishes afterwards. He used to play the violin. He was a passionate, funny, intelligent, ambitious, and sexy man who had stolen her heart. She began to wonder if she would ever see that man again.

Ben talked with me about his concerns for her. "I think she's getting depressed. More and more she is just screaming at the kids. She always looks tired and has a headache. Now she wants to have a fifth child. I don't think she can handle the four we've got now. We fight about it all the time. She grew up in this huge Catholic family and wants our family to be just like hers. I just don't know what we'd do if we had another baby."

They had another baby. Things got worse. Now the four-ring circus had expanded to five rings. Ben asked me to evaluate Joyce. He suspected that she had attention deficit hyperactivity disorder and might need treatment in order to control the "riot" at home.

Joyce agreed to an evaluation. I could find little evidence to support a diagnosis of ADHD except the high frequency of ADHD in her offspring. She appeared mostly to be exhausted.

Ben put two and two together: "If this is inherited, does that mean that I might have ADHD? I don't have any problem paying attention. I just can't think around noise!"

3
Neurobiology and Brainstorms

"In many years of work with animal as well as human subjects, researchers have advanced our understanding of the brain and vastly expanded the capability of mental health professionals to diagnose, treat, and prevent mental and brain disorders.

Now, in the 1990s, which the President and Congress have declared the "Decade of the Brain," we stand at the threshold of a new era in brain and behavioral sciences. Through research, we will learn even more about mental and brain disorders such as depression, bipolar disorder, schizophrenia, panic disorder, obsessive compulsive disorder, and attention deficit hyperactivity disorder. And we will be able to use this knowledge to develop new therapies . . ."

Sharyn Newirth (1990), National Institutes of Health

In 1989 then President George Bush signed a proclamation declaring the 1990s "The Decade of the Brain" and setting research in the neurosciences as a top priority. Many neuropsychiatric and neurobiological disorders are now thought to have their origins in genetically acquired, post-traumatic, post-infectious, toxic, or metabolic insults to the brain that lead to neurotransmitter dysregulations. Medications that aim to normalize target symptoms are thought to have their effects by normalizing neurotransmission in various neural circuits in the brain. Many medications have now taken their place as the cornerstones of medical therapy for disorders such as ADHD, depression, anxiety and panic disorders, obsessive compulsive disorders, motor tics and Tourette's syndrome, manic depressive illness, psychosis, Post-Traumatic Stress Disorder, and even personality disorders (including dissociative personality disorder). Such research has led to clarification and elucidation of the biological underpinnings of such medical disorders. A good example for us to begin to explore such evidence is attention deficit hyperactivity disorder.

EVIDENCE FOR NEUROBIOLOGICAL UNDERPINNINGS OF ADHD AND RELATED DISORDERS

ADHD continues to be classified as a "mental disorder" and more specifically as a "behavior disorder." It is considered to be an "idiopathic" disorder, meaning that the diagnosis implies no known cause. Most modern researchers and clinicians, however, believe that ADHD's foundation lies in the brain's neurobiology. Let's take a brief tour through some of the evidence for the neurobiological underpinnings of ADHD. The boundaries between psychiatry, psychology, neurology, and even such fields as gastroenterology and cardiology become increasingly difficult to define. Yet our official diagnostic nomenclature continues to perpetuate the obsolete notion that mind, brain, body, and even behavior are separable entities.

The dramatic and well documented response of ADHD to cortical stimulant medication has led to promising new research on brain neurobiological mechanisms that may underlie many neurobiological disorders. Such studies have focused on the hypothesis that stimulants affect catecholamines, their metabolism, or their action on receptor sites. It may be possible to understand the nature of these disorders through an understanding of stimulant drug action (Zametkin and Rapport 1987).

Thus far, no research has provided the ultimate proof of whether the dysfunctional behaviors or the emotional and cognitive processes of ADHD are primarily inherited, acquired from brain injury, or the products of experience and learning. The age old "nature or nurture" argument continues. Perhaps this is because the question is not a valid one. While organic deviations may produce ADHD symptoms, it is also possible that ADHD symptoms produce biological abnormalities (Conners 1977). The direction of causality between biochemical factors and behavior does not have to move one way only. Using PET technology, Schwartz (1996) found systematic changes in cerebral glucose metabolic rates after successful behavior modification treatment.

In the meantime, neurotransmitter and other brain research may help identify different types of ADHD, and help predict which will respond to specific treatments. At present this has not been completely elucidated, and treatment is still largely derived case by case on an informed "empirical" or trial and error basis. This is particularly true of response to medication. While medications often produce dramatic results, it is still difficult to predict which medication or what dose will be optimal without systematic trials. Such trials depend on the reliable and valid feedback of high-quality information from parents and teachers in the case of children, family members and co-workers in the case of adults, and ongoing reevaluation of the changing medical needs of the ever-changing and developing patient.

Positron Emission Tomography (PET) Scans

Zametkin and colleagues (1990) published a report on cerebral glucose metabolism in hyperactive adults in a widely heralded *New England Journal of Medicine* paper. Their studies showed that glucose metabolism, both global and regional, was reduced in a group of adults who were hyperactive since childhood. The largest reductions were in the premotor cortex and the superior prefrontal cortical areas earlier shown to be involved in the control of attention and motor activity.

Magnetic Resonance Imaging (MRI)

Recent research in the use of magnetic resonance imaging (MRI) techniques has revealed structural differences in the brains of individuals with ADHD. Hynd and colleagues (1990, 1991) demonstrated that the genu of the corpus callosum is smaller in groups of subjects with ADHD. This is a structure in the front of the brain that bridges the right and left frontal cortical areas and connects them. This is the pathway through which both sides of the frontal cortex are integrated. The striatal connections between the frontal lobes and corpus collosum are highly dopaminergic. The frontal lobe and frontal striatal connections are noradrenergic. It seems entirely logical that the findings from the PET scanning of decreased frontal orbital function should correlate with an anatomical difference in that area of the brain. These findings are also consistent with the believed effects of drugs like Ritalin in patients with ADHD that increase the release of dopamine and noradrenaline in the same areas. These MRI studies are among the first to measure such a difference in terms of brain anatomy.

GENETIC FACTORS

A fascinating new area of research in the understanding of ADHD and related neurobiological disorders comes from the field of human genetics. Genetics research has, in recent years, demonstrated that ADHD, as well as a wide spectrum of neuropsychiatric disorders, has its origins in genes.

An Autosomal Trait?

Clinicians have long been aware that ADHD is common among family members. Goldman (1995) reviewed research by Biederman and colleagues that showed between 35 and 45 percent of parents of children with ADHD currently have ADHD themselves or had it in childhood. Twin studies repeatedly find higher rates of ADHD in identical twins as compared to fraternal twins. The incidence of ADHD is also higher among siblings, grandparents, aunts, and uncles of children with the disorder. Among children with ADHD, the incidence of the disorder was 28 percent among their brothers and 34 percent among sisters. In families with ADHD children in which neither parent has the condition, the incidence was 20 percent among brothers and only 5 percent among sisters. These findings have led Biederman and colleagues to suggest that ADHD appears to behave like an autosomal dominant trait.

In 1980 David Comings, a well-known physician in the field of human genetics, and his wife, Brenda Comings, a psychologist, became interested in what was then thought to be a rare movement disorder, Tourette's syndrome. David Comings was editor of the *American Journal of Human Genetics* for eight years and president of the American Society of Human Genetics. It became apparent to them from their review of epidemiological studies that TS was much more common than generally thought (about one in 200), and that the majority of TS patients also had ADHD. A large percentage had conduct disorder, oppositional defiant disorder, and/or rage attacks.

The Dopamine D2 Receptor Gene: A Common Thread?

In 1991 a landmark study was published in the *Journal of the American Medical Association* by David and Brenda Comings who had coordinated a national team of researchers. This study considered the role played by a particular dopamine receptor in neurobiological disorders. The receptor, called the D2 receptor, is made by a particular gene, the DRD2 gene. This gene had earlier been reported to occur in 69 percent of alcoholics compared with 20 percent of controls, indicating that it plays a role in the hereditary basis for alcoholism. Comings and colleagues hypothesized that this gene might also be associated with a number of other psychiatric disorders frequently associated with alcoholism.

A sample of more than 300 people was examined. They determined that the mutated A1 allele of the D2 gene was found in about 25 percent of a general sample and in 15 percent of subjects known not to be alcoholics. (An allele is one of a pair of genes, situated on the same site on paired chromosomes, containing specific inheritable characteristics.)The frequency of the Al allele was significantly increased in patients with Tourette's syndrome (45 percent), ADHD (46 percent), autism (55 percent), and alcoholism (42 percent). These were the same other comorbid disorders that Biederman and colleagues (1991) had found associated with ADHD. These results suggested that the A1 allele of the DRD2 gene is associated with a number of behavior disorders in which it may act as a modifying gene rather than as the primary gene causing the disorder.

The researchers then compared a sample of ADHD and Tourette's syndrome patients and determined that, in addition, the D2A1 allele of the dopamine D2 receptor locus was significantly increased in both ADHD and Tourette's. Comings and colleagues explained that this gene was not the primary cause of these disorders. They believed other genes yet to be discovered were primary genes. The D2 gene again appeared to act as a "modifying" gene, a gene that makes some neuropsychiatric disorders worse if these disorders were already present.

Dr. Comings concluded that Tourette's syndrome and ADHD are the same disorder from a genetic point of view. He proposed that a wide range of polymorphous symptoms and disorders may have this genetic underpinning in common. When a single gene can produce a range of possible disorders, geneticists refer to it as a "spectrum disorder." This neuropsychiatric spectrum disorder, whether it is called TS with ADHD or ADHD with tics, seems quite possibly to be the Rosetta stone for understanding the genetics of a wide range of human behaviors.

Cohen and colleagues (1980) reported that clonidine, a drug that subdues noradrenaline, was useful in the treatment of Tourette's syndrome. By 1987 Hunt had extended this finding to the treatment of ADHD in children. Could the pharmacological data shed some light on the genetic findings? In 1990 Dr. Comings reported on his clinical experience using clonidine to treat the tics of Tourette's syndrome. He recommended that clonidine be the first drug of choice, and found the transdermal patch to be more effective than the oral tablet form of the medication.

He also found, as Hunt (1987) reported, dramatic improvement in symptoms of ADHD, including beneficial effects of clonidine on scholastic performance. However, for the severe ADHD child, stimulants often needed to be added. Cohen and colleagues (1979, 1980) and Hunt and colleagues (1985, 1987) had reported additional benefits of clonidine in decreasing symptoms of aggression, temper tantrums, depression, and obsessive compulsive behaviors. Dr. Comings then explored clonidine's effects on two disorders frequently associated with these symptoms: oppositional defiant disorder and conduct disorder. He noted dramatic improvement in these disorders with clonidine, that was particularly rapid in the case of oppositional defiant disorder.

The idea that such behavior disorders as conduct disorder and oppositional defiant disorder had a strong genetic basis was so new and upsetting to many professionals that these findings were received with some degree of controversy.

The final answers are certainly not yet in, but ongoing molecular genetics research has opened the door to a new era of highly sophisticated genetic research that will ultimately be able to specifically map out the genetic basis for ADHD and its links to other neuropsychiatric disorders.

The Dopamine B-Hydroxylase Gene: A Key to Oppositional Defiant Disorder and Conduct Disorder?

Recent studies have focused on another gene, the gene responsible for producing the enzyme dopamine B-hydroxylase. This enzyme converts dopamine into noradrenaline in the brain. Comings (1995) found that when his patients have a combination of the D2A1 allele of the dopamine D2 receptor gene and the B1 allele of the dopamine B-hydroxylase gene, their scores of oppositional defiant disorder and conduct disorder are significantly higher than those patients who have only one or neither of these two genes. This looks like strong evidence that oppositional defiant disorder and conduct disorder are largely genetic and polygenic in origin.

The possibility that these two alleles, in combination, may result in a syndrome that includes symptoms of hyperarousal and hyperreactivity seems entirely plausible. The striking convergence of the genetic and pharmacological data is striking to say the least. Coupling the facts that the newly identified B-hydroxylase gene that regulates the production of noradrenaline is associated with oppositional defiant disorder, and that clonidine, which decreases noradrenaline can, in many cases, make symptoms of oppositional defiant disorder disappear overnight, may provide a key insight into understanding the genetics, neuropathology, and effective pharmacological treatment of not only oppositional defiant disorder but a wide range of related disorders including conduct disorder, rage, and aggressive dyscontrol disorders.

In a more recent study, Comings and colleagues (1996) found that TS, ADHD, stuttering, oppositional defiant and conduct disorder, and other behaviors associated with TS appear to be polygenic, due in part to the three dopaminergic genes DRD2, D beta H, and DAT1.

These findings support the hypothesis that these highly associated symptoms represent a spectrum of disorders that are, to a significant degree, polygenetically acquired.

The genetic underpinnings are just beginning to be mapped out for such disorders as oppositional defiant disorder and conduct disorder. This already has profound implications for treatment. One such implication would indicate a shift in emphasis away from blaming parents toward providing sympathetic, supportive, and nonjudgmental suggestions on how to best manage the defiant, disruptive, and emotionally stormy child. Another might support the need for more integration of psychotherapeutic and neuropharmacologic methods.

In 1994 the National Institute of Mental Health (NIMH) launched a new, ambitious study to locate a primary gene that causes ADHD. The lead researcher, Alan Zametkin, and his colleagues recruited families with at least two affected members with ADHD. Each participant was asked to have a simple blood sample drawn to be used by the researchers to search for the gene causing ADHD. Ongoing studies such as these may someday identify the gene, or more likely genes, for ADHD and many related neurobiological disorders.

Where does this leave us in terms of characterizing such disorders as "mental" or "behavioral" versus medical illness based in abnormal biological functioning of the body? The insurance world still forces this split into "mental and nervous" versus "major medical." Where do such disorders as ADHD fall? Unfortunately they often fall in the crack between.

Parmelee (1992), chair of the department of child and adolescent psychiatry at the Medical College of Virginia, criticized Blue Cross and Blue Shield of Virginia's group policies that excluded from coverage: antisocial personality, sexual deviation, social maladjustment without apparent psychiatric disorder, group delinquent reaction of childhood, autistic disease of childhood, mental retardation, hyperkinetic syndromes (including attention deficit disorders), learning disabilities, conduct disorder, and oppositional disorder.

Parmelee compared the current battles over control of health care to struggles between multiple fiefdoms in Medieval England, "with the lands and peoples being swapped about to the most recent victor in seeming endless bloody battles. Today, American insurance companies are able to make proclamations that take territory, security, and hope away from families and children. Who is there to defend the many defenseless ones? . . . Some already imagine the day when administrative costs for the carriers may be more than the service costs for patient care. What will it take for a transformation to a post-feudal system?"

The genetic basis for many such neurobiological disorders may soon be mapped out. Our current diagnostic nomenclature, based in mind/body dualism, will then be stressed to the point of irrelevancy, if not absurdity. We will be forced, sooner or later, to adopt a more integrated conceptual framework. The primary and modifying genes that regulate the levels of the brain's neurotransmitters such as serotonin, dopamine, and noradrenaline may exist as inheritable variants that result in a syndrome that, at its core, involves hyperarousal and hyperreactivity. The additional contributions of numerous other genes, the impact of learning, the stresses and traumas of life, as well as the supports and opportunities provided by the community and family may ultimately determine whether this underlying stormy temperament develops into ADHD, Tourette's syndrome, oppositional defiant disorder, conduct disorder, anxiety or depressive disorders, and/or Mozart, Thomas Edison, Benjamin Franklin, or Albert Einstein.

4
Brain 101

I have found many patients, families of patients, their teachers, therapists, and so forth to be increasingly interested in understanding the complexities of the neurobiology that underlies many of the disorders they work with every day. It becomes more crucial to understand the biological aspects of a disorder as the relative contributions of biology to a given disorder increase. Nonmedical therapists, more than ever, need to understand how drugs work, how they are prescribed and monitored, and the nature and mechanisms of their effects and side effects to work successfully with patients afflicted with neurobiological disorders. This chapter aims to provide the basic foundation needed to begin to understand how various symptoms come about, how various medications are thought to work, and how these insights can guide the selection of medications and the understanding of their beneficial and adverse effects.

A basic understanding of the brain is becoming increasingly a matter of practical necessity. The age-old debate over "mind versus brain versus behavior" has become, in recent times, more than just an academic problem. Such tendencies by insurance companies to classify illness as either "mental and nervous" or "major medical" are having enormous impacts on access to medical care for millions of children, adolescents, and adults with various disorders. ADHD, for example, is frequently excluded from insurance policies, which view it as a disorder of "mind" or of "behavior" rather than of "brain dysfunction."

The term "mental illness" tends to lead patients and insurance executives to conceptualize disorders that are not physical. Its use fosters the common misbelief that such disorders are "all in the patient's mind," and that pharmacological treatment is only "covering up" symptoms and not dealing with the "real cause." [Popper et al. 1991, p. 261–262]

When exploring a more integrated, conceptual approach that incorporates biological underpinnings of human agony and ecstasy, we worry about unwittingly acting in the service of such reductionistic thinking. Some insurance companies, for example, have adopted the viewpoint that treatment for depression, to take one example, should consist only of using antidepressant medication. They assert that to consider developmental, psychodynamic, and marital-family system variables with a more integrative perspective only wastes time and resources. The "real" problem is due to a "chemical imbalance." We can only hope that a fuller knowledge of how mind, brain, symptom, medication, and various therapies all interact can counter such naive and dangerous points of view.

A broader and deeper understanding of the biological contributions to psychopathology should enrich perspectives that emphasize systems, complexity, and multiple treatment options. We can then proceed also to explore further the interplay of multiple factors, including biological, psychological, and social, that ultimately determine whether treatment with a given medication will succeed.

I often find my patients desire to understand the neurobiology of their symptoms and how the medications they take work. Compliance with medications can be greatly enhanced by such an understanding, and anxiety over side effects can be greatly reduced. Patients often quickly glaze over, however, with such explanations because of unfamiliarity with long Latin and Greek terms that sound complex and mysterious. This chapter briefly reviews some "brain basics." The reader should take the time to become familiar with the basic and essential terminology presented below.

A VERY BASIC ANATOMY OF THE BRAIN: INTRODUCING BOB

At this point let me introduce Bob (see Figure 4–1). Bob has volunteered his brain as a model for us to use in learning some basic anatomy.

The Cerebral Cortex

The brain can be visualized as looking a bit like an orange. The outer "peel" would represent the cerebral cortex (see Figure 4–2). This outer layer of "gray

FIGURE 4–1 Introducing Bob

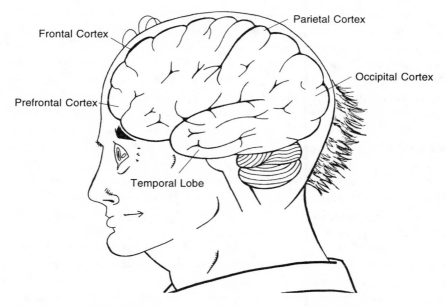

FIGURE 4–2 Bob's Cerebral Cortex (Side View)

matter" can be peeled off from the underlying "white matter" beneath. Our heads are bigger in proportion to other animals' largely due to our extensive *cerebral cortex*. The cortex is divided into right and left sides, and we refer to each region as a *lobe*. Our prominent foreheads are due to a fairly new expansion of the cortex (in evolutionary terms, the neocortex, or "new cortex") that contains our highest mental functions—those that make us distinctively human.

On the sides of our head is the *parietal cortex*. This is the cortical area where sensory and motor information is processed and motor output is planned and coordinated. A stroke here will produce loss of sensation in a part of the body, or loss of motor function in an arm or leg for example. Just beneath our temples are the *temporal lobes* which contain memory, the brain's library. These areas are responsible for recognition and association of information coming in from the senses. At the back of the head, the part that rests on the pillow at night, lies the *occipital cortex*. This is where vision is processed as information comes in from the retinas of the eyes. The part just behind your eyes and forehead is referred to as the *frontal cortex*. The most frontal part of this, right behind the forehead and just above the eyes, is called the *prefrontal* (or supraorbital) *cortex*.

The Frontal Cortex

The *frontal cortex*, or frontal pole, as it is sometimes called (like the North Pole of the earth), is the seat of the highest executive functions of the brain. This region of the cerebral cortex is responsible for analytic responses: judgment, planning, organization, inhibition, and selective attention. These areas allow us to delay, create direction, set priorities, analyze significance, and control volitional attention toward our chosen goals. It is much slower than the lower regions of the brain. This is the area of deliberation, of "premeditation." This highest and most recently evolved region regulates lower brain centers. Here resides our "working memory," similar to the random access memory (RAM) of a computer. These functions are fragile and easily disrupted. Frontal function can be overwhelmed by strong emotions of fear or anxiety. The result is impairment of attention, organization, planning, fine-tuning of mood and cognition, motor output, selection of perceptual input—what we collectively think of as "rational thought."

Much of what we know about the frontal cortex has been learned from traumatic brain injury. Injuries to the frontal lobes result in difficulties with attention, judgment, self-inhibition and-motivation, regulation of moods, persistence on task, frustration tolerance, impulse control, delay of gratification, and with preventing emotions from overwhelming abilities to think and empathize. This frontal lobe syndrome in many ways resembles the symptoms of ADHD. This discovery led to the earlier hypothesis that ADHD was the result of frontal traumatic brain injury, thus the original diagnosis of "minimal brain damage." At present, ADHD is considered "idiopathic" (cause unknown) in the current official diagnostic systems, though there is growing evidence that genetic and/or various neurobiological factors may be important contributors to the clusters of symptoms referred to as ADHD.

The frontal cortex appears to be an important area that has been implicated to explain not just attention problems, but problems with inhibition of unwanted thought and behavior. Information coming from the eyes, ears, skin, taste, and so forth comes to the frontal cortex by way of various tracks of white matter resembling bundles of electric wires referred to as the *striatum*. Incoming sensory information from lower parts of the nervous system is filtered to dampen out sensory "noise" for a cleaner "signal." In the frontal cortex a focus of attention is selected, other options are actively inhibited, and the intended focus is enhanced. Output tracks then carry intended thought and volitional output signals to the rest of the brain and body.

The Limbic System: The "Lizard Brain"

Deep in the core of Bob's brain lies another area of gray matter that is very old in terms of evolution. It is similar in many ways to that of the other animals. This limbic system, or "lizard brain," is the seat of primitive instinctual emotions and drives. The limbic system provides the wind that fills our sails; the frontal cortex, at the helm, harnesses this energy and steers us (see Figure 4–3).

The limbic system is made up of many structures, all with difficult names to pronounce and remember. We will refer specifically to only one in passing. The *hippocampus* is a structure that recognizes changes in incoming sensory information. We can habituate to sounds, for example, when they are steady (as with the noise from a machine), but tend to notice changes in volume, pitch, or quality. This is the principal behind "white noise" generators. These produce constant "masking noise" to cover changing noises such as doors slamming or sounds of cars going by when we try to read a book, study, or sleep. Bob has found that electric fans, air conditioners, even music can act as such a masking noise.

The Brainstem

The lowest part of the brain is referred to as the *brain stem*. It is the narrowing area that connects the brain with the spinal cord below, somewhat remi-

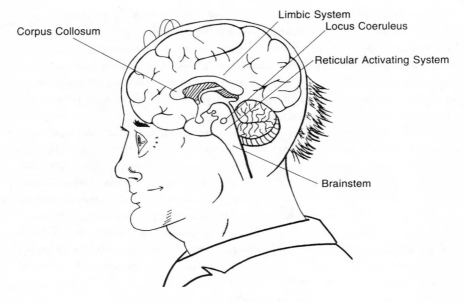

FIGURE 4–3 Bob's Brain (Inside View)

niscent of the stem on an apple. In this area the most basic functions of the body are regulated, such as breathing and temperature, arousal, sleep, and wakefulness. In the morning Bob's *reticular activating system* wakes him up and helps him stay alert most of the day. At night it organizes the transition to and maintenance of sleep. Dysregulation of this diurnal cycle results in poor sleep at night, and/or hyper- or hypoarousal during the day.

At the upper area of the brain stem, above the reticular activating system, is the *locus coeruleus*. This is the alarm system of the brain. When red flags go up signaling danger, the locus coeruleus increases its firing rate, and arousal immediately increases. This is part of the "fight or flight" reaction to danger.

NEURONS AND NEURAL CIRCUITS: THE BRAIN'S "WIRES"

Information in the brain is transmitted along long thin nerve cells called *neurons*, much like electricity travels along a wire, except that the signal travels along the surface of the neuron rather than down the core as in, say, a copper wire. When an electrical impulse reaches the end of a neuron, it is passed to the next neuron by means of chemical messengers crossing a narrow space, the synaptic space or "cleft" (see Figure 4–4). The process for the signal to cross the synaptic cleft is fairly complex, but understanding it is crucial to understanding a wide range of disorders and the various effects of medications.

When an electrical signal reaches the end of the sending or presynaptic neuron, it stimulates the release of chemicals into the synaptic cleft. These chemicals, referred to as neurotransmitters, are stored in small packets in the presynaptic neuron much like bunches of tiny grapes. These neurotransmitters are molecules that fit into receptors in the receiving or postsynaptic neuron much like a key fits into a lock (see Figure 4–4). When enough keys fit into enough locks, the postsynaptic neuron increases its firing rate and the electrical signal continues on its way.

Of the numerous neurotransmitters that have been extensively studied, we will focus here on three: dopamine, serotonin, and noradrenaline. There are other important neurotransmitters currently under vigorous study, including gamma amino butyric acid (GABA) that we will not be able to cover here.

If the foregoing discussion was not already familiar material to you, your head is probably spinning by now (if you are still reading and haven't skipped to

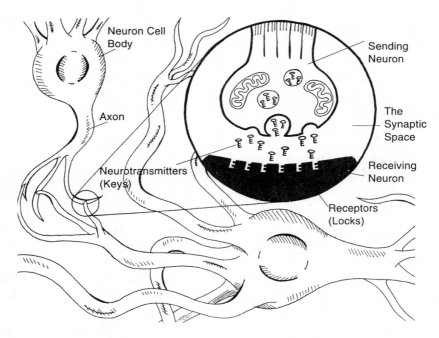

FIGURE 4–4 The Neuron and Neural Synapse

another section. Hang in there, it will be worth it!) Study of the brain involves a lot of unfamiliar and strange-sounding names and terms that can make even the simplest concepts appear mysterious and incomprehensible. Gaining familiarity with some basic lingo will pay off in large dividends, however, and is well worth some effort. The next sections use analogies to common machines that will hopefully put things in a more familiar context.

DOPAMINE, SEROTONIN AND NORADRENALINE: SELECTIVE FOCUS, INHIBITION, AND ACTIVATION

These three are not really neurotransmitters in the traditional sense, but are rather "neuroregulators" in that they modulate the state of processing throughout entire regions of the central nervous system. We will still refer to them with the generic term *neurotransmitters* for the sake of simplicity.

Dopamine: Selective Focus

Dopamine release appears to be critical to the integration of action in response to learned sensory cues. Dopaminergic neurons fire just prior to and during the execution of well-learned motor movement in response to an incoming sensory signal. Dopamine appears to facilitate the selection and organization of such sensory-motor associations.

Noradrenaline and dopamine together appear to improve the "signal-to-noise ratio" of the neuron. This results from a filtering out of the signal's "noise" and an amplification, or "enabling" of the neuron's response.

Bob's 35 mm Camera: Selecting the Breadth
and Depth of the Perceptual Field

Bob took a photography class. Now he considers himself a consummate photographer. In his class he learned all about how the camera worked. Now he can do lots of things with his camera. His camera lens focuses light to make an image on the film inside. With a wide lens aperture, Bob can produce a very fine photograph showing every detail of a single dew drop on a single flower petal. Such high resolution is great if he wishes to blow up the photo to a poster size. What is sacrificed for this high resolution is the depth of field. The wider the aperture and finer the resolution, the more shallow the depth of field becomes. This can be used aesthetically, as the background of a butterfly on a flower, only a fraction of an inch away but out of focus. Bob thinks it gives his pictures an impressionistic "Monet-like" quality to the background.

"Nora" - Adrenaline

"Dopey" - Amine

"Sarah" - Tonin

FIGURE 4–5 Three Important Neurotransmitters to Remember

On the other hand, if Bob is trying to take a picture of his aunt Judy standing in front of the ball at the Epcot Center, how can he get both Judy and the Epcot ball in focus? Bob knows that he can close down the lens aperture. This produces a great depth of field. Both aunt Judy in the foreground and the Epcot ball in the distance are in focus. Bob tried to enlarge the photo to give to Judy for her birthday. He was disappointed that, while the picture looked fine in wallet size, it looked fuzzy when enlarged. Bob forgot that the great depth of field he gained by narrowing the aperture sacrificed the fine resolution needed to produce a clear enlargement.

We can think of narrowing our attentional field in the same way, sacrificing attentional acuity in the cross-sectional plane for a longer span, or depth, of attention. Dopamine appears to control the aperture of this "lens" in our brains.

Bob's Video Camera: The Zoom Lens

The dopamine effects on attention can also be visualized as similar to the zoom lens of a video camera. Dopamine allows for zooming in by the lens, narrowing the field of interest and attention. We are constantly, second by second, zooming in and zooming out, like a video camera.

Bob got a video camera for Christmas. Now he is bringing it along to document his nephew's second birthday party. Bob hasn't figured out the automatic zoom lens yet. One second he sees the zoomed-out, wide angle look of all the guests and the decorations. The next second he is looking at a close up of a purple dinosaur smiling at him on the birthday cake.

It is the ability to flexibly adjust this zoom lens, to smoothly regulate the breadth and depth of the attentional field, that appears to be unreliable in many attentional disorders. Rather than being stuck zoomed-out or zoomed-in all the time, there is trouble flexibly controlling the zoom lens to fit the subject of interest.

This is very similar to the difficulty Bob is having with his video camera at the birthday party. When Bob tries to video the whole crowd, he suddenly finds the lens zoomed in on grandma's nose. He then tries to get a close up of grandpa's new pipe and suddenly the lens zooms back out and he ends up with the big wide angle shot again with grandpa lost somewhere in the crowd near uncle Billy.

Bob's Sensory Filters: Screening Out The Noise

Certain dopamine circuits can also be thought of as noise filters for screening out or subduing unwanted background perceptions (noise) and allowing the clearer signal to come through. At the unconscious and sensory level, they filter perceptions at the level of the eyes and ears, and so forth. They also allow us to habituate to noise that is constant.

Bob is often distracted by the bubbling of a fish tank, the humming of a refrigerator, or the dripping of a leaky faucet. After a brief time, though, he stops noticing them. If there is a change, such as when the refrigerator compressor stops, Bob suddenly becomes aware that the refrigerator had been making noise. He suddenly becomes aware of a change. He notices that the noise has stopped by the newness of the silence that follows.

Bob bought a "white noise" machine to help him cover up distracting noises when he was trying to read or sleep. He could habituate to the constant hiss of the white noise that covered up or masked other more distracting noises such as doors closing or voices down the hall. This helped Bob realize why he had liked to sleep on the floor as a child. Much to his parent's dismay, he could not sleep in his bed. Looking back, Bob realized that it was the sound from the vent in the floor that soothed him. The vent had served him as a white noise machine.

Dopamine also plays a role at the conscious level of perception. Once information rises up through the brain, gets to the top, and finally to the frontal cortex, it is consciously perceived. A conscious decision can now be made to select the focus of attention and sustain it over a span of time. Here dopamine plays a key role in this very important process of conscious selective attention.

In the frontal cortex there is active and conscious rejection of intrusive stimuli that interfere with the intended focus of attention. Such stimuli include various internal drive states and desires. Impulses to change the channel and attend to these by thought or action are actively inhibited to maintain directed attention.

The input tracks to the frontal cortex primarily use dopamine. The output tracks coming from the frontal cortex primarily use serotonin and noradrenaline. Dopamine is largely responsible for what gets access to the frontal cortex. The others control and fine tune what gets out. Output tracks that are important to the regulation of drive states are found in the third layer of the frontal cortex. These output tracks carry volitional behavior. They are not actively inhibiting drive states, but enhancing intentional drive states.

The Steering Wheel: Staying on Course

The steering wheel of a car is used to choose the direction of the car's movement. If the goal is to maintain a steady direction on the road ahead, it must keep this course and not allow the car to veer off one way or another. The steering wheel is what keeps the car on one course, out of the many directions available to the car. Bumps in the road, side winds, slanting of the road, and so on, quickly cause the car to drift without the control of the steering wheel. If the linkage is tight, a steady course is maintained, with numerous small corrections second by second. If it is loose, the car is sloppy and slow to respond. If the steering wheel fails, it would be easy to imagine how the car would soon end up in the ditch.

The "steering" mechanisms of the brain are regulated to a large degree by neural circuits located in the prefrontal cortex. These regulatory systems are mediated largely by dopamine neurotransmission. Dopaminergic circuits control selective attention. When these neural circuits are underactive, distracting perceptions are difficult to filter out and the focus of attention wanders from point to point. It is difficult to stick to one chosen path and pursue one chosen intention. Like a car with a loosely linked steering wheel, the brain has great difficulty maintaining a steady course toward a selected goal.

If dopamine neurotransmission is enhanced in the prefrontal area, we can narrow the field of attention while at the same time lengthening and deepening its span. Like the horse wearing blinders, we can restrict and hold our gaze to our intended goal.

Serotonin: Active Inhibition

<u>The Brakes</u>

Serotonin circuits in the frontal cortex are crucial to the modulation of thought, emotion, and movement. Here information is linked to motivation, the application of and sustaining of mental effort to a goal-directed focus, and the inhibition of competing impulses.

Let's look again at the example of the car. The brakes are used to actively inhibit forward momentum. This process takes energy not only from the driver's foot but from the hydraulic brakes that squeeze the pads onto the brake drums. If the brakes are worn, or there is not enough brake fluid in the brake lines, the car may be difficult to stop.

The brakes in our brain are serotonergic. Serotonin might be thought of as the brain's "brake fluid." Low serotonin transmission results in impaired ability to delay, to inhibit reactions, to tolerate frustration, to restrain one's drives. Serotonin is also important in regulating mood. When we tell others to "get a grip," "chill out," or "put a lid on it," we are asking their serotonin circuits to "put the brakes" on their emotions.

Serotonin circuits in the brain have calming, quieting, comforting effects. They subdue irritability and diminish and harness drive states. They allow us to suppress the urge to talk, touch, dominate, be too powerful. In other words, they allow us to maintain context-appropriate activity.

Noradrenaline: Activation, Arousal, Alertness, and Alarm

<u>Activation: Stepping on the Gas</u>

The gas pedal controls the energy applied to forward motion. Together with the brakes, it controls the speed of the car. The gas pedal in the brain is controlled by noradrenaline. This is the brain's "adrenaline." Outside the brain, in the periphery of the body, is found adrenaline. Inside the brain it exists in a slightly modified form called noradrenaline.

<u>Alertness: Vigilant Attention</u>

Noradrenaline is released in response to danger signals when a rapid response or rapid allocation of attentional resources is needed to be directed to specific signals coming from the external environment. Noradrenaline facilitates the focus on more salient sources of sensory information and the ignoring of others that are less pressing or require less immediate action.

Laid Back: Eating, Drinking and Grooming

The firing rate of the locus coeruleus, which uses noradrenaline, decreases during periods of calm or inactivity. It is very low during activities such as feeding, drinking, and grooming.

Arousal: Sleep–Wake Brainstem Neurophysiology

sleep that knits up the ravell'd sleave of care . . . balm of hurt minds, great nature's second course, chief nourisher in life's feast.

William Shakespeare
Macbeth, II, ii

Noradrenergic tone in the brain tends to be very low during sleep and is completely inhibited during REM sleep, when the neurotransmitter acetylcholine release is high. During waking, the brain is in a state of domination by noradrenaline circuits. These ensure a tonic inhibition of cholinergic release in the brain stem and maintain arousal.

Noradrenergic tone that is too low in the day results in sleepiness, lack of energy, and lack of alertness. Too much tone produces hypervigilance and hyperreactivity. At night, too much noradrenergic tone produces sleep that is restless and can even cause nightmares. Poor diurnal regulation makes for difficult transitions from waking to sleeping and from sleeping to waking.

When we wake up each morning, our brains rise from the depths of slumber as our brain's arousal system jump-starts our cold motors. This is a complex process. For simplicity, we will just say that our noradrenaline levels rise and start flipping the switches in our brain for wakefulness, alertness, and increased sensitivity to and perceptiveness of the world of sight, sound, smell, taste, and touch.

Some people are not morning persons. They take hours to wake up and their motor chugs along, like a motor trying not to stall on a brisk winter morning. Once awake, noradrenaline keeps us awake during the day. People who fall asleep in the middle of things, like conversations, are sometimes diagnosed as having narcolepsy. Milder cases occur in hypoactive ADHD, in which the person becomes sleepy and inattentive in situations that are mundane or repetitive.

Alarm: Fight or Flight

Adrenaline release from the adrenal glands affects various bodily organs and sets a metabolic state that is specifically geared to reactions of fight or flight. This is closely synchronized with noradrenaline release in the brain.

We have all heard of the fight or flight reaction to sudden danger. If we are walking along in the savannas of Kenya and a lion jumps in our path, we immediately feel a sudden rush of adrenaline in our veins. The lunch we were digesting is put on hold as our blood is rerouted from our stomach to our brain and muscles. Our heart rate, blood pressure, and breathing increases. We become extremely alert and focused. Thoughts about the past and future cease, and our attention is directed to the moment. We are hyperperceptive to every detail.

If we elect the flight plan, we retreat to safety and avoid harm. We run swiftly away. Our noradrenaline has activated our anxiety, our warning system. If we elect fight, our noradrenaline helps to activate our strength and aggression.

BOB'S CAR: A COMEDY OF ERRORS?

The following little one act play is offered as a challenge to test the reader's command of the subject matter of this chapter. (Table 4–1 reviews the basic terms used; see also Figures 4–2 and 4–3.)

It is 6:00 A.M. Bob drags himself out of bed and stumbles out the front door and down the driveway to his car. As he fumbles for his keys he mumbles to himself, "I've got to wake up. I guess I'm getting too old for these all-nighters." He turns the key in the ignition switch. The motor will not start. Bob has left the car lights on. The battery is dead, again. "Where was my brain last night when I needed it?" He grumbles, trying to wake up and think of what to do.

"Maybe I can push-start the car down this big hill! No, this is not my old Volkswagen that was a snap to start with a little shove. This is my new fancy car

TABLE 4–1. The Cast of Characters

Characters	Features
Reticular Activating System	wakefulness, alertness
Visual Cortex	receives input from eyes
Temporal Lobe	memory, recognition, significance
Locus Coeruleus	activate, energize, alarm
Motor Cortex	motor output to muscles
Frontal Cortex	selecting, organizing, prioritizing, planning

with the hydraulic steering and brakes. "If the motor doesn't start, the brakes and steering won't work. I'd be out of luck!" he realizes.

Bob goes inside and calls AAA for a tow truck to come out and jump-start his car. As he waits, he tries to jump-start his brain with a couple of cups of strong black coffee. Somewhere, deep in the base of Bob's brain, the reticular activating system stirs and opens its other eye. "Hey, you guys up there! Heads up! Look alive! Bob's hitting the road again!" Soon Bob is driving down the road humming "On the Road Again." He feels in control of the car now. The steering wheel is directing him toward his intended destination. Bob steps on the gas pedal a little harder and the car accelerates. "I'll make up the lost time in the air, he says confidently. He taps the brakes gently and the car briskly decelerates. "All systems are 'thumbs up!'" Bob yawns and rubs his eyes.

Suddenly, as Bob speeds down the hill, the traffic light at the bottom changes from green to yellow. The light flashes through the corneas to the retinas of his eyes; a signal shoots over the optic tracks to the back of his brain where the Visual Cortex registers it. "It's for you!" Visual Cortex says, and bounces the signal to the Temporal Lobe. "I recognize that," Temporal Lobe noted, "its a yellow traffic light. That means caution," and bounces the signal back to the center of the brain, to the small, pea-shaped Locus Coeruleus. "Hey, alarm system, here's a caution signal for you!"

Then things begin to hop.

Locus Coeruleus: Sound the alarm! Status, caution!

> Bob's motor cortex hears the alarm and sends instructions to his foot. Bob reflexively starts to hit the brakes. Then he thinks, "Should I go for it?" He pauses a split second to get a consultation from his brain. Somewhere behind Bob's forehead, just beneath the bill of his Atlanta Braves bill cap, the Frontal Cortex calls the team together.

Frontal Cortex: Listen up everyone, I need information, fast! Motor Cortex, hold that foot for just a second.

Motor Cortex: OK, Boss, but I'm a little low on brake fluid here.

Frontal Cortex: Bob's car is low on brake fluid?

Motor Cortex: No, I was referring to my brake fluid. You know, the neurotransmitter kind? I'm a quart low on dopamine and two quarts low on noradrenaline and fresh out of serotonin. Bob must have had a rough night. He didn't sleep long enough for us to refuel!

Frontal Cortex: I put in a purchase order already. Bob drank some coffee so you should at least be seeing some noradrenaline any minute. In the meantime, you'll have to make do with what you've got.

Motor Cortex: I'll do my best, Captain Kirk!

Frontal Cortex: Cut the comedy and get to work! Temporal Lobe, give me an update on the significance of the current situation!

Temporal Lobe: If my memory serves me well, Bob got a ticket the last time he tried to make it through a yellow light. The time before that he narrowly escaped a collision with an eighteen-wheeler. From my experience, I don't like the situation at all!

Motor Cortex: What's the word, Boss? Hold the foot or push the foot?

Frontal Cortex: Hold the foot for now! Where is the intentions report when I need it? Ah, here it is. Let's see, Bob intends to get where he's going on time.

Temporal Lobe: According to the record, Bob promised not to be late to his meeting this time.

Locus Coeruleus: I've been sending him alarm signals about that all morning. I blew a lot of noradrenaline just getting him out of bed. I had to resort to instigating a minor panic attack to get him moving. Now he's in a frenzy! He thinks he's going to get fired if he's late! It won't be easy to stop him now!

Frontal Cortex: We must be about out of time with that yellow light! Temporal Lobe, see what we're getting in from Visual Cortex. Tell it to keep an eye out for any signs of approaching cars and especially for eighteen-wheelers! Locus Coeruleus, don't push the panic button until you hear from me!

Temporal Lobe: I'm already on the case, Boss!

Frontal Cortex: What have you got?

Temporal Lobe: I'm still getting a yellow traffic light from Visual Cortex. That's good, at least Bob's got his eyes open, but that yellow means the light will turn red at any moment! I don't like that at all!

Frontal Cortex: Well, we've got about 10 milliseconds to help Bob make up his mind.

Temporal Lobe: Make up his mind? He couldn't even make up his bed this morning! This means Bob's in trouble! It's up to us now!

Locus Coeruleus: Time to panic yet, Boss?

Frontal Cortex: Not yet! Listen up, everyone! We owe it to Bob to help him with this, especially after how we dropped the ball with leaving the car lights on last night!

Visual Cortex: It wasn't my fault, I couldn't see a thing! Motor Cortex didn't keep Bob's eyes open!

Motor Cortex: I sent motor instructions that were not heeded, so don't blame me!

Reticular Activating System: Go ahead, say it! It's always my fault! Well, if Mr. Safe Guard over there wouldn't have whooped it up so much and blown so much noradrenaline, I would have had enough to keep Bob awake a little longer so he could have turned the car lights off!

Temporal Lobe: By the way, Visual Cortex, according to memory, I'm to remind you to monitor for approaching cars and, if I might add from my experience, police cars are especially significant. And oh, I almost forgot. Don't forget the eighteen-wheelers! I also recall a particular significance regarding the checking of the rearview mirror. You might pass that along to Motor Cortex to instruct the eye muscles accordingly to orient there.

Motor Cortex: Hey, who's giving the orders, anyway?

Frontal Cortex: Quiet, please! How's a Frontal Cortex supposed to think around here!

Locus Coeruleus: Excuse me, Captain, I'll need more noradrenaline to maintain the alarms. Can anyone spare a couple of cups?

Motor Cortex: Hey, Locus Coeruleus! Remember "Waste not, want not?" How about "A neurotransmitter saved is a neurotransmitter earned"? I get first crack at any noradrenaline delivery! My motor signal is going to need a voltage boost if Bob's foot is going to get the message!

Frontal Cortex: Noradrenaline is still on back order. You'll both just have to wait for that caffeine to deliver! And don't call me Captain!

Locus Coeruleus: Right, Boss.

Frontal Lobe: Now, where did I put the forecast report. I need to check on what Bob's outlook is this morning.

Temporal Lobe: You filed it in the right frontal cortical filing cabinet under "Mood."

Frontal Cortex: Thanks, here it is: The forecast calls for fair moods this morning. A low-pressure mass of serotonin moved in early this morning. Mood expected to be bright and optimistic. Outlook good: "No worries, no problems!" There will be a slight chance of brainstorms this afternoon from a high-pressure mass of noradrenaline causing a front of caffeine irritability to pass sometime late this afternoon. Hmm, Bob must have drunk a lot of coffee. I hope he didn't overdo it.

Temporal Lobe: I'm having trouble with the significance of the forecast report. Does it mean, "No worries, Bob will make it through the yellow light," or "No worries, Bob will get to his meeting on time"?

Frontal Cortex: I would guess it means both. With this serotonin high I expect the weather will continue to be clear and sunny. This would mean Bob is feeling quite optimistic. "No worries," remember? "Hakuna Matata!"

Temporal Lobe: With all due respect, the last time we got a "Pollyanna" forecast like that, Bob got a traffic ticket for speeding. Things sure got stormy then! You just can't trust the weather report anymore!

Frontal Cortex: Since you are the historian around here, maybe you can recall the time the forecast was "Outlook cloudy and pessimistic! There is a 75 percent chance of scattered disasters today with some possible major calamities." Remember how Bob stopped the car just in time to avoid colliding with that eighteen-wheeler? What significance do you give to that?

Locus Coeruleus: (interrupting): Impending panic! I'm warning you! While you're all quibbling, Bob is running the light! It's too late to stop! We're all done for!

Temporal Lobe: I'll be the judge of that!

Frontal Cortex: Thank you, that's enough, everyone! Locus Coeruleus, quiet down, now, I have an announcement to make! I've taken all of your input under advisement. You've all done an excellent job. I've tried to hear everyone out and be fair to everyone while considering the limited amount of time here, and have tried to make the most integrated and best decision for Bob. The recommendation to Bob is: STOP!

Locus Coeruleus: We're going to be killed! I *hate* government by committee!

Frontal Cortex: Motor Cortex, you may release that foot now. In fact, now you can step on it!

Motor Cortex: Aye, aye, Captain!

Locus Coeruleus: Panic time! Panic time! Five noradrenaline alarm!

Frontal Cortex: Hold off on that panic, Locus Coeruleus!

Locus Coeruleus: Easy for you to say! I've got noradrenaline coming out of my ears! I think the caffeine truck just delivered!

Stomach: (yawning): Hey guys, I just woke up. What's for breakfast?

Frontal Cortex: Don't bother me with that now, I'm busy! Who let the Stomach in here? Everybody hold on!

(Bob's foot hits the brakes and his car screeches to a stop. "I'm going to have to work on that reaction time," Bob says, shaking his head. "Or maybe I just need to get some sleep!")

Keeping the Balance between Brain Circuits

When Bob drives, he controls his speed by all three of these mechanisms: selection, inhibition and activation. Similarly, his brain regulates him by integrating many interacting systems. Now let's suppose Bob is driving his car down the road and he ends up in a ditch. Leaving Bob and his brain out of the analysis for a while, let's consider what might have gone wrong with his car.

If the steering wheel is a little loose and sloppy, the car is difficult to steer. At low speeds this may not be a problem. If the car travels at higher speeds, however, the capabilities of the steering wheel may be overwhelmed. A driver whose car has such weak steering must slow down by easing up on the gas pedal and/or braking more.

If the brakes are weak, the car must travel slower. Braking at slower speeds may be adequate, but at high speeds the brakes may be overwhelmed. If the gas pedal provides too much gas and the car tends to go too fast, better steering and brakes are needed to avoid an accident.

This analogy illustrates the concept of balance between integrated systems. The question is often not which system is dysfunctional, but are the systems in balance?

More fundamental neurochemical processes give rise to higher levels of integrated thought such as beliefs, values, interpretation of context and meaning, the formation of intentions, making plans, predicting, choosing and building the Taj Mahal. This makes for a complex neurobiology to understand and medically treat. Neurobiological issues can never be understood in isolation.

MIND VERSUS BRAIN

Our limited focus here on neurobiology is not intended to encourage naive or reductionistic thinking about the mind. To the contrary, this brief introduction should leave us with a humble appreciation of how much we still need to know about brain, mind, and behavior. The finely regulated balance of neurochemical systems in the brain provides the substratum on which psychological processes grow. This can be thought of as the prepsychological strata of the brain. Disorders of impulse control, noise filtration, regulation of arousal and sleep, of activity and reactivity, and so forth, may result in the spinning out of psychological problems involving beliefs, values, and meaning. From the time of conception and throughout our lives, we are continually becoming who we are as our inborn neurobiology continues to interact with the world around us. We must appreciate that the many integrated aspects of brain functioning that we explore in this book are only parts of the brain, which is only a part of the mind. We know this to be true just as we know that the steering wheel is only part of the car, which is only part of the journey.

5
Noradrenergic Regulation

BOB'S "MR. AROUSAL" MACHINE

Let's return to our method of instruction by whimsical analogy. Imagine that Bob has invented a "Mr. Arousal" machine. Bob has installed the control knob for Mr. Arousal on the side of his head. He wants to have better noradrenergic regulation of his brain.

The Mr. Arousal knob is handy because it allows Bob to turn his noradrenergic transmission up and down like the volume on his stereo. Bob wants to know if he can get a patent for this brainstorm of his. "This is my brainstorm to control my brainstorms!" he announces proudly. He decides to try out his new invention the next day.

Bob begins his day in quiet, deep sleep. The volume on his arousal knob is turned way to the left. He has installed a timer, borrowed from his Mr. Coffee machine, that turns the arousal knob a little to the right at 5:30 each morning. Then, at 6:00, the knob is briskly turned a quarter turn to the right. Bob's eyes blink open, and he hops out of bed. The coffee is not ready, but who needs it? Bob is awake and ready to meet the challenges of the day.

Bob has Mr. Arousal programmed to turn more slowly on weekends when he likes to sleep in and wake up more gradually. He borrowed a few parts from his heat pump's digital thermostat and added them to the Mr. Coffee parts. Now his house is always too hot or too cold, but Bob says its worth it. Before inventing Mr. Arousal, Bob needed several cups of coffee, cold showers, stimulation from sights, sounds, and expectations, and even worries and fears of the coming day to get him aroused, awake, and alert. Now his little Mr. Arousal knob does it all.

Bob used to depend on anxiety and fear to maintain optimal arousal during the day. "Oh, no!" he would say in a sudden panic, "I forgot! I have an appointment this morning. I'm late!" Bob's internal arousal knob, the locus coeruleus would alert the reticular activating system in Bob's brain stem and he would suddenly become awake and alert.

Anger also used to flick Bob's arousal knob. When he couldn't wake up in the morning, Bob would finally become angry at his wife, who kept "nagging" him to get up. Finally he would lash out at her, "Leave me alone! Stop trying to run my life!" Bob would then suddenly find himself awake and easily able to rise and get dressed. Bob's wife likes the Mr. Arousal invention, even though it looks funny sticking out of the side of his head, because he is not so grumpy in the morning.

During the day Bob can turn Mr. Arousal's control knob to the right or left according to the demands of each moment. If his noradrenaline sags a little, he becomes sleepy and less alert. Not a bad condition for siesta time, or for digesting a large pepperoni pizza from Tony's.

If Bob has an important meeting after lunch and needs to maintain his arousal, he can just give the knob a little turn to the right until he is at the most efficient state of vigilance for the meeting.

Bob finds that when he is reading he needs a state of quiet, restful, but alert attention. No problem for Mr. Arousal. Bob fiddles with the knob until he is less receptive to incoming stimuli from the world around him. Yet, if the house catches on fire, Bob will not be hyperfocused and will not fail to notice. He managed this by wiring Mr. Arousal into the security system of his home, which includes smoke detection. He is also wired into the television weather-watch channel. If there is danger, Bob will receive a jolt of noradrenaline and his attentional field will widen, like a lens zooming out for a wide view. He will scan his situation for clues, remaining on watchful, vigilant alert.

Bob is now ready to settle down in his recliner and focus on a good book.

No sooner does he get engrossed in his reading than the weather-watch channel announces a tornado sighting nearby. Mr. Arousal's knob begins to turn to the right. Bob's auditory acuity and receptivity are becoming very keen. He now has trouble concentrating on his book as every sound of the wind outside is captured by his ears and funneled into his brain. With each sound of the storm, Bob finds himself listening for signs of the tornado. Bob is now too distracted to read. "Well, at least Mr. Arousal passed the vigilance test."

Suddenly Bob is seized with feelings of apprehension, and finds himself reviewing his tornado plans as he tries to read. "If one comes, I'll head for the bathtub! I've always heard the bathroom is the safest place because of all the structure in the walls. . . ." The weather watch announces that the danger has passed. The knob turns back. Bob loses his hypervigilance, his ruminating, his apprehension, and his focus narrows again to his reading. Bob forgets about storms, about where he is, forgets even that he is reading as he becomes engrossed in a good book.

Now let's imagine what would happen if Mr. Arousal malfunctioned. What happens to Bob when the arousal knob gets turned up too high? Bob failed to remember that the thermostat he borrowed for Mr. Arousal had not been too reliable lately. The room temperature would wander back and forth from hot to cold.

Let's see what happens when this unreliable regulation is applied to Bob's arousal. Let's suppose that Mr. Arousal starts to wander like the thermostat. The arousal knob flicks a quarter turn to the right. Bob suddenly feels a sense of impending disaster. He senses something is terribly wrong, threatening him, and that he is unsafe. He looks around and nothing unusual is happening. He is just reading a book in his recliner. There is no reality to match Bob's emotional and cognitive state. He cannot find anything to account for this feeling of free-floating anxiety.

The knob flicks again, more to the right. Suddenly Bob is flooded with panic. He feels as if he were in an airplane, as if the wing had just exploded into flames and fallen off, and the plane is plummeting to the earth. Bob is seized with the emotional conviction that he is facing his imminent death.

Bob completely forgets about the book; he looks for escape, for some means of survival. But he is only sitting in a recliner holding a book. There is nothing else going on. This state of hyperarousal, however, helpful in the right circumstances, is totally out of context here.

NORADRENERGIC DYSREGULATION AND POST-TRAUMATIC STRESS SYNDROME

What are some other contexts that would require extremely high arousal? When soldiers stormed the beaches at Normandy on D day, their survival depended on a combination of fear, anger, feelings of being on a noble mission, patriotism, determination, a state of readiness for vigorous mortal combat, an anticipation, a thirst for battle, and an ability to unleash an aggression fueled by hate, love, fear, passion, and denial of vulnerability, a euphoric feeling of invulnerability in which the capacity to attack without reserve, even with glee, and to kill with pleasure the "evil" enemy is what was required from their instinctual armamentarium for them to survive. The soldiers who held back never made it off the beach that day.

One theory of the biological contributions to PTSD involves the sensitization of "triggers" which are experienced as "red flags" signaling the original danger and causing a rapid outpouring of noradrenalin. This returns the body to the original state of "fight or flight" when such a high arousal state was a reaction to a threatening and traumatic situation.

The post traumatic stress disorder (PTSD) resulting from combat experiences sometimes also hides a painful psychological secret. After extensive therapy one patient finally unburdened his guilt, confessing, "I cannot live with the way I felt as I killed. It was not the fact that I killed. It was the way I felt about it. In the heat of battle, I suddenly felt euphoric. I enjoyed it, and afterwards, I felt high. I enjoyed it and felt good about it. Once back in safety, glee turned to horror, and I knew I could never live with the shame of the beast I had been. This is a secret no one should know, not even me." Amnesia then cloaks the sin of the soldier's joy.

THE GOODNESS OF FIT BETWEEN STATE AND CONTEXT: HEALTHY VERSUS CRAZY

It seems that even the most abnormal states of mind and the stormiest of emotions would be normal and adaptive to some particular situation. What makes a symptom a symptom? A state could be considered psychotic rather than healthy not so much because of its character, but because of its misplacement. When we are prepared and ready to fight in mortal combat for the preservation of freedom, we are healthy on the beaches of Normandy, but we would be considered psychotic in our recliner reading a book on a Sunday afternoon.

Perhaps health is the capacity to realize the full range of possible human instinctual emotions, thought, and behavior, but also to have the ability to fine-tune the state to the context. It is the goodness of fit between state and context and the ability to flexibly adjust and regulate various states to maintain that good fit that defines a well-functioning brain. When the knob is turned all the way to the right, there is paranoia and manic psychosis. But can we say that, even in the most psychotic patient, we cannot imagine a hypothetical context in which, if the circumstances were true, the patient would not be reacting in the most adaptive way? Remember, "Just because you're paranoid doesn't mean they're not trying to get you." But if you're just in your recliner trying to read a good book, you're crazy.

Perhaps every human emotion, then, is a tool. Seen in this way, being adaptable is having a lot of tools and being able to use the right one in the right place at the right time. When we are restricted to only a few tools, we are limited in our ability to adapt flexibly and make the most of our opportunities. The person who inappropriately sees every situation in a pessimistic and risk-aversive way will miss opportunities to advance boldly and capitalize on opportunities. Over time, his hesitant and tentative posture will cause him to be left behind by his bolder, more assertive competitors who are willing to take the risk.

On the other hand, the person who is unrealistically optimistic is handicapped by an inability to realistically assess risk. Such a person may forget that they do not call it *risk* for nothing, and feel sure that "everything will work out fine." Many a fortune has been lost with these famous last words.

Is it healthier to be an optimist or pessimist, to see the glass as half full or half empty? Perhaps it is the ability to be both, and to flexibly change to fit changing situations. The capacity for fear may be what helps the courageous to survive. The capacity for grief may be what helps love to survive. The capacity for anxiety may be what keeps hope alive.

Are brainstorms, then, symptoms or tools? They could be either, depending on their goodness of fit with the demands of reality. If they represent a loss of adaptive regulation of state to context, they may be symptoms of a neurobiological syndrome, what I have come to refer to as the brainstorm syndrome. If they represent an intimate connection to a human experience based on a realistic appraisal of a situation, then they are the raw emotional and cognitive material of personal growth and newer ways of adapting to a newer world.

6
Diagnosis: The Current State of the Art

The term mental disorder unfortunately implies a distinction between mental disorders and physical disorders that is a reductionistic anachronism of mind/body dualism . . . unfortunately the term persists in the title of *DSM-IV* because we have not found an appropriate substitute. . . .

[*Diagnostic and Statistical Manual of Mental Disorders,*
4th Revision, 1994, p. xxi]

Biologically based brain diseases need a new nomenclature that can accommodate an integrated approach that does more justice to our current understanding.

[Popper et al. 1991, p. 261–262]

If hyperkinesis is symptomatic of an underlying disorder, the diagnosis of the underlying disorder is recorded instead.

[*International Classification of Diseases,*
9th Revision—Clinical Modification, 1991, p. 293]

THE CASE OF "SPARKY": SYNDROMES
THAT DEFY DIAGNOSIS

It was a cool, sunny West Virginia fall morning and the sky was a crisp blue. You could see far away on such a day when the humidity was low and the typical smoky haze was not obscuring the horizon. Danny and his best friend, Dale, were looking for a high place above the treetops where they could find out how far they could see. Why did they climb the electrical tower? Because it was there, and it was tall. It seemed to Danny like the thing to do at the time. Danny was 10 years old.

Dale was not as quick as his friend Danny, who was 40 feet up before he had barely made it off the ground. He was not as fearless as Danny. He was a bit timid and inclined to hold back and think things over before jumping in. Dale was not sure climbing the tower was such a good idea, but he didn't want Danny to know he was scared. Dale was worrying about what could happen. He paused and looked nervously up at his friend. Danny was smiling proudly, grasping the steel girders at the windy sunlit top of the tower. It occurred to Dale that his friend looked like he had just conquered Mt. Everest. Suddenly Danny was standing frozen in a shower of sparks. Then he was in the air. Two weeks later Danny woke up from a coma and found himself in a hospital. He had survived being electrocuted and falling off a 40-foot mining utility tower and landing on his head.

This dramatic experience followed Danny the rest of his life. It earned him the nickname "Sparky," a name he did not particularly appreciate. Embarrassed by a persistent right-side motor weakness, neither Danny nor his peers could ever forget that he was "brain damaged."

Danny was a young adult at the time he was presented to me for a forensic evaluation. There was apparently a settlement being negotiated between Danny and the mining company. I was asked to define Danny's specific symptoms and limitations and to make a determination of the degree to which they resulted from the head injury he sustained at age ten.

Danny had been evaluated numerous times as a child and adolescent following his injury and subsequent rehabilitation. His behavior was described as oppositional and defiant. As he reached adulthood, evaluations resulted in diagnoses of various sorts including various personality disorders, though he never met the diagnostic criteria for any specific personality disorder. Finally, his diagnosis was listed as personality disorder, mixed type.

As a teenager, Danny was described as inattentive, distractible, impulsive, and emotionally labile. He also had motor weakness on one side of his body. He displayed attentional and organizational problems, labile emotions, fine and gross motor planning difficulties resulting in a written expressive language disability, and a speech problem with stuttering.

Danny was described as often moody and had problems with aggressive behavioral dyscontrol. Motor tics were also noted but were mild and not frequent or numerous enough to qualify for a diagnosis of Tourette's syndrome. Other symptoms were numerous, and partially met criteria for a broad array of various psychiatric diagnoses. Most symptoms were not severe enough to satisfy any specific diagnosis, but appeared more as traits. Features of obsessive compulsive disorder (OCD) were manifested more as perfectionism or a meticulousness rather than the classical ritualistic behavior of hand washing, counting, and so on, and obsessive thinking took the form of chronic worrying and ruminating rather than the single intrusive thoughts of classic OCD.

Anxiety and depression tended to be mild but chronic, with an undertone of frustration and demoralization. Symptoms almost reached the level of a major depressive episode several times, but over the long run appeared to recede into a subtle but chronic depression that went unrecognized for several decades.

Danny's self-appraisal was characterized by a feeling of underachievement, of falling far short of his goals, even though by other standards he had been fairly successful. Danny had self-esteem difficulties dating back to childhood. He had not mixed well with others, though he complained of feeling lonely.

Danny had gotten married but his marital adjustment had been problematic, and he was on the verge of divorce. Kristin recalled her original attraction to Danny. " He was charming, an original thinker, spontaneous, had a sense of adventure, was funny, quick whitted, compassionate, sensitive, and enthusiastic." After several years of marriage, however, these traits became tiresome and the list of grievances began to grow longer. Spontaneity turned to unpredictability, unreliability, disorganization, and inability to follow through on goals and responsibilities. "He just can't or won't pull his own weight," Kristin complained.

With the birth of one and then a second child, both of whom began manifesting a similar symptomatic picture, the demands on Kristin increased and problems in the marriage escalated. But these two children had not been electrocuted, fallen 40 feet, and landed on their heads as their father had. Why did their symptoms so resemble their father's?

How Does a Sand Dune Disappear? One Grain at a Time

We see a cluster of symptoms that are mild and subtle, yet chronic. Over time, these symptoms can insidiously erode the lives of people who are afflicted with them. The results can be educational failure, occupational failure, social and marital failure, substance abuse, depression and anxiety disorders, criminality, and so forth. These lives seem to erode like grains in shifting sand dunes. Although these symptoms may not be easily labeled under existing diagnostic nomenclatures they, nonetheless, take their toll.

It had always been assumed that all of Danny's symptoms resulted from the head injury. His identity was largely formed around being a "head-injured child." When I asked to see any evaluation of Danny made before the accident at age 10, however, there were none. How could any determination be made of how his injury related to his subsequent symptoms if there was no information on what he was like before the injury?

I obtained Danny's school records prior to the accident. These indicated that Danny had been inattentive, distractible, impulsive, and hyperactive prior to the head injury. (Indeed, such symptoms as impulsivity and hyperactivity may have partially explained why Danny climbed a 40-foot electrical tower in the first place!) The family history suggested similar symptoms in the father. The school history was replete with teachers' documented comments, especially in the elementary school years. Danny's teachers complained of problems with attention, distractibility, disorganization, hyperverbalization, of his losing things, getting to class late, not turning in homework, and so forth. These had been forgotten, eclipsed by the drama of Danny's accident.

It was impossible to determine specifically how these prior symptoms might have been complicated by the head injury. The subsequent motor paralysis had been socially embarrassing to Danny. A dysfunctional family, divorce of the parents, and emotional abandonment by the father all must have played a role in the final complex of symptoms. The important issue clarified from a thorough history, however, was that the fall from the tower had not likely caused all of this child's difficulties, nor did a dysfunctional family situation. His problems appeared multidetermined by many complex and interwoven factors—neurological, psychological, and social.

It is important, when doing an evaluation for the court, to avoid forming any opinions relating to the legal issues in question, or, if a personal opinion results, to be careful that it does not interfere with the objectivity of the evaluation. What is fair or just is a determination made by the court. The medical evaluation and opinions should be confined to medical questions.

In real life, it is nearly impossible for anyone to totally avoid a human response to the predicament of a suffering person. We might wonder, for example, what the effect might be on Danny's life of receiving a large settlement from the mining company? Wouldn't this greatly benefit him? On the other hand, what role did the years of labeling him as brain damaged have on the development of "Sparky's" self-concepts? What role did the prospect of a large settlement someday play in the way his impairments were viewed by himself and others? We cannot know for sure. The important thing is not trying to avoid reacting in a human way but to make sure this reaction does not affect the objectivity of the professional opinion rendered.

Over the years, I have seen many such patients in my office practice who presented with clusters of symptoms that have been very difficult to fit into any existing psychiatric, neurological, or other medical diagnostic system. They seem not to fully meet the criteria for any specific diagnosis, but rather exhibit one or two symptoms from one diagnosis, another from a second diagnosis, and so on.

It may be extremely difficult to differentiate which symptoms are part of the original neurobiological disorder and how many are acquired or complicated over time. Often apparent "symptoms" that develop turn out to be compensatory strategies. A cluster of symptoms may actually be an adaptation to an underlying disorder and yet be mistaken as the primary disorder.

DIAGNOSTIC MANUALS: WHICH ONE TO USE?

The profession of medicine has been around since the dawn of human civilization. Modern psychiatry, however, is less than a century old. There are persons still alive today who were children when Freud, the founder of psychoanalysis, was writing *The Interpretation of Dreams*.

In the Middle Ages medical diagnosis was based largely on phenomenology, the "study of phenomena," which focuses on what can be observed objectively with the eye. Theories of causation are avoided in phenomenological diagnostic systems. Twentieth-century medical diagnostic nomenclature has benefited from discoveries ranging from germs to genetics, and most medical conditions today are defined on various levels of abstraction. For example, some diseases are defined by their structural pathology (e.g., myocardial infarction), others by the quality of the symptom presentation (e.g., migraine). Others are defined statistically by a deviance from a physiologic norm (e.g., hypertension), still others by etiology (e.g., pneumococcal pneumonia).

The Diagnostic and Statistical Manual of Mental Disorders (DSM)

The modern psychiatric tradition of diagnoses of "mental" disorders has not yet progressed beyond phenomenologically based diagnosis. The position of the American Psychiatric Association's *Diagnostic and Statistical Manual of Mental Disorders (DSM)*, since its third revision in 1980, has been that diagnosis should be made by clusters of objective behavioral symptoms that can be reliably observed (phenomenology) rather than by the cause of the problem (etiology). This led, for example, to the category of disruptive behavior disorders which lists behaviors as the diagnostic criteria. The diagnosis of a disruptive behavior disorder rests on the identification of specific problematic behaviors and their comparison to the official list of diagnostic behaviors. The restriction in the *DSM* to objectively observable and verifiable behavioral symptoms leads to diagnostic conceptual problems similar to those the rest of medicine struggled with in the Middle Ages.

Let's look again at the example of ADHD, a diagnosis coined by the *DSM* as a behavior disorder (see Table 6–1).

TABLE 6–1. *DSM-IV* Criteria for ADHD

Either (1) or (2):

(1) six (or more) of the following symptoms of inattention have persisted for at least 6 months to a degree that is maladaptive and inconsistent with developmental level:

Inattention:

    (a) often fails to give close attention to details or makes careless mistakes in schoolwork, work, or other activities

    (b) often has difficulty sustaining attention in tasks or play activities

    (c) often does not seem to listen when spoken to directly

    (d) often does not follow through on instructions and fails to finish schoolwork, chores, or duties in the workplace (not due to oppositional behavior or failure to understand instructions)

    (e) often has difficulty organizing tasks and activities

    (f) often avoids, dislikes, or is reluctant to engage in tasks that require sustained mental effort (such as schoolwork or homework)

    (g) often loses things necessary for tasks or activities (e.g., toys, school assignments, pencils, books, or tools)

    (h) is often easily distracted by extraneous stimuli

    (i) is often forgetful in daily activities

(2) six (or more) of the following symptoms of hyperactivity–impulsivity have persisted for at least 6 months to a degree that is maladaptive and inconsistent with developmental level:

Hyperactivity:

    (a) often fidgets with hands or feet or squirms in seat

    (b) often leaves seat in classroom or in other situations in which remaining seated is expected

    (c) often runs about or climbs excessively in situations in which it is inappropriate (in adolescents or adults, may be limited to subjective feelings of restlessness)

    (d) often has difficulty playing or engaging in leisure activities quietly

    (e) is often "on the go" or often acts as if "driven by a motor"

    (f) often talks excessively

Impulsivity:

    (g) often blurts out answers before questions have been completed

    (h) often has difficulty awaiting turn

    (i) often interrupts or intrudes on others (e.g., butts into conversations or games)

By design there is no reference to underlying causative factors. This is a bit like diagnosing a "breathing deficit disorder," or BDD. To carry this analogy further, one could then advocate a treatment by behavior modification, rewarding the patient for breathing more and punishing the patient for breathing less. While this may seem a bit ridiculous for an illness such as pneumonia, it becomes equally difficult to use phenomenological diagnoses to point the way to the types of treatment that are most likely to be beneficial for the patient. The main value of the phenomenological system is that it is easy to get agreement among a wide range of diagnosticians from widely different schools of thought. This is good for record keeping and statistical analysis of large numbers. What is sacrificed, however, is that the diagnoses are, in many cases, almost meaningless in terms of their clinical utility.

The mood instability, fine motor coordination problems, and various learning disabilities, so often seen with ADHD are not included as primary features of ADHD, but only as possible associated problems in the *DSM*.

Complicating the history of some patients are various episodes of insults to the brain such as closed head injuries, complicated viral encephalitis, and other toxic exposures such as lead. Many impulsive children are accident prone, and some younger patients may tend to eat leaded paint. Sustaining one or more concussions or other brain injuries may make it difficult to tease out how much of a child's difficulties was originally genetically acquired, how much is due to post-traumatic brain damage, and how much is acquired as psychological defenses to the neurological deficiencies. These may be further complicated by psychologically traumatic experiences such as child abuse or neglect. When we embrace the complex, we find less and less utility to the monochromatic concepts in the available diagnostic manuals. Even the multiaxial system of the *DSM* often fails to capture the most important aspects of the patient's difficulties.

The efforts of the phenomenology movement were directed at increasing reliability among clinicians and researchers across all settings—inpatient, outpatient, experienced clinician, novice clinician, and so on. Unfortunately, there is a well-known principle in statistics that has stood the test of time—that increased reliability almost always is purchased at the cost of decreased diagnostic validity and utility.

"Mental and Nervous" or "Major Medical"?

Although certainly not intended by those who crafted the recent versions of the *DSM* (III and IV), characterization of diagnoses by behavioral symptoms has unfortunately encouraged attorneys, insurance companies, and even some medical professionals to view behavioral symptoms as "the disorder" rather than behavioral markers for the real underlying neurobiological illness. In the United States, mental health reimbursement has thus continued to decrease as behavioral diagnoses have been viewed as trivial, imaginary, or too nonspecific, and impossible to document vis-à-vis the cost effectiveness of medical intervention. The management of medical reimbursement by nonmedical personnel, who often take diagnostic nomenclature quite literally, has led to a dichotomy. Most insurance companies in the United States currently separate medical problems into two groups for the purpose of determining reimbursement: "Mental and Nervous" and "Major Medical." "Major Medical" represents to these reimbursement experts disorders that arise from dysfunction of the body's physiology, including the organ in our head, the brain. "Mental and Nervous," however, is seen as "misbehavior" rising from poor parenting, learned asocial behavior, or simply a weak moral character, and is not viewed as having the same legitimate claim to resources as "real" medical problems.

Let's return to our example of ADHD. As ADHD has no stated cause, it can be trivialized as simply a problem of bad behavior, not worthy of neuropharmacological or other medical treatment. ADHD, like the hypothetical breathing deficit disorder (BDD), is such a nonspecific concept that it casts too wide a net and covers too many disorders.

Most medical scientists in the modern mainstream would agree, however, that ADHD represents a heterogeneous group of disorders, many of which have strong neurological underpinnings and genetically causative factors. Most types of ADHD respond dramatically and positively to medications such as the cortical stimulants, alpha agonists like clonidine and Tenex, or the wide range of other medications that include antidepressants and anticonvulsants. Nevertheless, this category of disorders or syndromes is considered a behavior disorder although many subtypes do not include problematic behavior at all.

The International Classification of Diseases

Hyperkinetic Syndrome of Childhood (314): Disorders in which the essential features are short attention span and distractibility. In early childhood the most striking symptom is disinhibited, poorly organized, and poorly regulated extremely overactive behavior. Impulsiveness, marked mood fluctuations, and aggression are also common symptoms. Delays in the development of specific skills are often present and disturbed, poor relationships are common. If the hyperkinesis is symptomatic of an underlying disorder, the diagnosis of the underlying disorder is recorded *instead*. [*International Classification of Diseases*, 9th Revision, 1991, p. 293], Clinical Modification.

The World Health Organization's ICD is the officially recognized diagnostic manual used by most of the world, including the United States. Most insurance companies recognize both the *DSM* and the *ICD*.

The *ICD* diagnostic criteria for hyperkinetic syndrome of childhood listed above is in marked contrast to the *DSM* criteria for ADHD. What is the relationship between the hyperkinetic syndrome of childhood and ADHD? Are they the same disorder?

The *DSM* recognizes a disorder that does not include the hyperkinetic symptom, ADHD without hyperactivity or impulsivity. To call this a hyperkinetic syndrome of childhood is thus odd, to say the least. Also notable in the *ICD* is the broader range of symptoms including emotional lability and many other features that are listed as associated features in the *DSM*. Perhaps most notable is the allowance and even requirement that if the clinician believes that the clinical picture is symptomatic of an underlying disorder, then the diagnosis of the underlying disorder is recorded instead.

The *ICD* requires that an underlying brain dysfunction manifesting neurocognitive, neuroaffective, and neuromotoric symptoms consistent with the diagnosis of hyperkineses would be listed as an encephalopathy instead. In the next chapter we will explore the encephalopathies in some detail.

7
The Static Encephalopathies

Static: At rest; in equilibrium; not in motion.

Encephalopathy: Any dysfunction of the brain.

Tabor's Cyclopedic Medical Dictionary,
13th ed., 1977, p. S-96, E-26.

MAKING THE DIAGNOSIS OF STATIC ENCEPHALOPATHY

A large and heterogeneous group of relatively benign and stable (static), though chronic, brain dysfunctions can be collectively referred to as encephalopathies. The term encephalopathy refers to "any brain dysfunction." We will focus here on a group of encephalopathies that we will refer to as the "static encephalopathies." The qualifier "static" refers to the quality of symptoms that appear to be stable over time or to improve mildly with age and maturity, but often to persist to a significant degree into adulthood. Some types of relatively benign static encephalopathies appear to involve neurotransmission dysregulation in a variety of brain neural circuits involving the regulation of attention, impulse control, motor activity, mood, arousal, and so on. Such symptoms are often exquisitely sensitive to manipulations of neurotransmission in these circuits. What I have come to think of as the brainstorm syndrome (BSS) may relate, in large part, to neural circuit dysfunctions involving the three key neurotransmitters we have focused on earlier: dopamine, serotonin, and noradrenaline. The brainstorm syndrome, then, may represent certain chronic, minimal, and relatively stable brain dysfunctions or static encephalopathies. We will continue to focus on this group of symptoms and these neurotransmitters in this chapter.

The Case of Hank

Hank first presented to me at age 4½. His parents were concerned that he appeared to be highly distractible, to have very poor concentration, and to be extremely affectively labile.

Hank was one of twins, delivered at thirty-six weeks. He developed respiratory distress syndrome at birth due to aspiration. This condition required a seven-day hospitalization in the pediatric intensive care unit. He received continuous oxygen and blood transfusions and a continual umbilical arterial line. He did not begin feeding until the sixth night. His weight dropped from 5 pounds 12 ounces at birth to 4 pounds 14 ounces.

Hank continued to have respiratory problems throughout his infancy. He had chronic sinus and middle ear infections. He had to breathe through his mouth at night. At 15 months of age his condition required an adenoidectomy and placement of tubes. His adenoids were removed because of airway obstruction. At the age of 3 his tonsils were also removed due to airway obstruction in combination with adenoid regrowth. Hank continued to have constant problems with asthma, chronic sinusitis, and otitis media. He contracted chicken pox with no apparent complications noticed then by his parents.

When Hank was 4½ his parents became increasingly concerned with his high distractibility, poor concentration, and emotional lability.

Evaluation of Hank

The diagnostic evaluation included a review of the past medical records, an office medical examination, and a review of the history and presenting problems with the parents. Standard teacher and parent checklist and rating scales were also obtained, scored and reviewed.

Initial Working Diagnosis: ADHD?

The initial tentative working diagnosis chosen was attention deficit hyperactivity disorder (314.01) as it fit some of Hank's symptoms, though he did not have the minimum required symptoms to meet the *DSM* diagnostic criteria.

As Hank's progress was monitored and additional historical information was gathered, it became clear that the diagnosis of attention deficit hyperactivity disorder (314.01) did not adequately capture the scope of Hank's symptoms. Although he did continue to manifest some of the behavioral symptoms listed in the diagnostic criteria, the behavioral aspects of his symptoms were not of primary concern, nor a primary focus of his medical treatment.

The *International Classification of Diseases Ninth Edition* (ICD-9) provided additional and alternative diagnostic possibilities. The *ICD-9* nomenclature included a broader range of symptoms in the list of diagnostic criteria for Hyperkinesis (*ICD-9*: 314.01). The stated rules of the *ICD-9* require that, in the opinion of the diagnostician, if the hyperkinesis is due to an underlying condition then the underlying condition must be listed *instead*.

Hank's Final Diagnosis: Static Encephalopathy

It was my medical opinion that Hank's symptoms were caused by such an underlying cortical neuroregulatory brain dysfunction. The diagnosis required and that best fit the constellation of symptoms was: *ICD-9-CM*: 348.3 Encephalopathy, Unspecified (static, chronic, benign). The etiology was left as unspecified as the relative contributions of the complicated neonatal course, subsequent respiratory disease, or other factors could not be specified. The diagnosis of an unspecified static encephalopathy was considered, then, to represent the most conceptually valid and clinically useful diagnostic nomenclature.

Hank's history was positive for (1) intrauterine distress from placental insufficiency, (2) a premature birth, (3) subsequent respiratory distress syndrome from neonatal hyaline membrane disease, (4) chronic sinusitis and otitis media, and (5) childhood viral illnesses including varicella.

Because his symptoms could be due to some or all of these known causative etiologic factors, the diagnostic code for encephalopathy was left as unspecified (348.3), even though the etiology is believed with a reasonable degree of medical certainty to be neurophysiological in nature. The qualifiers refer to the static or stable nature, chronic duration, and relatively benign course in terms of potential compatibility with a relatively normal quality of life with treatment.

Hank's brain dysfunction was likely related, in part, to the neonatal complications and/or represented a genetically acquired neurophysiological disorder. Similar brain dysfunctions have been reported as resulting from genetic variants of such neuroregulatory structures as the dopamine D2 receptor gene variant and/or the noradrenaline beta hydroxylase enzyme variant. The resultant symptoms originate from neurotransmitter cortical brain dysfunction. Typically there is a spectrum of neurocognitive, neuroaffective and neuromotoric systems manifested. One specific example is the dysregulation of fine motor planning in the premotor area of the parietal cortex, which can manifest as various fine-motor-planning difficulties involving speech (dysarticulation) or in writing (dysgraphia). Such cortical brain dysfunctions, whether idiopathic or of a specifically determined cause, often respond to therapy with cortical stimulants such as Dexedrine, Ritalin, or Cylert. The neurochemistry, neurophysiology, and neuropharmacological mechanisms by which these medications exact their effects appear to involve the normalization of neurotransmission, particularly in neural systems involving dopamine, serotonin, and noradrenaline.

Diagnostic Criteria for Static Encephalopathy

The term static encephalopathy will be used here as synonymous with the term *ICD-9-CM* encephalopathy (benign, chronic, static). The qualifiers benign, chronic, and static indicate that the brain dysfunction has three characteristics: (1) resulting functional impairment is relatively minimal compared to the degenerative encephalopathies; (2) the condition is typically present, to some degree, over the lifetime of the individual; and (3) the condition is neurologically stable over time. These qualifiers distinguish the static encephalopathies from the degenerative encephalopathies. The latter typically follow a progressive course resulting in varying degrees of deterioration and loss of functional capacity over time. The static encephalopathies remain stable or may improve with age and maturity.

The concept of an encephalopathy that is relatively benign, chronic, and static is reminiscent of the now archaic term *minimal brain dysfunction*. The abandonment of this term during an era emphasizing phenomenology was in some ways perhaps, unfortunate. A return to conceptualizing certain brain disorders by characterizing underlying neurobiological dysfunction may ultimately provide a more clinically useful and scientifically valid approach.

Social / Occupational / Educational Functional Impairments

Some impairment must be present in at least two of the following settings: home, school, work, and social life. There must be clear evidence of interference with developmentally appropriate social, academic, or occupational functioning. Functional capacity typically worsens in situations that require higher demands on the specific areas of neurophysiological dysfunction such as frustration tolerance, habituation to high levels of environmental stimulation, selective attention, and sustained mental effort. These difficulties are often perceived by others as bossiness, stubbornness, and excessive and frequent insistence that requests be met.

Symptoms that may be worsened by the above but also be part of the neurobiologically based symptom complex include: mood lability, dysphoria, rejection sensitivity, emotional intensity, and emotional hyperreactivity.

These neurobiological substrates may interact with social experience and contribute to: rejection by peers, demoralization, poor self esteem, academic underachievement, or oppositional behavior.

Inadequate self-application to tasks that require frustration tolerance is often interpreted by others as a poor sense of responsibility or laziness, or as oppositional behavior. Family relationships are often characterized by resentment and antagonism, especially because variability in the individual's symptomatic status often leads parents to believe that the troublesome behavior is willful.

Differential Diagnosis: What It Isn't

A differential diagnosis is a list of other diagnostic possibilities to be ruled out in the consideration of a particular diagnosis. For a static encephalopathy the following should be ruled out.

Progressive-Degenerative Encephalopathy

The benign and chronic static encephalopathies are in distinct contrast to the progressive and degenerative encephalopathies, such as Lou Gehrig's disease, which have a poor long-term prognosis.

Oppositional/Defiant Disorder

This is a behavioral diagnosis as defined in the *Diagnostic and Statistical Manual of Mental Disorders* (*DSM*). In oppositional defiant disorder the essential feature is the deliberate intent of the oppositional behavior to oppose authority. Individuals with oppositional defiant disorder may resist work or school tasks that require self-application because of an unwillingness to conform to others' demands. The symptoms of oppositional defiant disorder must be differentiated from the avoidance of school tasks seen in individuals with neurophysiological disorders.

Some individuals with such brain dysfunctions often develop secondary oppositional attitudes toward such tasks. They devalue their importance, often as a rationalization for their neurological incompetence and resultant failure.

Conduct Disorder

This is also a behavioral diagnosis as defined in the *DSM*. In the static encephalopathies, behaviors that secondarily result from underlying neurophysiological dysfunctions are typically less severe than those with primary conduct disorder. Behaviors may be incidentally disruptive but typically do not include premeditated and intentional aggression toward people or animals, destruction of property, or a pattern of theft or deceit, as in conduct disorder.

Primary Mood Disorder

The moods of the static encephalopathies are brief and labile, and not as chronic and pervasive as in the mood disorders as defined in the *DSM*. Major mood disorders may be a later psychiatric complication of untreated static encephalopathies. These appear to occur with increasing frequency in adulthood.

Comorbidity? The Lumpers versus the Splitters

The various static encephalopathies frequently are considered as comorbid (coexisting) with other medical disorders. When more than one disorder occurs, both should be diagnosed. According to Achenbach (1991):

> Apparent comorbidity may arise as an artifact of conceptual or diagnostic models that impute inappropriate boundaries between disorders. To draw firm conclusions about comorbidity, each disorder must be clearly distinguishable from others. Few behavioral or emotional disorders of childhood have been validated as separate diagnostic entities that can be reliably distinguished from one another. Rather than accepting reports of comorbidity at face value, we need to understand how particular conceptual and diagnostic schemas affect the perceived relations among disorders [p. 271–278].

There is often a family history of numerous diagnoses that seems to follow a certain family "pedigree" but takes on various forms in different members of the family. In addition, there is often a family history of suicides, criminality, or lives that failed in spite of recognized potential. Also, a family history of narcolepsy is more common.

Subtypes of Static Encephalopathy by Etiology (Cause)

In the *ICD-9 CM*, subtypes of encephalopathy are categorized based on the presumed etiology of the brain dysfunction. The following listing is based on this typology with additional comments and elaborations provided by the author.

Congenital Static Encephalopathy 742.9

The defining characteristic of the congenital subtype is that it is present at birth. There is rapidly growing research support indicating that many of the characteristic symptoms of the congenital encephalopathies are the manifestations of a polygenetically acquired central neurophysiological dysfunction. Some may represent a familial disorder. While the specific neurophysiological defects may not yet be determined, there is ongoing and vigorous study into the roles played by variants of genes. Studies of variants that code for neurotransmitter receptor subtypes as well as for various enzymes may provide key insight into the roles such genes play in the regulation neurotransmission.

Phenotypic manifestations may vary widely among members of the same family. They may still, however, share many common characteristics that can be related to dysfunction in neuroregulatory neural circuits, especially those heavily dependent on dopamine, serotonin, and noradrenaline. A positive family history for similar symptoms can be elicited by a thorough family history. Various members of the family with similar neurophysiological symptoms may have ended up with widely discrepant diagnostic labels, however.

There is a higher prevalence of similar symptoms in first-degree biological relatives. There is also a higher prevalence of Tourette's syndrome, ADHD, mood and anxiety disorders, learning disorders, substance related disorders, and antisocial personality disorder in family members. These disorders may share one or more common genes that contribute to a spectrum disorder characterized by unstable regulation of arousal and reactivity. There is usually a family history on one or both sides of depression, substance abuse, anxiety disorders, learning disorders, hyperactivity, motor tics, obsessive compulsive disorders, or other disorders.

Other cases of congenital encephalopathy appear to result from a variety of prenatal insults to the brain. Brain injury sustained during the birth process is coded separately as described below.

Post-Birth Injury Static Encephalopathy 767.8

The symptoms of post-birth injury encephalopathy may or may not be overt at birth but are usually apparent by 2 to 3 years of age. Many individuals, however, are diagnosed after the symptoms have been present for a number of years.

Lou (1996) found a significant association between prematurity and perinatal hypoxic-haemodynamic encephalopathy. Repeated hypoxic-ischemic events are particularly common in prematurity, a fact which seems to explain the high incidence of ADHD in this patient group. The magnitude of the problem is increasing with the increased survival rate among premature infants.

Post-Traumatic Brain Injury Static Encephalopathy 310.2

Post Concussion: Brain injury sustained from head trauma occurring after birth is coded separately. Symptoms appear to be acquired after a head injury. This may have been perceived as minor at the time, such as from a closed head injury sustained in an auto accident or a fall. In some cases neurological examination and/or laboratory data such as an Electroencephalogram (EEG) or neuropsychological tests may indicate brain injury. In many cases there are few overt or objectively measurable findings. Symptoms may have been present before the brain injury but to a milder degree.

The fact of an acquired brain injury per se does not preclude preexisting conditions such as a brain dysfunction present at birth (congenital encephalopathy). The clinical picture may be complex, making it difficult to determine which symptoms preceded the head injury. In many cases preexisting neurophysiological dysfunction is exacerbated by traumatic brain injury. This can be particularly complex where there is a history of multiple head injuries. Unfortunately, persons with such disorders may be more prone to the type of accidents that cause head injuries due to their functional limitations.

Post Encephalitic Static Encephalopathy: While Hank's symptoms were clearly caused by a brain dysfunction, or encephalopathy, the specific causative factors for such mild, nondegenerative static encephalopathies are usually difficult to specify with a high degree of certainty. Patients with similar symptom complexes have been reported to have an increased incidence of similar disorder in biological relatives, indicating possible genetic causative factors.

In other cases, a static encephalopathy is associated with a history of an acute encephalitis (*The Merck Manual of Diagnosis and Therapy, Sixteenth Edition*, 1992, p. 1472–1474). Encephalitis is an acute inflammatory illness caused by acute and direct insults to the brain. One example might be a viral encephalitis caused by viral invasion, or by hypersensitivity initiated by a virus or other foreign proteins. The exact incidence of specific complications of common viral illness has been difficult to specify, as many usually go detected, unless they follow a particularly fulminant course. The acute inflammatory illness may quickly and completely resolve and be diagnosed generically as a benign case of the "flu." Acute cerebral inflammation, however, may resolve, leaving a subtle sequelae of a more chronic postencephalitic encephalopathy.

In the case of herpes simplex encephalitis, localized cerebral dysfunction is more common in the temporal and frontal lobe cortical areas. Dysfunction in these areas has been associated with dysregulation of selective attention, affective modulation, and fine motor planning. Such resultant symptom complexes are not dissimilar to the difficulties Hank has struggled with, and it is not possible to rule out such factors given the data currently available.

Permanent cerebral sequelae are more likely to occur in younger children than in adults. The onset of Hank's difficulties was noted to be in his infancy, a time of the highest vulnerability. Postencephalitic encephalopathies have also been known to arise from noninfectious illness of the brain, and in parameningeal diseases such as chronic sinusitis and/or chronic otitis media. Infections may occur from complications of varicella (chicken pox), or various other common viral illnesses including measles, mumps, echovirus, coxacivirus, herpes simplex and zoster. Even reactions to vaccinations have been known to produce similar encephalopathies and are considered to have an autoimmune mechanism. Symptoms of the acute phases of illness may range from fulminating, resulting in death, or manifest overtly as only fever and the diagnosis missed entirely.

Resistance to Thyroid Hormone: Attention deficit disorders are a frequent manifestation of resistance to thyroid (RTH), a disorder caused by mutations in the hormone-binding domain of the human thyroid hormone receptor beta gene. Matochik and colleagues (1996) used positron emission tomography to measure cerebral glucose metabolism in regions known to be biological determinants of sustained attention. Performance on a continuous auditory discrimination task was severely impaired in the RTH subjects, while metabolism was higher both in the right parietal cortex and the anterior cingulate gyrus. Abnormally high functional activity of the anterior cingulate during sustained attention may be associated with a decreased signal-to-noise ratio for the neural processing of task stimuli on subjects with RTH.

Autoimmune Reactions Triggering OCD and Tic Symptoms: Allen and colleagues (1995) reported on a newly discovered, infection-triggered, autoimmune subtype of pediatric obsessive compulsive disorder and Tourette's syndrome. Their hypotheses is that infections with group A Beta-hemolytic streptococci, among others, may trigger autoimmune responses that cause or exacerbate some cases of childhood-onset obsessive-compulsive disorder or tic disorders (including Tourette's syndrome). The process may be analogous to that of rheumatic fever and sydenham's chorea, a movement disorder following an infection such as a strep throat. If this hypothesis is correct, then immunological treatments should lead to decreased symptoms in some cases. These researchers at the NIMH reported some success in treating cases with penicillin, plasmapheresis, immunoglobulin, and prednisone. At the time of this writing, a larger study was underway to further pursue these preliminary findings. A possible mechanism may be an autoimmune reaction against the anterior corpus collosum area of the brain. It is well known that Thomas Edison suffered from a severe bout of rheumatic fever as a child. Could such an autoimmune mechanism account for some of this great inventor's "brainstorms"? Does crafting 10,000 varieties of light bulbs seem a bit obsessive–compulsive? Again, we can only wonder.

Static Encephalopathy, Unspecified 348.3

When historical and clinical data are insufficient to point to a single clear and primary causative factor, the etiology may be listed as unspecified. This designation is appropriate if it is the opinion of the diagnostician that, beyond a reasonable degree of medical certainty, major causative factors are due to brain pathology.

Categories of Dysfunction within the Diagnosis of Static Encephalopathy:
Having Your Lumps and Splitting Them, Too

Categorical and quantitative models offer potentially complementary approaches to differentiating between disorders more effectively, a process that is essential for improving our knowledge of etiology and our assessment of the risks and benefits of particular psychopharmacological interventions.

[Achenbach 1991, pp. 271–278]

Following are important domains of neurological functions to assess as potential targets for medical intervention (see Table 7–1). A given individual patient may have varying degrees of impairment in one or more, or even all of these domains. Many patients have histories of receiving many diagnoses in the past as they were assessed by different clinicians over time.

A more detailed discussion of the dimensions that may be considered in the assessment and treatment of static encephalopathy will be presented in a following chapter. Each domain is believed to have its basis primarily in neurological dysfunction. Environmental factors may contribute in varying degrees to how much specific symptoms are amplified, modified, or whether they are expressed. Though treatment is primarily via pharmacological agents aimed at normalizing neurotransmitter function in the brain, environmental interventions and education may also play important roles in managing symptoms and augmenting medical treatment. In cases where psychiatric illness is comorbid or resulting as a secondary complication, psychiatric and psychological treatment should also be included as indicated.

MEDICAL OFFICE MANAGEMENT
OF MAJOR MEDICAL DISORDER

The following treatment summary is offered as one example of how a brainstorm clinical case might be documented in a major medical paradigm. The paradigm used is described in detail in the section entitled "Evaluation and Management" in the *Current Procedural Terminology* (*CPT*) manual published by the American Medical Association (1998, p. 1–42).

Hank responded well to an empiric trial with the cortical stimulant Dexedrine with significant reduction of his symptoms. As diagnostic studies were completed, the results were discussed with Hank and his parents, as were the results of analysis of the standard teacher and parent rating scales. Specific recommendations for reasonable and appropriate accommodations in the classroom

TABLE 7–1. Domains of Neurological Dysfunction

Category (symptom)	Regulation (function)	Dysregulation
I. Neurocognitive (prefrontal – organizational)	Selective attention Span of attention Anticipate consequences Goal-directed activity Plan/prioritize/sequence Error recognition/ correction	Distractibility Short attention span Cognitive impulsivity Short attention span Disorganization Errors of oversight
II. Neuroaffective (limbic – emotional/ drive)	Mood stability Security Aggression Motivation	Moodiness (mood lability) Anxiety/panic/worry Temper outbursts/violence Apathy/mania
III. Neuromotor (parietal)	Gross motor Fine motor	Dyscoordination (clumsiness) Motor tics, speech Dysgraphia (handwriting)
IV. Neurosensory (frontal)	Filter/habituate	Tactile hypersensitivity Impaired habituation
V. Arousal (reticular activating/ locus coeruleus)	Sleep/wakefulness Alertness/vigilance Stress/fight-or-flight	Insomnia Sleep apnea, narcolepsy, bedwetting Hypervigilance (watchfulness, fear) Anxiety/avoidance/ paranoia
VI. Neurosomatic	Gastrointestinal Cardiac Immune	Reflux esophagitis High blood pressure Coronary artery disease Allergies/asthma/respiratory infections Diarrhea/irritable bowel/ constipation

were discussed. These were deemed necessary and it was recommended that appropriate accommodations should be implemented at home and at school.

Parental concerns involved the long-term prognosis due to the probable chronic nature of Hank's problems. Long-term rehabilitative goals, including the prevention of or minimization of complications and resulting secondary disabilities, were explained and discussed.

In particular, his type of encephalopathy appeared to be stable, or static, as differentiated from progressive. It was explained that Hank could quite possibly have a fairly normal life depending on multiple factors, including his continued favorable response to medications, in particular the cortical stimulants.

The benefits versus risks and side effects of various treatment options were discussed and weighed. Informed consent was obtained from Hank's parents for the recommended treatment program.

Medical Office Visits

Office visits typically involved medical decision making of moderate complexity. This was due to the number of treatment options to weigh with Hank and his parents, the diagnostic complexities and the multiple dimensions of decision-making processes required to manage his medical care.

Since Hank's condition was chronic in nature, it was necessary to monitor his status at approximately monthly intervals to assure his rehabilitative progress. Office visits usually required thirty to sixty minutes. The primary focus of treatment has remained the medical management of the neurophysiological symptoms related to his diagnosis of encephalopathy, unspecified. Efforts during office visits are directed to the ongoing evaluation of 1) the various side effects of medication, 2) determination if there is the continued need for medication, 3) adjustment of the medication dosage and timing to assure adequate efficacy, 4) monitoring for the emergence of adverse drug effects such as the onset of motor tics, and so forth.

One example was Hank's continued difficulties with initiating the onset of sleep at night and with the transition to wakefulness in the morning. Such difficult state regulation is common in such encephalopathies and, together with constant difficulties "getting Hank organized," such problems have provided significant and ongoing stress for Hank and his parents. Disagreement between the parents over different management approaches to Hank's problems significantly stressed both parents and the marital relationship. There was an ongoing need to provide counseling and education for Hank's family as to: 1) what limitations they can expect from Hank's neurological problems, 2) what they may reasonably demand from him, 3) how to differentiate and adjust to various side effects of medication, and 4) maintenance of a balanced attitude of tolerance and acceptance for his limitations, and the positive alliance with health and education providers necessary to support his ongoing treatment.

Office visits have centered on the medical management of his neurophysiological problems. Interventions have primarily involved complex rational pharmacotherapy and a case management approach of the multiple factors that pertain to treatment of a chronic disorder in the context of the family, school, and community.

Treatment options have included nonpharmacological intervention as needed. This has involved ongoing discussions, in the context of Hank's ongoing development, of his relative handicaps and strengths, and how to differentiate normal behavior from behavior that is symptomatic of the underlying neurophysiological disorder.

In was my impression that Hank might meet the state criteria to receive reasonable and appropriate accommodations in his learning environment at school. His teachers reported that his symptoms significantly interfered with his alertness in class and his learning. Hank's parents were encouraged to become informed about his rights to a free and appropriate education. They were referred to school personnel and community agencies to help them with details of how to effectively advocate for Hank's best interests. They were counseled on how to form a therapeutic alliance with the school system.

Also included in Hank's treatment plan were specific instructions to the parents concerning the doses of medications and precise timing required to effectively use a very short-acting cortical stimulant such as Dexedrine.

Determination of the type of medication and the optimal regimen required empirical trials of different medications, doses, frequencies, and time intervals. Assessment required ongoing feedback from Hank's parents and teachers using standardized medication monitoring rating scales and checklists.

Hank's parents remained concerned about his small stature and the possibility of growth retardation, which has been reported in some cases with cortical stimulant use. The pertinent literature regarding this issue was referenced and Hank's growth was monitored and plotted on standard pediatric growth charts normed for sex and age. Hank has remained in the lowest percentiles of normal growth but has not shown an obvious pattern of growth retardation. His growth continues to be monitored and, referral for a pediatric endocrine evaluation will be made in the future should this become indicated. This has not been necessary to date. Additional topics of medical counseling with Hank and his family included the importance of compliance with prescribed medication schedules and other medical instructions, such as the recommended frequency of visits and the need for ongoing collateral information from teachers.

Teacher feedback was particularly important owing to the short duration of medication effects. Onset of action began abruptly after the morning dose and lasted only until about 2 or 3 o'clock in the afternoon. Hank's teachers were the only adults who would be in proximity to Hank during the periods of medication effects. Their cooperation in providing valid observations and feedback was crucial to the accurate appraisal and adjustment of the medication. Some considerable attention was focused on the importance of cultivating and maintaining a cooperative alliance with the school. It has been my experience that in cases where this alliance cannot be negotiated, the outcome is frequently treatment failure.

Such topics were reviewed on an as-needed basis as determined to be consistent with the medical management of Hank's problems and his family's needs. Coordination of Hank's care with other agencies was also discussed and implemented as needed. For example, a private educational consultant was retained at one point to consult with the school personnel to help make sure they understood and to appropriately accommodate specific needs arising from his medical condition. The consultant provided a liaison for the parents and the school. She was helpful in facilitating the formulation, implementation, and monitoring of reasonable and appropriate accommodations.

Hank has progressed well, especially with academic achievements in school. Currently, he is placed in the academically gifted program at his school. The prognosis is favorable for a normal life provided that medical treatment is maintained as needed.

Static Encephalopathy and the Third Party

An integrated approach to diagnosis and treatment of mind, brain and behavior can be confusing to some insurance companies. This is especially the case of managed care companies structured so they require assignment of all medical treatment from a given practitioner to either "Major Medical" or "Mental and Nervous" case managers.

The terms *major medical* and *mental and nervous* were constructed by the insurance industry and cannot be found in any medical terminology. There is no universally agreed upon meaning for these terms by medical or insurance experts. Even efforts to define their meaning in court litigations have not resulted in less vague or consistent definitions. (In one such situation, a major insurance company offered its definition of mental and nervous conditions as "those conditions that mental health professionals treat"!)

Such an artificial and ambiguous dichotomy of mind and body is an unfortunate artifact of the way health care management companies are currently organized. This will change, I hope, as they become more sophisticated.

The Risks to Patients of Diagnostic Labels

"Can we synthesize our many dimensions and integrate our newly developing concepts into one language? The implications of finding a new term could be widespread. Clinicians want a word that does not present a grave threat to the self-esteem of children and that helps achieve self understanding."

[Popper et al. 1991, p. 261–262]

In rethinking and attempting to broaden the interpretations of the diagnostic nomenclature currently available, I have not done so with any intent other than to accurately and realistically represent what I see and understand in my daily treatment of my patients. The perspectives offered here were not derived quickly as an academic exercise. They developed slowly over many years of dealing with the realities of treating thousands of such patients.

Most important, by modifying and/or expanding the range of available diagnostic nomenclature, we potentially influence how our patients are labeled and viewed by others. By placing emphasis on the neurobiological basis for certain syndromes, we help enlighten the world that our patients must face. We do this by helping to broaden understanding so that their handicaps are no longer seen as resulting from a lack of morality, character, proper parenting, poor teaching, TV, or Nintendo. We help clarify that "behavioral management" paradigms that encourage shaming, punishing, and blaming will never provide solutions, as they clearly have not in the past. We can help to shift the focus toward what is good, courageous, and of great value in so many struggling people.

8

The Dopamine–Serotonin–Noradrenaline (DSN) System: Diagnosis by Target Symptoms

GROUPING SYMPTOMS BY NEUROTRANSMITTER DYSFUNCTION

I have found it more useful in my work with patients to define domains of neurophysiological dysfunction rather than to focus on a diagnosis. Addressing each of these domains allows for a detailed and clinically useful organization of the diagnostic data and facilitates a conceptual organization that is more useful in guiding treatment.

An instrument I developed for use in my practice and have found useful in my clinical work is included in this chapter, the *Dopamine-Serotonin-Noradrenaline Questionnaire© (DSNQ)*. While not empirically validated, its use has greatly increased my "hit rate" of trials with medications. Rather than relying only on trial and error, I have effectively used this instrument as a tool to provide a more educated guess regarding selections of medications. Symptoms are grouped and scored according to neurotransmitter functioning. Medications can then be chosen to compliment the DSNQ profile.

For example, a syndrome characterized by symptoms associated with low dopamine, low serotonin, and high noradrenaline (inattention, agitated dysthymia, hypermotoric) might respond best to Cylert (to increase dopamine), Zoloft (an SSRI to increase Serotonin), and clonidine (an alpha-2 agonist to decrease noradrenaline).

TABLE 8–1. Examples of Neurotransmitter Dysfunction Symptom Groups

I. Dopamine Low	DL	Inattentive, distractible, disorganized, novelty bias, easily bored, late, creative, digressive
II. Serotonin Low	SL	"Looking at the world through poop colored-glasses," moody, disinhibited, obsessive, worried, migraines, insecure, needy
III. Noradrenaline Low	NL	Low energy ("out of gas")
IV. Noradrenaline High	NH	Over aroused, sensitive, fearful, intense emotions, indignant, angry, hypermotoric, impatient, insomnia, slender, sensitive stomach
V. Serotonin Low Noradrenaline Low	SL NL	Under aroused, pessimistic
VI. Serotonin Low Noradrenaline High	SL NH	High energy, impulsive, agitated depressed
VII. Serotonin Low Noradrenaline Low Dopamine Low	SL NL DL	Pessimistic, under aroused, inattentive, distractible, disorganized
VIII. Serotonin Low Noradrenaline High Dopamine Low	SL NH DL	Inattentive, distractible, disorganized, overaroused, disinhibited, tics, moody, impulsive

USING THE DOPAMINE–SEROTONIN–NORADRENALINE QUESTIONNAIRE (DSNQ): BOB'S BAD BRAIN DAYS

I. Dopamine Low (DL)

At times Bob tends to have low dopaminergic function in his prefrontal cortex. He may have great difficulty working around certain noises and other distractions. This is due to impaired filtering of sensory input from the sense organs of his body that rise upward to his brain and project into his prefrontal cortex. Processing of such input involves selective attention. Dopaminergic output from the prefrontal area maintains selected intention and volition. Low dopaminergic tone results in digressive thinking and multiple parallel lines of thought.

At these times Bob's conversation seems to ramble to others who sometimes get impatient with him when he does not get to the point. His friends might complain that he is getting off the subject. Bob thinks he is just trying to give a complete explanation. When others try to talk with him, he has trouble listening. He may stop listening to someone and, without realizing it, become lost in his thoughts. When listening to presentations, lectures, or sermons, Bob catches his mind wandering and thinking about something else. It is difficult for him to concentrate while reading unless the material is very interesting to him. When he is really involved in an activity, he tends not to hear when people address him.

Bob tends to think about many things at the same time, like a juggler with many balls in the air, or a person watching several or more TV channels at the same time. He has great difficulty attending to just one thing at a time.

Bob tends to be afflicted with a novelty bias. He has lots of enthusiasm for beginning a project, but loses interest once the newness wears off. He then gets sidetracked by the next new thing that blows by and hijacks his attention.

Bob is often late. He tries to be on time, but has great difficulty keeping track of time. He knows it is time to come out of the shower when the water turns cold.

Bob needs to be in hot pursuit or on the hunt of some important goal and to see some immediate results to keep interested in a job. Otherwise he tends to lose interest. On the job, Bob has to do or learn a lot of things that are intensely boring to him. He needs things to be changing constantly to keep from getting bored. Bob is very good at coming up with creative and original solutions to problems, but has trouble following through with them.

Bob is a pack rat. He hates to throw something away that he may later need. He has great difficulty keeping his room, house, or office neat. Some days he just can't seem to get organized. He has trouble pacing himself with long projects. He tends to wait until the last minute and then tries to do it all at once. When Bob has a list of things to do, it is difficult for him to decide what is most important and what sequence to do them in.

Bob has great difficulty conforming to rules if they don't make sense to him or if he doesn't agree with them. Bob often makes mistakes because he acts before considering the potential consequences.

Once Bob has been interrupted from working on a task, he finds it hard to get started again. He often fails to get something done because he got sidetracked and ended up doing something else. On "bad dopamine days" Bob seems to have two left feet. He is clumsy and accident-prone. The world seems like one big banana peel just waiting for his foot. His fine motor coordination is also poor. His handwriting is messy and his speech is awkward. He gets his words all jumbled up when he tries to speak.

Using the DSNQ Self Rating Scale

Please rate whether the characteristics below describe you as compared with most people you know. Use the following scale:

0 Not at all (Does not apply to me)
1 Just a little (Not much of a problem)
2   Pretty much (Somewhat of a problem)
3 Very much (A target symptom for treatment)

Self Rating for DL

001 _____ I have great difficulty working around certain noises and other distractions.

002 _____ I often think about many things at the same time, like a juggler with many balls in the air.

003 _____ I tend to have a lot of enthusiasm for new projects, but I lose interest when the newness wears off.

004 _____ Others get impatient with me when I do not get to the point.

005 _____ I seem to be late often, even though I try to be on time.

006 _____ I stop listening to someone talking and, without realizing it, get lost in my thoughts.

007 _____ I keep a messy room, desk, house, or office.

008 _____ I need to be in hot pursuit of some important goal and to see some immediate results to keep interested in a job.

009 _____ I am easily bored.

010 _____ I need things to be constantly changing to hold my interest.

011 _____ I am very good at coming up with creative and original ideas, but have trouble following through with them.

012 _____ I tend to toss written instructions aside, preferring to figure it out my own way.

013 _____ I am a pack rat. I hate to throw away something that I may later need.

014 _____ I have trouble with organization.

015 _____ When listening to someone talk, I catch my mind wandering and thinking about something else.

016 _____ It is difficult to concentrate on something unless the material is very interesting to me.

017 _____ I tend not to hear people addressing me when I'm busy.

018 _____ I have difficulty conforming to rules if they don't make sense to me.

019 _____ I have trouble pacing a long project. I wait until I have to cram at the last minute.

020 _____ I tend to act before thinking through the possible consequences.

021 _____ It is difficult for me to decide what things are most important to do or what order to do them in.

022 _____ I often lose track of time.

023 _____ People complain that I am "getting off the subject" when I am just trying to give a complete explanation.

024 _____ I find it hard to get started again after being interrupted from a task.

025 _____ I often fail to get something done because I become sidetracked into doing something else.

026 _____ I work best when I do things my own way.

027 _____ I quickly run out of steam if a task takes too long.

028 _____ Once I get into doing something, I find it difficult to stop and change to another activity.

029 _____ I often say what's on my mind before considering the situation, the timing, or how others might react.

030 _____ I tend to be accident-prone.

031 _____ I have difficulty getting my thoughts down on paper.

II. Serotonin Low (SL)

Bob has "low serotonin days" too. On these days he has difficulty supressing thoughts, urges, appetites, worries about the future and feels insecure and emotionally needy. He is more distracted by his thoughts than noise from the world around him. He can't seem to control his thoughts. He can get a thought stuck in his head that plays over and over like a broken record. He can't seem to keep worrisome thoughts from intruding into his thinking. He worries about whether there will be enough money, enough security, enough safety, whether things will turn out all right in the future. His friends tell him that he shouldn't wear himself out needlessly worrying, but Bob can't escape the feeling that he needs to be very mindful of these things to make sure the future is secure.

He feels he can't keep himself from repeating certain actions over and over even though he knows they are not necessary (washing hands, checking locks, counting things). He often has to go back and check things, such as a lock, several times before he can feel confident that it is secured "right." He feels an intense need to check over and over to make sure he did certain things "just right."

At times he becomes too preoccupied with cleanliness or orderliness to concentrate on what he is supposed to be doing. He often feels emotionally insecure, fragile, and vulnerable. He feels such strong cravings for something that he can't stop thinking about wanting or needing it. He seems to have very little will power. He often finds it difficult to suppress even small urges to do certain things that he knows he really doesn't want to or shouldn't do.

On low serotonin days Bob can be such an extreme perfectionist that he has difficulty finishing a task on time. At these times his friends accuse him of being stubborn. Bob just works best when allowed to do things his way.

On such days Bob is moody. He can never predict what mood he'll be in from day to day. He feels he is not the person he should or wanted to be. He feels he has achieved less than he was capable of. He often doesn't feel confident enough to take a risk that he knows he needs to take. Once Bob starts arguing, he finds it very difficult to stop himself. He can't seem to "chill out" or "put a lid on it." Even though he wants to stop, he cannot resist the urge to have the last word.

Bob tends to worry about whether others are critical and rejecting of him. He needs a lot of reassurance to feel accepted and appreciated. He often feels a strong need for someone or something to make him feel emotionally secure. At such times Bob feels that he would put forth more effort if he felt it would make any difference in the long run. He feels things will turn out the same in the end no matter what he does.

Bob feels an intense longing for something or someone, to make him feel safe and secure, less lonely and empty inside. He experiences strong cravings, and gets preoccupied with feelings of wanting or needing something. Bob has erratic mood swings. He can easily get in a negative mood. Like the proverbial pessimist, the glass always looks half empty on a low serotonin day. He worries that he is not competent and successful enough. He worries that things will not work out right.

Self Rating for SL

032 _____ I am almost always worrying about something.

033 _____ I have frequent mood changes.

034 _____ I have certain thoughts that I can't stop thinking over and over.

035 _____ I can be such a perfectionist that I have difficulty finishing a task on time.

036 _____ I have frequent headaches.

037 _____ I can't help repeating certain actions over and over (washing hands, checking locks, counting things, etc.).

038 _____ I can become too occupied with cleanliness or orderliness to concentrate on what I am trying to do.

039 _____ I often feel emotionally insecure, fragile, or vulnerable.

040 _____ I can have such strong cravings for something that I can't stop thinking about wanting or needing it.

041 _____ I seem to have very little will power.

042 _____ I never know what mood I'll be in from day to day.

043 _____ I often feel that I am not the person I should or wanted to be.

044 _____ I feel that I achieved far less than I am capable of.

045 _____ I often don't feel confident enough when I have to take needed risks.

046 _____ Once I start arguing, I find it difficult to stop. I seem to have to have the "last word."

047 _____ I often have to go back and check something several times before I can feel confident that I did it right.

048 _____ I easily feel rejected and need a lot of reassurance to feel accepted and appreciated.

049 _____ I often feel like things will turn out the same in the end no matter what I do.

050 _____ I often feel an intense longing for something, or someone, to make me feel safe, secure, and less lonely.

051 _____ I can easily get stuck in a negative mood (pessimistic outlook).

052 _____ I often find it difficult to stop talking "on and on" about something that's really not that important.

053 _____ I am often more distracted by my own thoughts than things going on around me.

054 _____ I tend to worry about future things that aren't really a problem yet.

III. Noradrenaline Low (NL)

Bob begins his "low noradrenaline days" with difficulty waking up from the night's sleep. He then continues to have trouble throughout the day staying alert for long periods of time without becoming sleepy, tired, or disinterested. He has difficulty sustaining effort for tasks that take a long time. He just runs out of steam before the job is finished. He has difficulty staying awake if he's not active, such as if he has to sit for a long time. He feels he has no energy at all, even for thinking or doing ordinary tasks that should be easy. He has to keep on the move during the day. If he doesn't stay active he becomes sluggish and sleepy. He feels the need for a highly stimulating experience to make him feel awake, clearheaded, and alive. He feels as though he doesn't fully wake up during the day. At times Bob is too tired or just doesn't have enough energy to restrain his emotions.

Self Rating for NL

055 _____ If I don't stay active I become sluggish and sleepy.

056 _____ I feel like I seldom ever fully wake up.

057 _____ At times I'm too tired or just don't have enough energy to restrain my emotions or behavior.

058 _____ I crave excitement to make me feel awake, clear headed, and "alive."

059 _____ I have difficulty waking up in the morning.

060 _____ I often have trouble staying alert for long periods of time without becoming sleepy, tired, or disinterested.

061 _____ I am a deep sleeper.

062 _____ At times I feel I have no energy at all, even for thinking.

063 _____ I often find that the more tired I get the harder it is for me to settle down and go to sleep.

064 _____ I can drink caffeine and go right to sleep without any difficulty.

065 _____ I tend to gain weight easily.

066 _____ I have difficulty staying awake when sitting for a long time.

067 _____ Drugs that make most people sleepy, such as Benadryl, tend to speed me up instead.

IV. Noradrenaline High (NH)

Bob has "high noradrenaline days." At these times he has an extremely high level of energy and activity. He can, however, become jittery, nervous, restless, all keyed up, and impatient. Everything seems urgent to him and needs to be done yesterday.

Alarm: At these times Bob can experience a sudden attack of fearfulness, of a sense of danger, without being aware of any specific reason. He easily gets defensive, and will argue a point just for the principle of it. He tends to make mountains out of molehills. He has a hot temper with episodic outbursts of intense anger. Bob has great difficulty keeping quiet about situations that he perceives as unjust or unfair, even if he knows it will get him into trouble to argue about it.

Instinctual Drive Activation: On the other hand, his friends tell him he is too tender hearted, that he shouldn't take things to heart so much. He cries at the sad part of movies and his moods are intense. He can become too emotionally intense over what others see as no big deal.

Peripheral Autonomic System: Bob has a lot of gastrointestinal problems. His appetite fluctuates, he gags easily, is prone to nausea, diarrhea, and reflux esophagitis (heartburn). His sleep is fitful and irregular.

Self Rating for NH

068 _____ I have a "hot" temper.

069 _____ It doesn't take much caffeine to make me nervous or unable to sleep.

070 _____ I am too "tender hearted." I shouldn't take things to heart so much.

071 _____ I have intense moods.

072 _____ I have nightmares.

073 _____ I tend to be impatient.

074 _____ I am a light sleeper.

075 _____ I am a picky eater.

076 _____ I tend to gag easily.

077 _____ I am prone to nausea.

078 _____ I am prone to reflux esophagitis (heartburn).

079 _____ I tend to be highly reactive to situations that I see as unjust or unfair.

080 _____ At times I have an unusually high level of energy.

081 _____ At times I get jittery, nervous, restless, "all keyed up."

082 _____ I tend to develop diarrhea, especially under stress.

083 _____ I tend to lose weight easily.

084 _____ Caffeine can make me nervous and keep me awake at night.

085 _____ Drugs that make most people drowsy, such as Benadryl, make me drowsy as well.

086 _____ I often feel scared in ordinary situations.

087 _____ I will tend to argue a point "just for the principal" of it.

088 _____ I tend to "make mountains out of mole hills."

V. Serotonin Low, Noradrenaline Low (SL, NL)

At these times Bob tends to struggle with feeling unmotivated. He becomes depressed, feeling that life is just too much trouble, that things will never get better. Even ordinary activities seem to require too much effort. He finds himself thinking, "it's no use to try." Bob feels helpless and hopeless, that things will never get better. He feels just "sick and tired of feeling sick and tired."

When Bob's brain is "out of gas" he just doesn't have the energy or even the inclination to restrain his thoughts, feelings and behavior. At these times he is like a steam pot that leaks too much to hold any pressure at all.

Self Rating for SL and NL

089 _____ I often feel helpless.
090 _____ I often feel hopeless, that things will never get better.
091 _____ I often struggle with feeling unmotivated.
092 _____ I often feel that "it's just no use to try."
093 _____ I tend to easily become constipated.
094 _____ I often feel I feel it will take too much effort to do even ordinary activities.
095 _____ I often feel "sick and tired of feeling sick and tired."
096 _____ I often feel that life is just too much trouble.
097 _____ I often feel I can't muster the energy to control my thoughts, emotions, or behavior.
098 _____ The more tired I get, the more restless I become.

VI. Serotonin Low, Noradrenaline High (SL, NH)

At these times Bob has a low tolerance for frustration. His emotional intensity often creates problems with others. He tends to be emotionally overreactive. He displays outbursts of temper.

Bob is oppositional to authority or rules. He is argumentative and tends to be critical of others. Small imperfections can really get on his nerves. He is very demanding and not easily satisfied. He tries not to overreact so much, but he usually doesn't realize he's overreacting until its too late. Bob is quick to become very emotional. He experiences extreme mood swings. In a split second he can become extremely happy or excited. Then, in an instant, he can as rapidly become sad or upset. Once Bob gets upset, he finds it hard to cool down until he has blown off steam. He gets angry too quickly and blows his top, but then gets over it and forgets it just as quickly. This is disconcerting to his friends who cannot brush off these emotional outbursts so easily.

At these times Bob is tense. It is hard for him to suppress the urge to move around and fidget when he is supposed to be sitting still. He has great difficulty keeping himself from moving too much and talking too much. He experiences migraine headaches and abdominal pains and at night he has difficulty relaxing and great difficulty getting to sleep. He seems to have just too much energy that won't shut off.

Bob experiences sudden rushes of intense feelings that something bad is about to happen. He feels apprehensive and on the lookout. He is quick to get defensive when he feels someone is being critical of him. He tends to be suspicious of other people if he doesn't know what they're thinking. He feels he can sense that someone is being critical of him, or blaming him even when they don't come out and say it. His friends tell him not to be so paranoid. This really upsets him. He gets upset and defensive too quickly when criticized, but he can't help feeling attacked.

Bob feels such strong needs for certain things that he can't help giving in to. He may seem argumentative to others, but he feels that he is just sticking up for what he thinks is right. He is very shy. He is so cautious that he often misses opportunities because of holding back too long and not striking while the iron is hot.

Bob feels "keyed up," but in an angry and hostile way. He is a powder keg waiting for a spark. He becomes argumentative with the first person who happens to walk in the room. Minor frustrations fire him up and he overreacts to situations. Once upset, he finds it hard to "chill out" or "get a grip." He escalates into an intense emotional outburst, "blowing up" as if venting a tremendous amount of steam out of his head similar to a steam pot failing to contain too much pressure.

Self Rating for SL and NH

099 _____ I have difficulty relaxing.
100 _____ I tend to be greatly annoyed by the mistakes of others.
101 _____ Small imperfections can really get on my nerves.
102 _____ I tend to have difficulty getting to sleep.
103 _____ I often have stomach or intestinal pains.
104 _____ I tend to be very demanding and not easily satisfied.
105 _____ It is hard to suppress the urge to move around and fidget when I am supposed to be sitting still.
106 _____ I tend to become a "motor mouth" when I get excited.
107 _____ I am quick to become emotional (e.g., happy, excited, sad, upset, etc.).
108 _____ I tend to be suspicious of other people's motives.

109 _____ I am quick to get defensive when someone is critical of me.

110 _____ I often have more energy than I can control.

111 _____ I often feel strong urges that I can't resist.

112 _____ I am very shy.

113 _____ I am "too cautious."

114 _____ When I feel down I tend to get very agitated.

115 _____ I am too emotionally intense for some people.

116 _____ I can easily lose my temper.

117 _____ I am argumentative.

118 _____ Once upset, I find it hard to cool down, to "chill out."

119 _____ I have a low tolerance for frustration.

120 _____ I tend to overreact.

VII. Serotonin Low, Noradrenaline Low, Dopamine Low (SL, NL, DL)

At these times Bob is much like V (SL, NL), but with the addition of cognitive difficulties (inattention, distractibility, disorganization) which compound his problems.

Self Rating for SL, NL, and DL

121 _____ I often just don't have the energy or even the desire to get organized.

122 _____ I become easily fatigued and unable to function around distractions.

123 _____ It takes a great effort to concentrate.

124 _____ I often feel lonely, lost, and defeated.

125 _____ I often wander from task to task and accomplish nothing.

VIII. Serotonin Low, Noradrenaline High, Dopamine Low (SL, NH, DL)

At these times Bob is much like VI (SL, NH), but with the addition of cognitive difficulties (inattention, distractibility, disorganization) which, again, compound his problems.

At these times Bob feels agitated, all "keyed up." He is exquisitely sensitive to certain types of stimulation such as sights, sounds, and touches. The tags in his shirt irritate him and he can't habituate to the stimulation. Even the seams in his socks drive him crazy. He is physically touchy and if someone touches him, even as a kind gesture, he reflexively pulls away from what feels aversive to him. He can become aggressive when angry. Though he doesn't get physically aggressive, he can look pretty scary during one of his furies. He is easily annoyed and upset, or emotionally "touchy." He then can be stubborn and inflexible. Once he gets onto a negative track he has trouble getting off. He can get stuck on a negative way of seeing things and ruin the rest of the day. He doesn't realize at the time that he is overreacting; he perceives himself as the victim of others' mistreatment. He tends to get on the opposite end of a bone. He is difficult to calm down once upset.

On these days Bob is constantly worrying about something. He is compulsive about doing everything "just right." He has difficulty adjusting easily to minor changes in his expected routine and tends to avoid new situations. He tends to procrastinate or avoid tasks that are most important, worrying about how well he will do.

Bob finds that he cannot suppress urges to scratch, twitch, sniff, or stretch. He is constantly aware of some uncomfortable sensation that he can't supress the urge to respond to.

Self Rating for SL, NH, and DL

126 _____ I tend to procrastinate or avoid tasks, especially when I am worried about my performance.

127 _____ I can get aggressive when angry.

128 _____ I am very stubborn (excessively persistent).

129 _____ I get stuck on an idea, feeling, or activity and have difficulty letting it go.

130 _____ I often don't realize I'm overreacting until it's too late.

131 _____ I tend to be oppositional to authority or rules.

132 _____ Seams in my socks or tags in my clothes often irritate me.

133 _____ I tend to pull away when someone touches me when I don't expect or initiate it.

134 _____ I find it hard to suppress the urge to move certain ways (scratch, sniff, stretch, twitch, blink, clear throat, etc.).

135 _____ I am over sensitive to certain types of stimulation such as sights, sounds, and touches.

136 _____ I can become physically aggressive when angry.

137 _____ I tend to be emotionally touchy (easily annoyed and upset).

138 _____ I have difficulty adjusting to changes in my routine.

139 _____ I tend to withdraw, avoid, or feel negatively toward new situations.

TABLE 8–2. Medications for Neurotransmitter Dysfunction Groups

Symptom Group	Medications	Examples
I. DL	DOP stimulant	Adderall, Dexedrine, Desoxyn, Ritalin, Cylert
II. SL	SSRI	Zoloft, Prozac, Paxil, Luvox
III. NL	NA stimulant	Adderall, Dexedrine, Desoxyn, Ritalin
	NA antidepressant	Desipramine, Effexor
IV. NH	Alpha-2	Clonidine, Tenex
V. SL NL	SSRI + NA stimulant	Zoloft + Adderall
	SER + NA antidepressant	Imipramine, Effexor, Wellbutrin
VI. SL NH	SSRI + Alpha-2	Zoloft + Clonidine
VII. SL NL DL	SSRI + NA & DOP stimulant	Zoloft + Adderall
VIII. SL NH DL	SSRI + Alpha-2 + DOP stimulant	Zoloft + Alpha-2 + Cylert

9

The Medical Management of the Brainstorm Syndrome

There is a lot more to effective treatment using medications than just determining which medications to use in which persons for which symptoms. There are many additional and crucial issues that come into play and that are necessary to address if the medications are to be allowed to do their work.

THE MUSHROOM COLLECTORS

I heard a story years ago during my medical training. The source is unknown to me. The story, as I recall, concerned a group of people who belonged to a mushroom collecting club in the Northwest in the late 1960s. These collectors of natural varieties of mushrooms would go on excursions into the forest to gather exotic varieties. They would then cook their favorite mushroom recipes and have a big potluck dinner. They were well acquainted with the poisonous varieties and careful to avoid them.

On one fateful trip, however, some psilocybin (hallucinogenic) mushrooms were gathered by mistake and the group enjoyed a full dose in the potluck dinner that followed. When the hallucinogenic effects of the mushrooms began to take effect, the group concluded that they must have picked some of the deadly variety by mistake. Panic ensued, ambulances were called, and they all ended up in the community hospital emergency room "deathly ill." (I would not be surprised to hear that some members of this club have never eaten another mushroom to this day!)

To their surprise, however, as the news spread, flocks of hippies came questing for the magic mushrooms and inquiring as to where they could be found. The victims of the mushroom "poisoning" could not understand why anyone would want to subject themselves voluntarily to such an experience. The hippies, however, considered this a consciousness-expanding, even a religious experience. This story illustrates the power of expectations in shaping response to medications.

Medications come to symbolize many things. One is the expectations and hopes of the physician who prescribes them, or how a therapist who works directly with the patient views the symptoms, side effects, role of the medication, expected benefits, and possible risks. If the patient experiences these persons as respectful, genuinely interested, and projecting a vision of a better future for the patient, then this is the message in the pill. This is what gets incorporated with each swallow.

(*Note*: This book is not intended to replace appropriate diagnosis and/or treatment, when indicated, by a qualified physician. Do not alter any medication treatment program without the explicit approval and direction of the treating physician.)

THE MEDICINE MAN: SCIENTIST, SHAMAN, OR SORCERER?

The Case of Timothy

An angry adolescent was brought to me by his parents. Timothy was a tall, thin, soft-spoken teenage boy with a handsome, gentle puppy dog face that was trying to hide under a fragile, adolescent cool. He had been thrown out of a treatment program because of his passive resistance to treatment. He refused to take any medication, became sleepy and bored with any discussions, and was refusing to talk to anyone about anything.

Timothy's parents agreed to bring him weekly for a while. Their job was to get him there. Beyond that, discussions would be strictly confidential. They were not to ask him about what was discussed during the visits. They were also not to ask him whether he was taking his medication.

Timothy came, arms crossed, and made it clear that we would not accomplish anything. He gave only brief, one-word answers. He watched the clock and reminded me of how much time we had left. He asked if he could leave a little early because he was meeting some friends. He arrived late for his appointments and often forgot them entirely.

His parents kept the faith and stuck to their job of doing their best to remain supportive of his visits with me despite his efforts to sabotage them.

The sessions consisted mainly of my flying an airplane on the computer. Timothy went along, humoring me, watching me try to fly under the Golden Gate Bridge without crashing into it. In time he could not keep from wanting to try. Soon a laugh escaped his lips every now and then. We never talked about any of his problems.

Timothy was used to any communication with an adult resulting in blame and advice about how he needed to "shape up." The experience of shared experience in a casual and free-flowing fashion seemed novel to him. Soon he began to forget the time and seemed disappointed when the visit ended. At the end he would remember his bravado, reestablish his cool, and saunter out the door.

After about six visits Timothy's parents called to let me know that whatever we were talking about in the sessions was paying off. Timothy appeared much more relaxed, his mood had improved, and they believed he was now taking his medication regularly. The reports from school indicated that his behavior there had improved greatly. What kind of science, wisdom, or sorcery had I employed to help Timothy?

Had Timothy's parents known that we were flying an airplane on the computer they might have responded with, "Is this what we're paying you for? To have fun with him? Why aren't you discussing his problems with him?"

The relationship between a patient and one having knowledge of the healing arts is as old as human experience itself. Whether one is a scientist, shaman, or sorcerer, some fundamentals of this relationship remain the same.

I have found that when the rapport with a patient is good, the patient will usually be compliant with the treatment plan, including prescribed medications. It is important that a medication symbolize my positive regard and hopes for the patient. Too often the label on the bottle is perceived as a sign around the patient's neck that says "defective" and "shame" in neon lights for all the world to see.

Often a therapist will work with a prescribing physician. In the case of nonmedical therapists, it is still important to cultivate knowledge and insight into the purposes, mechanisms, side effects, risks, and mythology of a given medication. The patient is always susceptible to how the therapist perceives or misperceives medication whether this is explicitly revealed or not. When there is a good foundation of knowledge regarding medical treatment, and the therapeutic rapport is sound, the patient may then begin to reveal previously unstated fears and misgivings. These may relate not only to medications but to other concerns as well.

This finally happened with Timothy one day, after a crisis brought him in for a visit. On that occasion he suddenly talked freely and directly about his concerns. After that, we usually didn't get to the airplane and didn't seem to need it anymore (although we did take it up for a spin occasionally just for fun!).

"UNLABELED" USES OF APPROVED MEDICATIONS: COMMON MISCONCEPTIONS

We will take time here to address an extremely important issue related to the medical treatment of brainstorm syndromes. This relates to the use by physicians of Food and Drug Administration approved drugs for so called "unlabeled" purposes. It is a common misconception among insurance companies, and even among some physicians that it is not "right" to prescribe outside FDA guidelines. Afraid of assuming liability, many insurance companies refuse to reimburse for so called off-label uses of medications. It is generally not appreciated how much of common and accepted practice includes uses of FDA "approved" drugs for "unapproved" purposes. This is especially true in the field of psychopharmacology and even more so in pediatric populations.

To put this very important issue in perspective, it is necessary to understand a bit about the basic steps of new drug development, the mission of the FDA, what the *Physician's Desk Reference* is, and what "indication" means in these contexts. The above concerns are addressed in a letter published in the FDA Drug Bulletin of April 1982, under the title "Use of Approved Drugs for Unlabeled Indications," reproduced below:

> The appropriateness or the legality of prescribing approved drugs for uses not included in their official labeling is sometimes a cause of concern and confusion among practitioners.
>
> Under the Federal Food, Drug, and Cosmetic (FD&C) Act, a drug approved for marketing may be labeled, promoted, and advertised by the manufacturer only for those uses for which the drug's safety and effectiveness have been established and which FDA has approved. These are commonly referred to as "approved uses." This means that adequate and well-controlled clinical trials have documented these uses, and the results of the trials have been reviewed and approved by FDA.
>
> The FD&C Act does not, however, limit the manner in which a physician may use an approved drug. Once a product has been approved for marketing, a physician may prescribe it for uses or in treatment regimens or patient populations that are not included in approved labeling. Such "unapproved" or, more precisely, "unlabeled uses" may be appropriate and rational in certain circum-

stances, and may, in fact, reflect approaches to drug therapy that have been extensively reported in medical literature.

The term "unapproved uses" is, to some extent, misleading. It includes a variety of situations ranging from unstudied to thoroughly investigated drug uses. Valid new uses for drugs already on the market are often first discovered through serendipitous observations and therapeutic innovations, subsequently confirmed by well-planned and executed clinical investigations. Before such advances can be added to the approved labeling, however, data substantiating the effectiveness of a new use or regimen must be submitted by the manufacturer to FDA for evaluation. This may take time and, without the initiative of the drug manufacturer whose product is involved, may never occur. For that reason, accepted medical practice often includes drug use that is not reflected in approved drug labeling.

With respect to its role in medical practice, the package insert is informational only. FDA tries to assure that prescription drug information in the package insert accurately and fully reflects the data on safety and effectiveness on which drug approval is based.

The History and Mission of the FDA

In 1938 the FDA was given authority by the federal government to approve drugs. Drug manufacturing companies had to get approval concerning the safety of new drugs. In 1962 requirements for approval were expanded so that the company must also establish the effectiveness of a new drug before it can make claims about its effectiveness in its advertising and package labeling.

It is not the role of the FDA to suggest new uses of old drugs, nor does the FDA do any drug development research. The issue is not whether the FDA is concerned with public welfare; it is not charged with taking the initiative for new drug research and development. The FDA is strictly a regulatory agency for drug manufacturing companies and advertising agencies.

New Drug Development

Today most new drug research and development is in the hands of private drug manufacturing companies. The mission of these companies is profit. The aim of new drug development is to invent or discover a new drug for which a patent can be obtained. Drug patents are awarded to the company for a set number of years and then other companies may make generic versions and compete with the original company. Once a new drug is found to have a potential market and is patented, the race is on. Many millions of dollars and the better part of a decade are invested in going through the process of obtaining FDA approval.

Once the new drug is approved and marketing begins, there is little incentive to continue to research additional indications for its use. By the time approval could be obtained by the FDA for a new use, the patent would usually be close to expiring. Once a patent expires, other companies may then manufacture inexpensive generics which decrease the drug's profitability. Manufacturers are reluctant to invest money in a drug only to have competitors reap the benefits. The commercialization of new drug development has shifted the primary motive for drug research and development away from the best medical interests of the patient to the best financial interests of the pharmaceutical companies.

Keeping Up with the Medical Literature: 10, 000 Journals!

The primary responsibility for advancing research on new indications for existing drugs rests in the hands of academic research institutions such as universities, schools of medicine, and government-sponsored institutions such as the National Institutes of Health (NIH). Results of new research are published in the more than 10,000 medical journals that circulate to physicians who try to keep abreast of new developments in their respective fields. It is common practice for physicians to prescribe medications for new uses that have not gone through the process of FDA approval, if such uses are adequately supported by such literature.

Physician's Desk Reference or Manufacturer's Liability Reference?

In accordance with FDA requirements, a summary of information about each drug is contained in the drug label. This information is too extensive to actually fit as a label on a medication bottle. Instead, the label is inserted in the box in which the medication is shipped. Most patients never see the drug label. Some may refer to the collection of labels or package inserts of currently available drugs which comprises *The Physician's Desk Reference (PDR)*. The *PDR* does not review so-called "unapproved" uses of medications. It also tends to list so many possible adverse effects of a given medication that one is left with the impression that all medications can cause all possible adverse outcomes. The *PDR* does little to help in weighing the potential benefits versus risks necessary to make an informed decision and to give an informed consent. It's main value to the pharmaceutical industry is the legal protection it affords manufacturers. Many physicians prefer to use other sources that are written specifically for the prescribing clinician, such as the American Medical Association's *Drug Evaluations Annual*.

Informed Consent for "Off Label" Uses of Approved Drugs

Appendix A includes a form that I use in my practice to document the informed consent for "unapproved" uses of FDA-approved drugs. While this form cannot substitute for legal counsel, it provides an illustration of some key points. It is important to remember that informed consent for medical treatment is not simply a process of having the patient sign a form. Consent forms only aide the documentation of a process. The real process of informed consent is the result of an active collaboration and ongoing dialogue between physician and patient.

THE RESPONSIBILITY OF THE PHYSICIAN TO TREAT EFFECTIVELY

Since the time of Hypocrites, the oath of the physician has been to "first, do no harm." To many, this means that to withhold effective treatment may not help the patient, but at least it does no harm. Risk-aversive physicians thus argue that they are not willing to assume any risk in treating their patients and will use only very conservative approaches. The risks of not using an available and effective treatment, and of failing to control a disabling problem are less often discussed. Risks of treatment are emphasized, risks of not treating are not.

In an age of escalating malpractice litigation, more and more physicians are opting for very conservative treatments to protect themselves from liability. A malpractice insurance underwriter recently made the recommendation to me never to prescribe outside the *PDR* guidelines or I would be extremely vulnerable in a lawsuit. The subtleties of the FDA guidelines would be lost on a jury made up of lay "peers."

If enough scientific evidence exists to support that a specific unlabeled use of a drug may control otherwise seriously disabling symptoms and pose minimal and manageable risk, is it the ethical obligation of the physician to discuss this option with the patient? Is it ethical to withhold this treatment for the "best interests" of the physician or insurance company rather than the patient? At this point in the history of medicine, each physician is left to struggle with his or her conscience.

RATIONAL COMPLEX PHARMACOTHERAPY

Given that, in current psychiatric practice, there is a lack of specific treatments directed at etiology, the practitioner is often left with the use of nonspecific treatments for syndromal disorders or target symptoms.

Meltzer (1987)

At the time of my medical training, a popular idea in the use of medications was that the best treatment used only one medication for a single diagnosis. This followed from the antibiotic era when it was that there was only one assumed cause for one diagnosis. A single medication (e.g., Penicillin) was thought to target a single cause (e.g., pneumococcus). The term polypharmacy was used pejoratively to refer to the "bad" practice of using multiple medications to treat "one" diagnosed disorder.

Today we have come a long way. Choosing a medication is often based more on target symptoms than on diagnosis. Medications such as the selective serotonergic reuptake inhibitors (SSRIs) target clusters of symptoms that do not define any specific diagnosis. Instead these symptoms appear to define syndromes that span many diagnostic categories.

Many disorders are complex, involving multiple causes and dimensions. Often much better effects can be attained using smaller doses of several medications that have complementary mechanisms of action or that target different symptoms.

The need to use combinations of medication has arisen out of the often less than satisfactory response to single agents and the apparent synergistic effects of certain combinations of medications. The old term polypharmacy is now being replaced by the more modern term, *rational complex pharmacotherapy* (Wilens et al., 1995, p. 110–114).

It is hoped, of course, that a patient will respond to a single medication. In complex cases this may be the exception rather than the rule. This presents a need to understand the additive and interactive beneficial effects and adverse effects of a large number of potential combinations of medications.

We will not make a comprehensive review here of the vast array of available medications that can be helpful in treating neurobiological disorders. There is an ample supply of excellent texts that have done this well. We will focus here on a few of the finer points of using these medications in concert.

The Cortical Stimulants: "Squeezing the Sponge"

The cortical stimulants, or "psychostimulants"—Ritalin, Dexedrine, Cylert, Adderall, Desoxyn—are usually short-acting "releasing agents" that increase the release of neurotransmitters from the nerve terminal and into the synaptic space. This is a bit like squeezing a sponge and leads to a rapid onset of effect and a "rapid fall-off" or short withdrawal period. This results in a bell-shaped curve of effects with therapeutic, peak, and withdrawal effects. The rapid-withdrawal phase often produces a time commonly referred to as the "rebound period."

The cortical stimulants are most often used for increasing: alertness, focus of attention, span of attention, fine motor coordination (writing, speech), cognitive organization, and for decreasing: impulsivity, hyperactivity, fidgetiness, and distractibility. Table 9–1 provides a "thumbnail sketch" of the therapeutic effects and side effects of medications that increase the release of dopamine, serotonin, and noradrenaline.

Increasing Dopamine: Selection, Filtering, Span of Attention/Intention

This is like tightening up the steering, stepping on the gas, and stepping on the brakes. The engine runs a little hotter and the rpms are up, but there is more control of this energy. It can be directed along the desired trajectory toward the desired destination. Speed can be controlled by active braking.

Increasing Serotonin

This will be explained in more detail in the section on SSRIs. Briefly, the release of serotonin results in increased mood stability, confidence, and optimism, and decreased impulsivity, hyperactivity, anxiety, irritability, and mood swings.

Increasing Noradrenaline

This will be explained in more detail in the section on noradrenaline. Briefly, the release of noradrenaline results in increased arousal, alertness, short-term memory, mental and physical energy, and decreased hyperactivity. In cases where attentional problems are caused by lack of alertness and vigilance from underarousal, attention is improved by increasing arousal resulting in improved alertness and vigilance.

Rebound and Withdrawal Side Effects

"Rebound" problems may occur if the three neurotransmitter effects wear off (out of sync). Dopamine and serotonin effects often wear off first, leaving a high noradrenaline level. In other words, "The brakes give out, the steering wheel gives out, but the gas pedal is still stuck to the floor."

TABLE 9–1. Effects of Dopamine, Serotonin, and Noradrenaline

Dopamine	selection, filtering of distractions, intentionality
Noradrenaline	energizes, activates alarm
Serotonin	mood control, balance of optimism/pessimism, inhibition of impulses

TABLE 9–2. Effects of Enhancing Dopamine, Serotonin, and Noradrenaline Neurotransmission.

Neurotransmitter	Therapeutic Effects	Peak Side Effects	Rebound Side Effects
Dopamine	selective attention; filtering of distractions; intention; percision of fine motor control, (writing, articulation)	hyperfocused; perseveration; detachment; hypersaliency	poor selective attention; distractible; noise intolerance; disinterest; poor sustained attention
Serotonin	mood control; balance of optimism/pessimism; impulse control; cognitive control	emotional flattening; nausea; euphoria; silliness; mania suppressed ejaculation; appetite changes	agitated depression; mood swings; negativity; pessimism; impulsivity; emotionality; OCD symptoms
Noradrenaline	increased mental, physical, and emotional energy; increased cognitive, emotional intensity; goal directed behavior; appraisal of threat, libido; appraisal of fairness; enhanced dopamine effects	expansive; grandiosity; decreased fatigue; insomnia; anxiety (fearful type); paranoia; hostility; aggression; defensiveness; self-righteous indignation	mental, physical, emotional fatigue; apathy; impulsivity (low arousal type); irritability (low arousal type); low vigilance; stimulation-seeking; hunger; sleepiness; anergic depression

Outbursts of energy in the forms of temper or other emotional releases (e.g., crying) can be common occurrences during the rebound period. A child, or even an adult, may vent an enormous amount of energy, which usually takes the form of verbal hostility rather than physical aggression. The emotional storm disappears as quickly as it came, leaving an unexpected calmness and serenity. This perplexes those who do not understand it as an adverse effect of the medication. Extended release formulations decrease rebound effects by wearing off more gradually. Adderall, for example, is an extended release amphetamine that appears to have a uniquely smooth and prolonged effect. The patients that I have treated with Adderall have been virtually free of rebound side effects.

Selective Serotonin Reuptake Inhibitors (SSRIs): Plugging the Synaptic Drain

The mechanism of action of this family of drugs—Zoloft, Paxil, Prozac, Luvox—involves blocking the reuptake pumps on the nerve surface that reabsorb serotonin back into the cell after it has been released into the synaptic space. This is a bit like putting a plug in the bathtub drain.

Some effects of serotonin release were mentioned earlier. When a medication is used to enhance serotonin neurotransmission a broad range of possible symptoms is targeted.

The SSRIs are most often used for decreasing: mood swings, depressive symptoms, anxiety, obsessive and compulsive symptoms, emotional rebound from the cortical stimulants, appetite suppression from stimulants, insomnia, impulsivity, irritability, and symptoms of overarousal.

Although most often referred to as antidepressants, these drugs may relieve many symptoms related to low serotonin. There are at least fourteen known subtypes of serotonin receptors and the number continues to rise as more are constantly discovered. Serotonin is like a key that fits these different locks. Low serotonin is associated with mood dysregulation, anxiety, impulsivity, obsessive-compulsive disorders, eating disorders, sleep disorders, motor tics, and aggressive behavior.

These drugs have the advantage of being highly selective for increasing serotonin. Older agents had varying degrees of noradrenaline effects that, when not needed, could lead to side effects of too much noradrenaline, such as rapid heart beat.

Serotonin-enhancing drugs are taking a more central role in the treatment of certain types of attention problems. Many persons describe attention problems due to obsessive thoughts. When they try to sustain their attention, intrusive thoughts distract them. They are also distracted by intrusive impulses compelling them to do things. They are less distracted by external stimuli, and thus the problem is less a result of poor dopaminergic noise filtering. Stimulants may increase or decrease obsessive and compulsive symptoms in such individuals.

Addition of an SSRI often improves attention by allowing the person to actively inhibit intruding thoughts and impulses and thus maintain the intended focus of attention.

The Alpha-2 Agonists: "Turning Down the Steam"

The alpha-2 agonists—clonidine and guanfacine—inhibit certain noradrenergic circuits such as those in the locus coeruleus and reticular activating system. Recent interest has focused on effects in the frontal cortex that normalize memory function. Chapter 10 is devoted to clonidine; we will not repeat that information here. We will elaborate here how clonidine and similarly acting alpha-2 agonists may be coordinated with other medications.

The alpha-2 agonists are most often used to decrease overarousal, hyper-reactivity, hypervigilance, frustration intolerance, irritability, distractibility, anxiety, hyperactivity, aggression, motor tics, stuttering, and symptoms of somatic overarousal (hypertension, irritable bowel syndrome, etc.).

BALANCING DOPAMINE, SEROTONIN, AND NORADRENALINE EFFECTS

Cortical stimulants and Alpha-2 Agonists

Some people do not tolerate the cortical stimulants because of symptoms of overstimulation. Such persons are often already high on noradrenaline. They have too much energy, and this is the basis for high distractibility, reactivity, hyperactivity, anxiety, aggression, rapid heart rate with palpitations, and so forth. Stimulants can make this worse.

If an attention problem is due to not enough alertness, the noradrenaline effects from the cortical stimulants wake up the individual and allow normal vigilance. If the medications cause the person to become overstimulated, a state of hypervigilance results. Increased sensitivity to stimuli results in increased distractibility and reactivity. This puts more of a burden on the dopamine filters. Motor activity increases and energy is vented through movement or outbursts of silliness, giddiness, anger, or the like.

Higher noradrenaline activates anxiety, fear, and panic. Persistence is increased, and when the person is frustrated, this energy is redirected and vented by explosive emotional outbursts. In such cases it is often possible to isolate the needed dopamine effects without causing too much of a noradrenaline effect. A useful approach is to combine a noradrenaline-subduing drug such as clonidine or Tenex with the cortical stimulant. This resembles lifting the foot up a bit from the gas pedal, while still preserving the braking and steering power.

Clonidine decreases distractibility, hyperreactivity, anxiety, hostility, and irritability, and improves, for example, frustration tolerance, whether these are primary symptoms of the disorder or produced as side effects from a cortical stimulant. Excessive doses of clonidine, however, produce a loss of energy and dizziness from lowered blood pressure. Achieving a balance with the addition of a cortical stimulant helps to normalize selective attention and arousal.

Cortical stimulants, SSRIs and Alpha-2 Agonists

I have found the following tables useful in balancing effects when using combinations of medicine or when matching a medicine to a particular symptoms profile. The relative magnitude of effects is only a rough approximation based on clinical experience.

Solutions to Common Problems

The information in Table 9–3 can be very helpful in guiding decisions about medication adjustments. It is therefore much easier to make an educated guess directed at maximizing desired effects and minimizing undesired side effects (see Table 9–4).

TABLE 9–3. Approximate Relative Effects of a Range of Medications on Dopamine, Serotonin, and Noradrenaline

Drug	Dopamine	Serotonin	Noradrenaline
Amphetamine*	+++	+	+++
Ritalin	+++	+	++
Cylert	+++		
Clonidine		+	− − −
Tenex		+	− −
SSRIs**		+++	
Desipramine		++	++
Imipramine		++	++
Elavil		++	++
Wellbutrin, Effexor	+	++	++
Buspar		− − (1A receptor)	

*Amphetamine = Dexedrine, Adderall, Desoxyn
**SSRIs = Prozac, Zoloft, Paxil, Luvox

Legend: Relative magnitude of effects
+	=	Mild increase
++	=	Moderate increase
+++	=	Very Much increase
− − −	=	Very Much decrease
− −	=	Moderate decrease
−	=	Mild decrease

TABLE 9–4. Potential Solutions to Some Common Medication Problems

Problem	Solutions
Overstimulation from stimulant	Change to less noradrenergic stimulant Add alpha-2*
Underarousal not remedied with stimulant	Change to more noradrenergic stimulant Add desipramine
Extreme motor hyperactivity rebound from stimulant	Change to extended release formulation Add tapering dose of stimulant Decrease dosage Add alpha-2
Extreme emotional rebound from stimulant	Change to extended release formulation Add tapering dose of stimulant Decrease dosage Add SSRI**
Weight loss from stimulant	Add alpha-2 Decrease dosage Omit afternoon stimulant dose Take afternoon stimulant dose earlier (3–5 p.m.) If using extended release in afternoon, change to regular release Add alpha-2 at bedtime
Waking in the middle of the night	Add alpha-2 at bedtime
Waking in the middle of the night from clonidine tabs at bedtime	Add extended release oral clonidine Clonicel®*** or Tenex at bedtime
Anxiety from stimulant	Change to less noradrenergic stimulant Add alpha-2
Sedation from clonidine tablets	Decrease dose Divide dose into 4–5x/day Change to transdermal patch Change to Clonicel® Change to Tenex

*Alpha-2 (alpha-2 adrenoreceptor agonist) = clonidine or Tenex
**SSRI = Selective serotonin reuptake inhibitor
***Clonicel® = compounded oral extended release clonidine

10
Clonidine: "Turning Down the Steam"

If attention and activity were a steam engine, [Ritalin] increases the heat and applies the brakes; clonidine turns down the heat.

[Hunt 1988 (in Copeland 1991, p. 237)]

Experience with clonidine in clinical practice has shown it to be a very useful medication. Clonidine appears to be exquisitely sensitive in targeting and diminishing symptoms that arise from an overactive and/or overreactive central autonomic nervous system.

A BRIEF HISTORY OF CLONIDINE AND ITS USES

Treating Hypertension

Clonidine has been widely used in medicine since the 1970s for reducing excessive sympathetic tone and resultant autonomic physiologic effects such as elevated blood pressure. It has been approved by the Food and Drug Administration, and the safety of its use has been well documented in extensive literature dealing with adult hypertension.

In recent years many new and thus more profitable antihypertensive medications have been developed, patented, and marketed. The result has been that clonidine, now off patent and inexpensive, has lost the enthusiasm of the manufacturers, who prefer to promote new products still under patent. Clonidine, still very effective and useful, has tended to be overlooked. Important roles remain, however, and new ones appear continually, for such alpha-2 agonists as clonidine.

115

TABLE 10–1. Target Symptoms of Clonidine

impulsivity	frustration intolerance
motor hyperactivity, tics	inattention
over excitability	hyperarousal, hyperactivity
outbursts of anger or aggressivity	underweight
obsessive ideas	anorexia
compulsive behavior	delayed growth
speech difficulties	insomnia
behavioral blocking	mania
argumentativeness	stress reactions
oppositionality, defiance	migraine
irritability	asthma, allergies
anxiety, panic, PTSD	nicotine withdrawal
paranoia	hypertension

Oster and Epstein (1991) believed that these newer medications were, in some respects, inferior to clonidine. They considered this to be the case not only in the treatment of hypertension, but in a wide array of problems relating to autonomic hyperactivity.

Considerable evidence suggests that hyperactivity of the sympathetic nervous system is implicated not only in the pathogenesis of essential hypertension but also in several blood pressure-independent complications of essential hypertension. Even with the advent of newer antihypertensive agents, including angiotension-converting enzyme inhibitors and calcium antagonists, the centrally acting sympatholytics (alpha-2 adrenoceptor agonists) remain a valuable group of medications for the management of hypertension of all grades of severity. [p.1638–44]

THE RAPID EMERGENCE OF NEW OFF LABEL USES

As clonidine waned in the treatment of hypertension, it was being rediscovered as a very useful aid in managing the symptoms of a wide range of neurobiological disorders. What these disorders appear to have in common is a hyperreactive central autonomic nervous system, particularly involving the noradrenergic system. What clonidine contributes to the treatment of these clinical syndromes is a reduction in the symptoms of excessive activation and arousal. Clonidine's effectiveness is a function of the degree to which the clinical symptoms are related to such noradrenergic dysregulation (Hunt 1991).

Clonidine, both alone and in combination with stimulants and other medications, has gained widespread acceptance in the clinical treating community. Johnston et al. (1995) estimated, for example, that more than 100,000 children in the United States were on a methylphenidate-clonidine combination. Clonidine's popularity has grown in spite of the fact that the type of formal clinical trials necessary to gain FDA approval for uses other than in treating adult hypertension have yet to be done. Following is a brief review of the medical and research literature currently available relating to the many emerging "off label" uses of clonidine.

Motor Tics

Clonidine has been used to treat motor tics since 1979. Motor tics are experienced as irresistible, often exacerbated by stress, suppressed for brief periods of time during sleep, occur in bouts several times a day, and have their onset before age 21.

Motor tics appear to reflect high noradrenaline and probably low serotonin as well. Tics often increase with any increase in arousal such as anxiety, or excitement. They can be inhibited voluntarily for short periods of time with conscious effort. A student who is focused on suppressing motor tics, however, is not paying attention to much else.

Medications can have dramatic results in controlling tics. By either decreasing noradrenaline with clonidine, and/or increasing serotonin such as with a serotonergic antidepressant, tics usually are diminished. The older approach of using dopamine receptor blocking agents such as haloperidol (Haldol) also decrease motor tics, as hyperactive motor pathways controlled by dopamine are involved. Clonidine has been found to be an effective and much safer alternative to the more traditional dopamine blocking neuroleptics. Clonidine has distinctive advantages in that it is not known to pose a risk for causing tardive dyskinesia. This is a serious and potentially irreversible movement disorder (Comings 1990) associated with most dopamine blocking agents. The blocking of dopamine receptors may also sacrifice attention and decrease learning and cognitive proficiency. Dopamine blocking agents are now avoided if possible. They are still used in controlling more severe symptoms when other treatments have failed and when the potential benefits outweigh their risks.

Tourette's Syndrome

Tourette's syndrome (TS) is a neurobiological disorder characterized by changing motor and vocal tics, with associated symptoms of obsessive-compulsive ideas and behaviors, and attention deficit disorder with hyperactivity.

Genetic factors seem to play a major role, but the precise mode of inheritance is still not known.

Cohen and colleagues (1979, 1980) first reported that small doses of clonidine improve TS in children. Clonidine was observed to ameliorate the disorder in the majority of 25 patients who could not tolerate or did not benefit from treatment with haloperidol. Clonidine had a gradual onset of action. Compulsive behavior, frustration intolerance, speech difficulties, behavioral blocking, attentional problems, and tics were responsive to treatment. These results suggested that the noradrenergic system may be involved, primarily or secondarily, in the expression of the genetic predisposition to TS.

Leckman and colleagues (1991) noted that TS patients experienced substantial, long-term symptomatic improvement with minimal side effects when taking clonidine. There was also significant improvement in motor and phonic tics. Associated behavioral symptoms appeared to show the most consistent improvement with maximum benefit achieved after 4 to 6 months of treatment. There were no serious side effects and tolerance to clonidine did not develop.

As with simple motor tics, TS had most often been treated with the dopamine receptor blocker haloperidol until the 1980s. In studies by Borison and colleagues (1983), clonidine was shown to be equally efficacious with haloperidol, but did not produce adverse central nervous system side-effects.

Singer and colleagues (1985) found that haloperidol improved tic symptoms in 50/60 patients, but side effects often nullified these benefits. Clonidine was helpful in 47% and caused few side effects.

Attention Deficit Hyperactivity Disorder (ADHD)

Hunt (1985) extended this research to a group of children with ADHD. A controlled clinical trial demonstrated clonidine's usefulness in treating the symptoms of hyperarousal and hyperreactivity in certain children with ADHD. Hunt demonstrated that clonidine improved frustration tolerance and task behavior, and decreased motor hyperactivity, emotional over excitability, hyperreactivity, and outbursts of anger or aggressivity. A comprehensive review of the practical uses of clonidine in children and adolescents appeared in the *Journal of Child and Adolescent Psychopharmacology* (Hunt 1990). Steingard and colleagues (1993) provided further support of a role for clonidine in the treatment of children with ADHD, particularly for those with comorbid tic disorders.

Clonidine appears to be useful when used alone or in combination with other medications, such as cortical stimulants, antidepressants, and so on. In many cases of ADHD, hyperactivity, impulsivity, emotional over excitability, argumentativeness, oppositionality, low frustration tolerance, aggressiveness, irritability, emotional outbursts, anxiety, and so forth are the symptoms that most interfere with normal adjustment. These are the problems that most frequently bring preschoolers and young children to medical attention. For such a child, clonidine alone may be sufficient and better tolerated than a stimulant.

Sleep Disorders

Wilens and colleagues (1994, 1995) reported on the benefits of using clonidine for treating sleep disturbances associated with ADHD. This has been an increasingly common use of clonidine in clinical practice.

Managing Side Effects of Cortical Stimulants: Anxiety, Anorexia, Insomnia, Weight Loss, and Rebound Overarousal

The side affects of the cortical stimulants have been problematic. These typically include decreased appetite (Kalikow and Blumencranz 1996), insomnia (Wilens et al. 1994), potential for increasing motor tics, delayed growth, and numerous "rebound" adverse affects. Patient compliance with Ritalin has long been known to be poor (Firestone 1982) in spite of its beneficial clinical effects.

Referring again to our car analogy, medications like Ritalin improve the steering, step on the gas, and improve the braking power. All together this results in increased arousal and alertness, and improved impulse control and selective attention. Stimulants, however, can have their problems. After several hours, as the effects wear off, things can get out of balance. For a brief time the person may resemble a car that has lost its steering and brakes but still has the gas pedal still stuck to the floor. Impulse control may decrease, but arousal and reactivity may still be high. The stimulus barrier may decrease, resulting in increased reactivity and irritability. Outbursts of anger are a frequent side effect of stimulant use, usually occurring during the rebound period, which is often in the late afternoon or typically about four to five hours after a short-acting dose is taken.

Peak side effects may also result from increased arousal. Higher noradrenaline results in hypervigilance and the fight or flight state. Breakthrough of aggressive outbursts may occur that can be more intense, fueled by the high arousal state.

Suppression of appetite may eventually result in weight loss, usually a temporary effect early in treatment, but sometimes problematic. While the issue of "stunted growth" produced much concern in the past, this issue has pretty much been laid to rest today. Growth slowing, even when significant, is temporary and does not alter the final height achieved in adulthood.

Many children with Tourette's syndrome (TS) are handicapped more by difficulties with inattention, impulsivity, and hyperactivity than by their tics.

However, stimulant medications used to treat attention-deficit hyperactivity disorder (ADHD) can exacerbate tics.

Clonidine may be effectively combined with a stimulant. Stimulants appear to be exquisitely sensitive in targeting and improving selective attention and attention span. Clonidine, on the other hand, serves more to decrease impulsivity, motor hyperactivity, over excitability, outbursts of anger or aggressivity and improve frustration tolerance. (Hunt et al. 1991, 1992). Using clonidine in combination with a psychostimulant appears to result in a synergism of therapeutic benefits, enhancing the effectiveness of both drugs, but also decreasing the side effects of both medications as well. In other words, the therapeutic effects are additive, but the side effects tend to cancel each other out.

Aggression

There is currently no FDA-approved medication for the treatment of aggression. Beta blockers such as propranolol have shown some usefulness as reviewed by Connor (1993). Lithium (Campbell 1995) and Carbamazepine (Silva 1996) have also been used, among many others. Kemph and colleagues (1993) found clonidine to be significantly effective in reducing symptoms in overly aggressive children. Clonidine may thus hold promise as one of the few medications helpful in treating aggression.

Autism

Many autistic children have associated problems of inattention, impulsivity, hyperactivity, and aggressivity that limit the feasibility or effectiveness of educational and behavioral interventions. Clonidine has been shown to be helpful in reducing these symptoms.

Jaselskis and colleagues (1992) examined autistic children with excessive inattention, impulsivity, hyperactivity, and oppositionality. Subjects that had not tolerated or responded to neuroleptics, methylphenidate, or desipramine showed significant improvement with clonidine treatment.

Anxiety Disorders

Generalized Anxiety Disorder (GAD)

Symptoms of generalized anxiety disorder (GAD) such as palpitations, shortness of breath, sweating, dry mouth, hot flashes, abdominal distress, and trouble swallowing may be due to sympathetic autonomic hyperactivity. For some time the beta receptor blocking agents such as propranolol (Inderal) have been shown to decrease such symptoms, especially those involving peripheral adrenergic overexcitation. Clonidine also shows a muting of the autonomic manifestations of anxiety, and appears to have central effects as well. Its effect in decreasing anxiety appears independent of its sedative properties. Clonidine has an advantage over the beta blockers in patients with asthma: the alpha agonists do not pose the risk that the beta blockers do in precipitating an asthma attack.

Social Phobia and Selective Mutism

Seriously symptomatic patients who suffer from social phobia demonstrate marked anxiety in social situations. It is believed that the anxiety symptoms are likely mediated by an adrenergic hyperactivity. Clonidine could be used as an adjunctive treatment for social phobia with other medications: SSRIs (Zoloft), the benzodiazepines (Xanax), and buspirone (Buspar), combined with psychotherapeutic methods.

Panic Disorder

Liebowitz and colleagues (1981) found clonidine to be effective in treating both panic disorder and panic attacks with agoraphobia. Uhde and colleagues (1989) found the antipanic effect did not persist in their study subjects. Clonidine's potential efficacy is based on the possibility that panic disorder is a dysregulation of brain alpha-2 adrenoceptor sensitivity. It is unclear why an initial antipanic effect would not be sustained. The clonidine dose may need to be increased periodically to maintain an antipanic effect. This has been found to be the case when treating many conditions with clonidine and other drugs that are metabolized by the liver. The rapid initial tolerance that appears to plateau slowly after a few weeks or months is most likely due to initial increase in liver enzymes that speeds up the clearance of clonidine. Other limitations of clonidine in panic may be due to its rebound hyperarousal, often experienced when the short-acting oral tablet dose wears off. Rebound hyperarousal could contribute to precipitation of panic. If this were the case, extended release formulations of clonidine would be expected to more clearly provide sustained benefit. (See section on Clonicel® later in this chapter.)

Post-Traumatic Stress Disorder (PTSD)

Genetic studies by Comings and colleagues (1996) examined Vietnam veterans in an addiction treatment unit who had been exposed to severe combat conditions. They found that a DRD2 variant appeared to confer an increased risk for post-traumatic stress disorder (PTSD). The absence of the variant of the gene for making the dopamine receptor was associated with a relative resistance. This suggested that dopamine receptors play a role in PTSD. PTSD symptoms are also believed to be related to noradrenergic hyperarousal, as Nutt (1989) and others (Southwick 1993) have explained. Orr and colleagues (1995) found abnormal physiologic responses to loud tones in Vietnam veterans with post-traumatic stress disorder. Such studies would suggest a potential benefit from treatment with clonidine. Clonidine has been used to treat Cambodian patients with PTSD (Kinzie and Leuing 1989). Hansenne and colleagues (1991) explored the use of clonidine response as a test in evaluating post-traumatic stress.

I have found clonidine useful in my practice as an adjunctive treatment to diminish some of the physiologic hyperreactivity that occurs upon exposure to events that trigger PTSD symptoms. I have found similar benefits from clonidine in treating dissociative disorders such as multiple personality disorder, when related to past traumatic events. The diminution of a conditioned or sensitized autonomic responsivity serves to make memories that induce fear and panic easier to access and detoxify.

Bipolar Disorder (Manic Depressive Illness)

Lithium remains the first line and most effective medication for treating bipolar disorder. Other medications found to be effective include Valproate and Tegretol. Based on the catecholamine hypothesis of mood disorders, the manic phase of bipolar disorder may reflect an extreme state of noradrenergic hyperactivity. A subduing effect on mania by clonidine would certainly support this view. Clonidine has shown some efficacy in treating the manic and mixed phases of bipolar disorder, with minimal side effects (Kontaxakis et al. 1989).

Post-Traumatic Brain Injury (TBI)

There is a broad spectrum of neurophysiological symptoms that characterize the post traumatic brain injury (TBI) syndrome (Gualtieri 1990). Manic syndromes can follow various brain injuries and can greatly complicate rehabilitation and treatment outcome (Starkstein et al. 1988). Bakchine (1989) and other researchers noted that after brain injury there is an increase in noradrenergic transmission that could be a factor in the precipitation of organic mania. Clonidine has shown usefulness in the rapid reversal of the manic symptoms in patients with focal brain damage, especially after bilateral frontal or right temporoparietal lobe lesions.

Psychosis

Several studies have documented the effectiveness of clonidine in treating certain types of schizophrenia characterized by problems with arousal. Clonidine's efficacy supports a role for noradrenaline in the etiology of schizophrenia. It is not surprising that paranoid schizophrenia responds most to treatment with clonidine as this paranoid state is one involving extremely high noradrenergic states similar to those noted in mania. Clonidine may not be a good antipsychotic per se, but it may contribute to stabilizing the overaroused, paranoid aspects of the psychosis. In doing so, clonidine might indirectly potentiate the effectiveness of an antipsychotic.

Conduct Disorder

Schvehla and colleagues (1987) found clonidine to be beneficial in a group of prepubertal boys who had dual diagnoses of attention deficit hyperactivity disorder and conduct disorder. These children responded to clonidine after they failed trials of conventional drug therapy, consisting predominantly of psychostimulants.

Obsessive Compulsive Symptoms

Obsessive and compulsive types of symptoms are associated with a wide range of disorders. They can be selectively targeted by SSRIs in combination with other medications such as clonidine (Cohen et al. 1992). Clonidine may be particularly useful when the OCD symptoms are associated with high arousal states such as excitement, anxiety, and reactions to stress. Hewlet and colleagues (1992) compared the efficacy of clomipramine, clonazepam, and clonidine in the treatment of obsessive-compulsive disorder.

HIV Encephalopathy

Cesena and colleagues (1995) reported on the behavioral manifestations in the a case of a 4-year-old child with acquired immunodeficiency syndrome (HIV). Initial manifestation of central nervous system involvement consisted of a sudden onset of impulsivity, hyperactivity, initial insomnia, and aggressive behavior. This clinical picture suggested an initial presentation of HIV-1 encephalopathy. Clonidine was helpful in ameliorating these behaviors.

Asthma and Allergies

Lindgren and colleagues (1987) compared the effects of clonidine and guanfacine on the histamine liberation from human mast cells and basophiles and on the human bronchial smooth muscle activity. Clonidine, but not guanfacine, inhibited the antigen-induced histamine release from human basophiles and mast cell preparations. Clonidine and guanfacine had no effect on the basal bronchial muscle tone. It was suggested that the inhibitory effects of clonidine on allergic reactions and on excitatory nerve transmission in human airways may be useful in the treatment of asthma or allergies.

Migraine

Clonidine has been used for the treatment of headaches and for the prevention and reduction of narcotic use in migraine patients (Bredfelt et al. 1989).

Narcotic Withdrawal

Clonidine has been used to diminish the signs and symptoms of morphine, heroin, and other narcotic withdrawal (Jasinski 1985, Kleber et al. 1987, Spencer and Gregory 1989).

Potential Benefits for Prefrontal Cortical Deficits

Alpha-2 receptor agonists such as clonidine and guanfacine may reduce prefrontal deficits in working memory, executive function, and focused attention, with relative sparing of episodic short term memory, in patients with Korsakoff's disease, attention deficit disorder, or schizophrenia. These agents appear to have little therapeutic value in patients with dementia of the Alzheimer's type (Arnsten et al. 1996).

BASIC PHARMACOLOGY

Mechanisms of Action

Alpha Receptors

In the brain, the central noradrenergic receptors can be divided pharmacologically into alpha-1 and alpha-2 subtypes. The alpha-1 are postsynaptic receptors, and the alpha-2 are both pre- and postsynaptic receptors. Clonidine activates both subtypes, with preferential activity at the alpha-2 adrenoceptors. Alpha-2 receptors have an autoregulatory function. Their activation appears to have a direct inhibitory action that tends to reduce central noradrenergic activity and decrease noradrenergic transmission.

Locus Coeruleus

The noradrenergic terminals, most of which originate at the locus coeruleus (LC), are widely distributed throughout the brain. Although noradrenergic neurons represent less than one percent of the total population of brain neurons, their high collateralization makes each neuron have as many as half a million terminals. Consequently, the importance of the noradrenergic neurons is great despite their relatively smaller numbers (Moore 1982). Electrophysiological and neurosurgical lesion studies with experimental animals have implicated the ascending dorsal noradrenergic bundle of the locus coeruleus system in cognitive process such as memory, learning, and selective attention (Coull 1994).

Synchronization of Central and Peripheral Autonomic Arousal

The LC is synchronized with the peripheral autonomic system through nuclei in the brainstem. An alerting response in the LC results in immediate changes in the body's heart rate, blood pressure, respiration, skin temperature, sweat glands, and so forth. Measurements of such changes comprise the polygraph test, the interpretation of which depends on the theory that one is more vigilant when fabricting than when remembering. This inference has not been empirically validated and polygraph findings are not currently admissible in court. In medical assessment, interest is focused directly on arousal. Raine and colleagues (1990) found that low arousal, as measured by electrodermal activity, predicted future criminal behavior, supporting the theory that criminality is associated with decreased central autonomic arousal (Eysenck 1977). In my practice I find electrodermal measurements during computerized continuous performance tests (CPTs) help me to better predict medication response.

Prefrontal Cortex

Noradrenaline appears to play a crucial role in the cognitive functions associated with the frontal lobes, particularly the prevention of distractibility by irrelevant stimuli. The alpha 2–receptors of the prefrontal cortex appear to be of particular importance in this respect. Affinity for the alpha-2A adrenergic receptor is associated with improved working memory and attention regulation in the aged primate (Arnsten et al. 1996).

The aged primate brain is prone to profound catecholamine depletion in the prefrontal cortex as well as degeneration of the locus coeruleus. Elderly monkeys show deficits in performance of the delayed response task, which can be reversed directly by both clonidine and the alpha-2 agonist guanfacine.

These results can be explained by an attenuation of the distracting properties of irrelevant stimuli following stimulation of noradrenergic activity. Conversely, distractibility is magnified whenever noradrenergic activity is reduced.

Similar findings have been reported in studies of healthy humans. The exception to this is when the locus coeruleus is firing in response to stress or when novel stimuli are encountered. By decreasing locus coeruleus firing on such occasions, clonidine counteracts the effects of stress on task performance. Such effects, however, may be beneficial or deleterious. Some amount of stress may improve task performance. Too much, however, can interfere from locus coeruleus overdrive.

Bob's Mr. Arousal machine (see chapter 5) again provides us with a common example of this mechanism. Bob knows that test performance anxiety gave him the extra "edge" that helped him stay focused. "Before 'Mr. Arousal,' I couldn't seem to pay attention unless I was a little scared," he acknowledges. At times, however, Bob's anxiety got out of control. "At these times I would freeze, lock up, block, become too distractible and even confused. I couldn't remember things on a test that I knew I had learned. When the test was over I could remember the answers," he laments, "but then it was too late. But Mr. Arousal has fixed all that!"

In real life, where there is no Mr. Arousal machine, medications such as clonidine and various anxiolytic medications can be beneficial in decreasing the deleterious effects of excessive performance anxiety.

Pharmacodynamics

Clonidine is well-absorbed after oral administration. It's bioavailability is nearly 100 percent. The peak plasma concentration and the maximal hypotensive effect are observed in one to three hours after an oral dose. The elimination half-life ranges from six to twenty-four hours with a mean of about twelve hours. This appears to be much shorter in children and adolescents, probably due to more rapid hepatic metabolism. About half of an administered dose can be removed unchanged from the urine, and in patients with renal failure the half-life may be increased. There is good correlation between the plasma concentration of clonidine and its pharmacological effect. The clonidine transdermal therapeutic system (Catapres-tts) patch provides a constant release rate for a week and takes three to four days to reach steady-state concentrations in plasma. Plasma concentration remains stable for about eight hours following the patch removal.

Hazards from Combining Ritalin and Clonidine? A False Alarm from National Public Radio

In 1995, the public radio network, based on information from the Food and Drug Administration, circulated a story about a possible link between the combination of clonidine and methylphenidate and cases of unexplained sudden death in several children. The FDA had received four reports of such deaths in children during the previous year (Fenichel 1995).

A review (Popper 1995) of the four individual cases revealed that other factors (recent anesthesia, a history of cardiac fibrosis and heart murmur, apparent multidrug overdose, history of syncope) were sufficient to cause the reported deaths without implicating clonidine.

The normal rate of sudden unexplained deaths in the general population is estimated to be about 1 per 10,000 children yearly (Denfield and Garson 1990). Estimations of the rate of reported sudden unexplained deaths for children on a clonidine-psychostimulant combination are about the same, or 1 per 10,000 children yearly (Swanson et al. 1995). Because the two rates were essentially the same, there was no basis for concluding that there was an increased risk from being treated with a clonidine-methyphenidate combination. The FDA decided that the available data did not support the theory of an increased rate of sudden unexplained deaths. No further action was deemed to be warranted beyond continued monitoring.

Despite these conclusions, an unsubstantiated panic rapidly spread by way of newspapers and the National Public Radio Network. There were many unwarranted discontinuations of what had been effective and necessary treatments with clonidine and methylphenidate. This raised ethical questions about what defined responsible journalism (Popper 1995).

Cantwell and colleagues (1997) reviewed four cases in which minor adverse reactions were noted in patients treated with clonidine. In two cases, the combination of methylphenidate and clonidine was associated with minor cardiovascular effects and EKG abnormalities, both of which disappeared when the clonidine dose was reduced. In the third case, the patient skipped an evening dose of a clonidine tablet and had an apparent rebound overarousal which resolved without complications. Such problems with rebound overarousal occur much less frequently with the transdermal clonidine patch and, in my experience, with oral extended release clonidine (Clonicel®). The last case concerned the sudden death of a patient who had a history of exercise-induced blackouts prior to starting clonidine treatment. Clonidine was not determined to have been a contributing factor in his death. These reports, like prior ones, were frightening at first, but on closer examination turned out to be nonconclusive.

Risk versus Risk: Finding a Balance

The other side of the risk equation is rarely discussed. How many lives were saved by the successful management of a potentially hazardous medical condition? This is a number much more difficult to accurately measure or even define. Untreated persons may die in automobile crashes or other accidents from failed vigilance. It has long been appreciated that it is common for untreated people to self-medicate. The adverse and even lethal effects of chronic nicotine, caffeine, and alcohol use (Blouin et al. 1978) are well known: lung and a host of other cancers, coronary artery and other heart diseases, sclerosis of the liver, pancreatitis—the list goes on and on. Marijuana and cocaine and unsupervised stimulant use are also common forms of self-medication. Suicides from the complications of failed lives, untreated depressive illnesses, drug misuse, impulsive and risk-seeking behaviors all contribute to an unknown rate of death and misery (Loney et al. 1981, Mannuzza et al. 1993). This undetermined rate is rarely considered in risk assessment of a given treatment.

One example may suffice. A young child patient of mine, when he was two and a half years old, had lost his mother in a single automobile accident. She was not under the influence of any drug, was driving normally, the weather was fine. Her car simply ended up in a ditch for unexplained reasons. This boy's mother had been known as a bubbly, friendly extrovert. She was always the life of the party. She was very personable and successful as a pharmaceutical representative. Her friends affectionately teased her, however, about being a dumb blond or a space cadet because she was forever looking for her keys, purse, or where she parked her car. She was always late, or showed up at the wrong place or at the wrong time. She was a good driver. When she talked on her car phone, however, she would become so overfocused that she would miss turns or exits and get lost. She often found herself in a town different from the one she had intended to drive to. In school she had been a bright student with poor grades and had been diagnosed as having learning disabilities. She was constantly in trouble for socializing too much in class. Her gift of gab and engaging personality turned out, in the end, to make an important contribution to a successful career that depended on good "people skills."

Why did my young patient lose her to an unexplained automobile crash? No one will ever know for sure. No one ever considered that she may have had a neurobiological disorder that placed her at significantly increased risk for death. Barkley and colleagues (1993) reported on such driving-related risks and outcomes of attention deficit hyperactivity disorder in adolescents and young adults. More recently a study in New Zealand (Nada-Raja et al. 1997) found that adolescents with ADHD were more likely than their peers to commit driving offenses. Female subjects, in particular, were more likely to be in crashes.

This is a sad topic to ponder, but important to acknowledge if helpful and necessary medical treatments are to be protected from one-sided arguments about risk assessment. As in all treatment planning, a careful weighing of all potential risks and benefits must be completed in collaboration with the patient, and an informed consent accomplished and documented (Krener and Mancina 1994) (see Appendix A).

EXTENDED-RELEASE ORAL CLONIDINE: CLONICEL®

This section briefly summarizes my clinical experiences in developing and using an extended-release oral capsule of clonidine, Clonicel®.

Problems With Clonidine Oral Tablets: Roller Coaster Effects

While clonidine has proved to be an extremely powerful and useful medication for a wide variety of conditions, significant problems with the traditionally available preparations (oral tablets and transdermal patches) have unfortunately limited its use. These problems have mostly involved the ease of administration and the control of side effects.

The beneficial effects of a dose of oral clonidine in children tend to last only 2 to 4 hours, necessitating the administration of the oral tablets at least three or four times per day. Even with this frequent dosage, "peak and trough" side effects of sedation and rebound hyperarousal can be problematic. Clonidine's clinical effects appear with its rapid absorption. A sharp peak of effects occurs about one hour after ingestion and then rapidly falls off. Patients often report transient periods of drowsiness about one hour after taking a dose and may even fall asleep and nap for ten or fifteen minutes until this passes. Four or five hours after taking the dose there can be a rebound period with hyperactivity, anxiety, and emotional outbursts. If this period occurs in the middle of the night, there can be nightmares and insomnia.

In the original use of clonidine—for the control of high blood pressure—rebound effects in the form of sudden rises in blood pressure could be dangerous. Such a rebound could result in middle-of-the-night or early-morning blood pressure surges. Abrupt discontinuation of high doses of clonidine, without tapering, can present a hazard for a malignant hypertensive episode. Such adverse blood pressure effects have not been reported, however, in individuals who are normotensive (do not have high blood pressure to begin with).

Blood pressure does not appear to be significantly affected in normotensive patients. Rare cases of sudden death have not been conclusively attributed to any use of clonidine. The concern has been raised, on theoretical grounds, that the rebound noradrenergic overdrive which may occur with abrupt discontinuance of clonidine, may pose risks to patients with undiagnosed cardiac disease. For this reason, routine cardiac and blood pressure screening and monitoring is considered prudent until this issue is clarified.

Other "peak-trough" side-effects are usually more unpleasant than dangerous. The rebound in noradrenergic tone may result in rapid escalation of hyperactive and hyperreactive behavior. Outbursts of anger can be disruptive enough to result in the abandonment of an otherwise effective treatment.

Clonidine has been found to be very effective for the treatment of sleep disorders in ADHD children (Wilens et al. 1994). The drug may wear off in the middle of the night, however, causing sudden awakening, nightmares, and even night terrors (Horacek 1994). It has been my practice to have parents fill out a checklist prior to a child's visit to rate various symptoms and medication side effects. Included are items regarding changes in sleep patterns. Parents have rarely reported nightmares and middle-of-the-night wakenings associated with short-acting Clonidine tablets.

When a child is asked directly about sleep problems during the one-on-one interview, a different picture emerges. He or she often reports fairly specific and compelling descriptions of middle-of-the-night rebound hyperarousal, wakefulness, nightmares, and anxiety, which are experienced by the child as problematic. Frequently, when parents are brought into a discussion regarding this, they are surprised that they had been unaware of these problems. Even when the parents are aware of the onset of nightmares that result in the child's routinely seeking safe harbor in their bed during the wee hours of each morning, they often do not attribute this as a side effect of clonidine. More typically they attribute the symptoms to psychological factors, a "phase," or normal behavior (Horacek 1997).

Not included in their report is the adverse effect of a rebound hyperarousal in the middle of the night. This may occur about four to five hours after the bedtime dose of clonidine (Horacek 1994). This may manifest as simply wakening, or as more troublesome nightmares, or even night terrors.

In cases where the patient is a child, this rebound can result in an anxious child showing up in the parents' bedroom every night like clockwork. I have seen this problem misinterpreted as a behavioral problem and dealt with as such, when it was clearly an unrecognized adverse effect of the medication.

The Search for Alternatives

The clinical experience with clonidine suggested that it had potentially beneficial effects for a wide array of disorders. The limitations in the use of clonidine appeared mostly related to its short duration of effects, peak and trough effects, and rebound noradrenergic overdrive from rapid withdrawal. This prompted the search for alternatives to the oral clonidine tablet.

The Clonidine Skin Patch (Catapres-tts)

To address the peak and trough problems of clonidine in the treatment of adult hypertension, a transdermal skin patch, Catapres-tts, was developed by the Boehinger-Ingelheim pharmaceutical company. This innovation provides a more constant blood level of clonidine. The idea of using controlled release medications was novel in the area of antihypertensives. Presant (1992) believed this to be a promising contribution to the treatment of hypertension:

> Although novel controlled-release drug delivery systems have been used in other areas of medicine, their application in the treatment of hypertension has been relatively recent. . . . It is possible that future research will prove that the agents that provide complete 24-hour control may reduce the cardiovascular events associated with the early-morning blood pressure surge. [p. 45S–55S]

As use of the Catapres-tts patch extended to the treatment of children with ADHD, motor tics, and Tourette's syndrome, it was discovered, through clinical usage, that the clonidine dose delivered by the patch could be determined exactly with the help of a pair of scissors. If a whole patch produced too much initial sedation, the patch could simply be cut in half, or even in quarters, without interfering with its effectiveness. By providing a constant blood level and a dose that could be fine-tuned to the child's need, this approach resulted in virtual absence of sedation.

Problems With The Transdermal Patch: Skin Rashes

The clonidine skin patch turned out to have its own unique problems, however. My experience was similar to that of others who reported that more than 50 percent of patients eventually developed severe skin irritation (contact dermatitis) from the adhesive used to make the patch stick to the skin (Hunt 1992). The incidence of skin irritation had been reported in the adult hypertensive literature to be only 5 percent. The reasons for this difference are surely important, though still obscure. The higher prevalence of allergies associated with ADHD, including ectopic skin rashes and reactions to bandages and surgical tape, may be a factor.

Such intolerance by the skin of the patch's adhesive is the most common reason that my patients elect to discontinue using it. This is so even after the Catapres-tts patch has proven clearly effective in controlling the target symptoms. This complication became particularly frustrating when the clonidine patch turned out to be the only medication that could effectively control symptoms that were very important to control. For several years heroic attempts using various topical steroid creams, rotating patch sites, frequent patch changes, and so forth, provided only a small additional percentage of my patients who could tolerate the skin patch.

Tenex (Guanfacine)

Animal research (Arnsten 1988) had showed that another alpha-2 agonist, guanfacine (Tenex), could improve memory and learning in aged monkeys. Hunt questioned whether Tenex might prove to be of similar usefulness as clonidine for treating symptoms of overarousal.

Chappell and colleagues (1995) found that Tenex was associated with significant decreases in both impulsivity and inattention in children with both TS and ADHD. In addition, Tenex caused a significant decrease in severity of motor and phonic tics. The most common side effects were transient sedation and headaches.

Clonidine Verses Guanfacine

Hunt and colleagues (1995) explored the use of Tenex as an alternative to clonidine because its' duration of effects is several hours longer than clonidine's. Their study supported the use of Tenex as a beneficial and useful treatment of ADHD, reducing hyperactive behaviors, and enabling greater attentional ability with minimal side effects. They reported that Tenex appeared to have less sedative side effects than clonidine and hypothesized that this might be due to a more selective receptor binding profile for Tenex.

Comparison of Side Effect Profiles

A more detailed look at the comparative side effect profiles of Tenex and clonidine, however, suggests a different explanation (Table 10–2 and Figure 10–1). When Tenex is compared to clonidine given as an oral tablet, there is a marginal advantage in the side effect profile in favor of Tenex. If, however, we add clonidine given as a transdermal skin patch, we see this form of clonidine produces less side effects than Tenex. This data suggests that side effects with the clonidine tablet may be primarily due to its short half-life, with peak and trough effects and more rapid withdrawal. A sustained release of clonidine actually is better tolerated than Tenex. This is consistent with my clinical experience in using an oral extended release clonidine (Clonicel) which, in my experience, has minimal side effects similar to the clondine skin patch.

A Comparison of Mechanisms of Effect

Clonidine

Clonidine can decrease spontaneous locus coeruleus firing and restore stimulus-evoked responsivity in situations characterized by very high rates of baseline locus coeruleus firing. Clonidine normalizes locus coeruleus-regulated arousal and responsivity to relevant stimuli. There are at least two important mechanisms for these effects:

1. Stimulation of noradrenergic presynaptic receptors results in a potent and *direct* autoinhibitory feedback to the locus coeruleus. This results in decreased baseline spontaneous locus coeruleus firing and increased firing rates in response to relevant stimuli.

TABLE 10–2. Side Effect Profiles for Clonidine versus Tenex (*PDR* 1994, p. 1904)

Side Effect	Tenex (n = 279)	Clonidine Oral Tabs (n = 278)	Clonidine Patch (n=101)	Placebo (n=59)
Dry mouth	30%	37%	25%	0%
Somnolence	21%	35%	12%	8%
Dizziness	11%	8%	2%	8%
Constipation	10%	5%	1%	0%
Fatigue	9%	8%	6%	2%
Headache	4%	4%	5%	8%
Skin Irritation	na	na	51%	

Side Effects of Clonidine tablets, Tenex and Clonidine Skin Patch

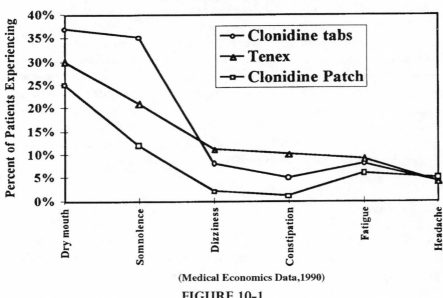

(Medical Economics Data,1990)

FIGURE 10-1

2. Stimulation of noradrenergic postsynaptic receptors results in a less potent and *indirect* feedback inhibition via PFC tracks which project back to the locus coeruleus.

Tenex

In contrast to clonidine, which has actions at both presynaptic noradrenergic projections from the locus coeruleus and post synaptic PFC neurons, Tenex is relatively limited to post-synaptic effects in the PFC. Tenex has only very mild affinity for presynaptic receptors. The milder decreases in locus coeruleus firing associated with Tenex appear to result from less presynaptic direct autoregulatory feedback to the locus coeruleus as compared to clonidine. Tenex's contributions appear more confined to indirect post synaptic feedback to the locus coeruleus via PFC pyramidal neurons.

Tenex's Weaker Effects as Compared to Clonidine

This relative lack of presynaptic affinity and agonist effect of Tenex as compared to clonidine may account for the milder clinical effectiveness noted in my practice.

Tenex's weaker effects were noted in animal studies as early as 1980. From results of their studies in mice and rats, Iizuka and Imai (1980) concluded that the central effects of Tenex, while resembling those of clonidine, were generally weaker than those of clonidine.

This finding was repeated in human research in the same year when it was found that Tenex had a lesser CNS depressant action than clonidine when administered in equipotent hypotensive doses (Kugler et al. 1980). In three double-blind studies in young normotensive volunteers, Spiegel found that central effects were less pronounced and occurred later, after Tenex than after clonidine (Spiegel and DeVos 1980). Yamadera and colleagues (1985) found effects observed after Tenex treatment to be qualitatively similar to those after clonidine, but were of considerably lower intensity. Nakagawa and colleagues (1982) found Tenex to have an equal potency towards the pre- and postsynaptic alpha 2-adrenoceptors as clonidine but is weaker as an alpha 2-agonist than clonidine. Clonidine was found to be about 12 times more potent than Tenex in inhibiting autonomic symptom of [opiate] withdrawal (Buccafusco et al. 1984).

Clonicel®: An Extended Release Oral Capsule of Clonidine[1]

In my clinical practice I use an extended-release oral form of clonidine, Clonicel®, which I have compounded by a local pharmacist. On the basis of my uncontrolled clinical observations in treating over 500 patients, this extended-release formulation appears to be easier to administer, has virtually no side effects of sedation or rebound hyperarousal, and has better patient satisfaction and compliance. The end result is that the percentage of successfully treated clonidine-responsive cases has been greatly increased.

TABLE 10–3. Comparison of Onset and Duration of Effects (Medical Economics Data 1994)

	Avg. half-life (hours)	Range (hours)	Peak levels (hours)
Clonidine tabs	12	6–20	3–5
Tenex tabs	17	10–30	1–4

1. Clonicel® is the trademark for the patented technology of oral extended-release forms of clonidine. Its preparation and/or use of the name Clonicel® is restricted to licensed parties in accordance with specific standards of formulation and quality control.

Clonicel® has properties identical to those of clonidine tablets or patch with the added benefit that it maintains a steady blood level and good patient compliance. In other words, its lack of peak-and-trough properties and skin-irritating properties results in a medication now acceptable to the patient. This brings about better compliance and translates ultimately into more successful treatment. Every clinician knows that no medicine works well if the patient won't take it. Clonicel's® innovation is in providing a delivery system for clonidine that affords the therapeutic effects of clonidine, and yet is easy enough to use and free enough from side effects that patients will actually use it.

I have used Clonicel®, typically in doses ranging from 0.025 mg to 0.3 mg, two or three times per day in more than 300 children who were clinically diagnosed to have ADHD. These children were treated in a private practice setting, with assessments of therapeutic effects, adverse effects, and compliance based on the feedback of the children, parents, and teachers (and using some standardized checklists). In most of these children, the medication was used as an adjunct to psychostimulant therapy when residual behavioral symptoms (hyperactivity, impulsivity, aggressivity, or emotional hyperreactivity) remained problematic. In some cases clonidine was used alone, primarily in hyperactive children who did not tolerate psychostimulant side effects or who had more prominent behavioral than cognitive symptoms.

Adverse effects of extended-release clonidine appeared identical to commercial forms of clonidine, resembling the side effect profile of the clonidine skin patch. Mild sedation was frequently seen but easily managed by decreasing the dose and then gradually increasing as tolerated. The orthostatic effects were of minimal clinical significance. Rebound hyperactivity, rebound hyperarousal, nightmares, and insomnia did not appear to be induced by the extended-release formulation.

From my observations in using it clinically, Clonicel® provides a reliable clinical effect that is maintained for about 8 to 10 hours, permitting a dosing schedule of 2 or 3 times per day. In my patients this has provided beneficial effects as stable and reliable as those of the transdermal patch but without the problematic side effects of the patch. The sedation and rebound problems of the oral tablets were not noted with Clonicel®.

One additional and highly advantageous benefit of Clonicel® has been the absence of the nightmares and wakening in the middle of the night from rebound hyperarousal that I found to occur in as many as a third of my patients using the regular tablet form at bedtime. In some cases such nighttime problems reached the proportions of night terrors and/or resulted in a scared child refusing to leave the parents' bed and sleep alone. As a chronic pattern became established, efforts to resolve it from traditional psychotherapeutic methods inevitably failed. This was because the sleep problem was perceived as a psychological one, and was approached as such instead of being recognized as an adverse effect from the medication (Horacek 1994). In virtually every such case in my practice, the middle-of-the-night problems immediately resolved when the clonidine tablets were replaced with Clonicel®.

The Ancient Art of Compounding

Clonicel® is not currently being manufactured and is not available commercially. In my practice the pharmacist prepares the compounded formula locally, in compliance with a prescription order from the physician, within the scope of lawful compounding practice[2]. Clonidine® has, of course, been approved by the FDA for commercial manufacturing, distribution, and use in patients under medical care. The pharmacist uses generically manufactured clonidine tablets and pulverizes them into an extremely fine powder. This powder is mixed with a methylcellulose extended-release polymer, specifically hydroxypropylmethylcellulose (HPMC) of a specific molecular weight and viscosity. This particular polymer has broad clearance from the FDA as a direct food additive. The compounded clonidine is then placed into a gelatin capsule or tablet.

The "gold standard" for validating the effectiveness of medications is the experimental method of the double-blind placebo controlled randomized clinical trial (RCT). All other types of information on therapeutic benefits to patients of various medications and/or treatment are highly susceptible to various biases. Unfortunately, in medicine, very little gets well validated by these rigorous standards and we are left to look at the best information available and use the best clinical wisdom we can muster to make therapeutic decisions that cannot wait for the ultimate answers that may never come.

It is a good habit, therefore, always to take such information as anecdotal reports, small "open-label" studies, and summaries of clinical experience, as presented here, with a grain of salt. However, we must be cautioned not to keep our minds open so much that our brains fall out! Often the best we can offer is the process of "informed consent," in which dilemmas and uncertainties of the "state of the art" are shared with the patient who participates as a well-informed collaborator.

---

2. Individual prescriptions are filled at Stanly Labs, Charlotte, NC. There is no financial relationship between Stanly Labs and this author.

For example, Clonicel® was used in ADHD children who had previously responded positively to clonidine, but had been overly sedated by the commercially available tablets (or had developed contact dermatitis with commercial transdermal formulations). In these cases the children and parents were often frustrated to see the clonidine significantly useful but be limited by the practical problems in drug administration. Parents provided specific informed consent for the specially prepared formulation of clonidine, having previously given informed consent for the use of commercially available forms of clonidine.

In the manufacturing world, new drugs are scrutinized by controlled experimental studies to assess the reproducibility and/or reliability of their effects. Although no such studies have yet been done on Clonicel®, I did not encounter any clinical problems with batch-to-batch variability or within subjects over time. I did not obtain plasma clonidine levels (after fixed times) to measure bioavailability in comparison to the commercially available formulations. More generally, the pharmacokinetic features of extended-release clonidine were not measured. It would be expected that the elimination half-life of clonidine would not be changed, but the rate of absorption over time would presumably be longer (i.e., increased absorption half-life). Finally, as I did not conduct a controlled comparison between the various formulations or obtain a placebo contrast group, my current data cannot be considered to have demonstrated the efficacy of the extended-release formulation.

Among the variables that can affect rate and reliability of drug release in such compounds are effects of particle size, polymer solution viscosity, proportion of polymer versus inert ingredients, and drug solubility. It is important, therefore, to standardize preparations so that there is consistency and quality control. Until such factors can be adequately standardized, there is no way of reliably predicting the clinical responses of patients who are administered other locally-prepared formulations. Therefore practitioners are advised not to infer that any other locally-prepared formulation would have the clinical properties anecdotally described here. I hope that this brief report will stimulate more formal research and the development of extended-release forms of clonidine so their potential benefits can be more readily and widely available.

11
Beyond Medications

The medical management of brainstorm syndromes often involves coordination of care with other agencies and providers, such as therapists, physicians, the workplace (in the case of adults), or the school (in the case of school-age patients). This often involves educating key personnel or staff about the nature of the brainstormer's problems to the extent necessary to make reasonable and appropriate accommodations in the work or learning environment.

The most difficult problems that my patients meet with in such settings involve the misinterpretation of their symptoms as reflecting an immoral or uncooperative attitude. A conceptual framework that is based on false assumptions concerning the patient's intentions can lead to disaster. An example is the assumption that a behavior at question is motivated by willful and intentional defiance, laziness, and disrespect. The repeated interpretation of malicious motives when the real issue involves more innocent oversight often leads to chronic frustration and, ultimately, a state of mutual contempt between the brainstormer and the authority. Misperception of symptoms as resulting from moral deficiency quickly poisons the relationship, often irretrievably.

Fortunately, the intentions of those involved are usually honorable, though misguided. I have often found such situations to be surprisingly easily to salvage. A little knowledge can lead to the desired "paradigm shift."

What is this magic that I see so often unfold before my eyes? How can people totally change their attitude about something they have lived with for so many years in a matter of seconds?

PARADIGM SHIFTS

The End of the Rope: Annie and the Birthday Cake

"I'm at the end of my rope!" Annie's stepmom announced. "Ever since we've been married she has not liked me. She has no respect for me, and thinks she can simply defy me. I have no more patience for her. I've never seen anything like it. You should have seen the way she talked back to me. Now she's upstairs pouting and won't come down, as if I was mean to her!"

"What happened?" Dad asked.

"I left to go to the store," said stepmom. "She wanted to decorate your birthday cake. I told her she could use the white frosting. She wanted to know if we had any more decorations and I told her that we didn't. I said she should use the white frosting and that will be fine. When I got back, she had pulled out that old frosting that's two years old that I've been meaning to throw away and used it. When I asked her why she had disobeyed me, she argued that the frosting was still good and that frosting doesn't go bad. That wasn't the point. The point was that she thinks she can make the rules and do whatever she wants, no matter what I say. I'm through with her! From now on you can handle her."

Dad went wearily upstairs. Annie was lying on her bed, red-faced, staring at the ceiling. "What happened?" dad asked.

"She's always so mean to me. She walked right in the door and the first thing she did was start criticizing me," cried Annie.

"What was she mad about?" said Dad.

"I don't know, I guess she was mad because she thought the frosting I used was spoiled, but it wasn't. I found it in the cupboard. I didn't want to just give you a plain white cake, and I thought there must be something around I could use. I found some frosting stuck way behind everything."

"Did she tell you not to use anything but the white frosting?" Dad asked.

"No," said Annie. "She said we didn't have anything but the white frosting."

"Well, sounds like a misunderstanding. Why doesn't everybody cool off for a while, and then we'll have some ice cream and cake." Dad went downstairs and took a look at his birthday cake. It was a meticulous job, the frosting was perfectly swirled with little white frosting flowers. Along the upper rim were tiny fresh purple violets. On the top was one small candle flanked by two small green frosting flowers. It was a work of art.

Dad walked back up to the master bedroom where Stepmom was already feeling guilty. "She says you told her we didn't have any decorations, not that she couldn't use any."

"Well," stepmom's resolve was already weakening, "she hears what she wants to hear. I told her to use only the white frosting. She found that old colored decorating stuff I've been meaning to throw away. It's over two years old."

Dad, brokenhearted by this simple tragedy and hoping to gently forge a peace, said, "I don't think she was being defiant. She worked so hard on that cake, to make it special for me. She was proud of it and excited to show you. She wanted you to be pleased. When you came in the door and were immediately angry with her she didn't have a clue as to why."

Stepmom rallied, "She doesn't need to know why. She just needs to accept that when I tell her something she doesn't always have to argue with me about it. If I say she can only use the white frosting, then she should just accept that, and when I reprimand her for disobeying she should not talk back and get such an attitude."

Dad tried again, knowing his wife's tough stance was made of butter ready to melt, "She thought you were arguing about whether she poisoned the cake with stale icing. She maintains the icing was good, that she's not as stupid as some people seem to think."

"Well, that's not the issue at all. She needs to learn a little respect, even if she thinks I'm the bad stepmother," said Stepmom.

"The real issue," Dad gently explained, "is that she didn't hear what you said, or didn't understand what you said. She made no conscious or deliberate decision to defy you. She had no idea you would be mad. She was looking forward to showing it to you. She had no money or opportunity to buy me a present, she spent hours making me a birthday card, and wanted to decorate the cake in a special way. If she made a mistake, it was an innocent one. She's brokenhearted now. Sure, she blames you. She's convinced she meant no harm, so that only leaves you. She's convinced you don't like her."

"Well, you're right and I'm sorry," agreed Stepmom. "I've just never seen anything like her. She only comes to visit for a while, its not like she lives here all the time. How am I supposed to understand her in such a short time and know how to deal with her?"

"I don't know. I wish she did live here all the time. I fear for her. I don't think many people will understand her. It's going to be hard for her. I understand her because I was just like her myself. It was hard for me, and it still is. When I try to explain what is going on to her she just tunes me out. I know its because she has so much difficulty listening. I wish her mother could accept the diagnosis. If she's going to get any help, her mother is going to be the key. But when we talk on the phone we just argue. Maybe if I wrote her instead of trying to talk on the phone it would help," explained Dad.

"Well, its your birthday, and its getting late. Why don't you get Annie and we'll have some ice cream and cake," said Stepmom. In a few minutes the three were sitting around the beautiful cake. "Annie, I'm sorry for our disagreement. I think the cake is beautiful."

Annie didn't say anything. She hung her head and her face flushed with shame and gratitude. Her eyes watered but no tears fell. "Are you going to apologize and be friends again?" Dad said with a subdued melodrama that forced a hint of a smile from Annie. "Sorry," she said, in an inaudible whisper, not looking up.

Stepmom winked at Dad, "Good, now let's cut the cake!" Annie immediately brightened and within seconds it was if the whole episode had never happened.

Dad sat munching on his carrot cake and feeling very satisfied with himself. "I did a terrific job handling that situation. I'm sure glad I took my Adderall."

That is a paradigm shift. It is the heart and soul of the healing process once the diagnosis is made. The therapist's job is to nudge this process along. Sometimes it's funny. Other times it's poignantly sad as those involved realize all the moments lost to such misunderstandings. The good news is that future moments now have a much better chance.

In working with parents, siblings, spouses, significant others, coaches, friends, bosses, and co-workers, the magic of understanding these disorders for what they are is powerful. Perhaps the most powerful effects are on the patient as an individual. This is particularly true of the adult patient. A process often begins of reliving one's life, moment by moment, and suddenly, for the first time, understanding what happened, as one paradigm shift after another casts a life laced with perplexity and pain in a bright new light.

Billy: Rebel Without a Clue!

"We're at the end of our rope!" the parents told me as they sat together on the couch in my office. "We've taken everything away from him, there's nothing left to threaten him with. Instead of making him behave he's only worse, as if he's going to prove to us that no one can make him do anything he decides he's not going to do."

"What happened?" I asked.

"He got suspended again," said Dad. "He refused to do his assignment in class and was disrespectful and defiant to the teacher. She sent him to the office to see the principal. The principal gave him the choice of doing the assignment there, in his office, or being suspended. He still would not do the assignment, so we got a call from the school to come and get him. I have to take off work and go pick him up. When we asked him to explain himself, he refused to talk about it."

"For his punishment he does not get to go on the class trip to Florida," explained Mom. "He's got to learn that there is a price for his stubbornness. We knew he had been looking forward to this trip, and we were hoping that he'd finally make some friends by going. It was the only thing he had left of any value that we could take away. Now we're not sure it was a good idea, but we feel, right or wrong, we need to stick to our decision to show him we will not back down."

"Let me talk to him," I said, and they ushered themselves out and down the stairs. In a minute the little hoodlum sauntered in and plopped down in the computer chair.

"Are we going to fly the F-15 today?" he asked, hoping to avoid the topic.

"Sure," I said. He booted up the game and in seconds was flying over Iraq on an Operation Desert Storm bombing run.

After he demolished several targets of key military importance, I asked, "So what's new?"

He gripped the joystick and went into a skillfully executed barrel role. "Oh, not much. I got suspended from school, but its not a big deal."

"What happened?" I asked.

"I got sent to the principal's office and he suspended me."

"For what?" I probed.

" I don't know—for refusing to do something, I guess," he said shyly.

"And what was it that you refused to do?"

"Some assignment. So my teacher sent me to the principal and he said if I didn't do it there he would suspend me. I didn't do it so he suspended me. My parents are pissed. They said I couldn't go on the class trip to Florida. It's a pretty stupid trip anyway. I really didn't want to go that much."

"What was the assignment, anyway?" I asked.

"What?"

"What exactly was the assignment that the teacher told you to do."

"I don't remember."

"Did you know at the time what it was?"

"Not really."

"You didn't know what the assignment was?"

"I wasn't listening when she said what it was."

"Why didn't you ask her for some clarification?"

"She gets really pissed when I do that. I used to ask her at the beginning of the year but she always gets mad and says if I paid attention, she wouldn't have to repeat herself."

"Are you telling me that when you were refusing to do the assignment in class, you didn't know what the assignment was?"

Billy looked embarrassed. "Pretty much," he said, and dropped a few scatter bombs on a radar installation somewhere near Baghdad.

"What happened then?" I asked.

"The teacher got more and more pissed at me, and threatened to send me to the principal. I got so mad, I finally just put my feet up on my desk and put my hands behind my head. Then she sent me to the principal."

"What did he say?"

"He said I could do the assignment in his office. If I didn't he would suspend me."

"So then what happened?"

"He suspended me."

"Why?"

"For not doing the assignment."

"Did you know what the assignment was?"

"No."

"How could you refuse to do something if you didn't even know what it was that you were refusing?"

"I don't know."

"Did you tell the principal you didn't know what it was you were supposed to do?"

"No."

"Why?"

"I don't know."

"Did you tell your parents?"

"We haven't talked about it much."

I see these simple tragedies played out every day. By the time of the family's first session with me, they have already placed an application to a military academy or filed for a divorce. There are no villains here, merely a clash of assumptions.

The parents consciously or unconsciously might be thinking the following: "We need to get tougher with him for his own good. If he grows up like this he will be a failure in life. Sure, its hard to see him suffer, but he needs to stew in his own juice or he'll never learn. It's a battle of wills that we can't lose, for his sake. If he grows up to be a no-good, we will have failed as his parents.

Whatever happens now is crucial. As the twig is bent, so grows the tree. If he doesn't do well now, he will fall into an endless pattern of failure. It's our job to take control, and to force him into submission."

The child, consciously or unconsciously, might be thinking the following: "Every day people are always telling me how smart I am, how I can get straight A's if I wanted to. They say I can do anything I set my mind to. But what they don't know is that I want to get good grades. They try to scare me with warnings of how terrible my life will turn out if I don't do well in school. They don't know that I'm already scared of being a loser. If I'm so smart, then why am I always doing stupid things? Maybe I'm not smart at all. Maybe I'm really retarded. They say I'm just lazy, but when I try I always mess up somehow. I would rather they think that I'm a smart person who just doesn't care than have them discover that I'm really just stupid. Whenever I don't try, they seem to forget what stupid things I did and start telling me how smart I am. I need to keep faking that I'm smart but lazy so they won't figure out my secret, that I'm just plain dumb."

No one in the family is usually aware that there is an explanation that has not been considered. Is there really a choice between smart versus dumb, or compliant versus defiant, or lazy versus industrious, or respectful versus irreverent? Another possibility is that the child might be suffering from a neurobiological disorder.

A child might miss instructions due to an attention problem. When confronted, it may be his temperament to hyperreact and to escalate rapidly. What makes this a vicious cycle is that both sides of the battle are invested in it. The parents feel a moral duty to "hang in there" for the child's own good, and the child needs to maintain the smoke screen of defiance to hide the "real" issue of his feared intellectual inadequacy.

The only solution to this tailspin is to understand and accept the situation for what it is and to shift paradigms. It is surprising how quickly all concerned understand this, as if somewhere deep inside they suspected it all along, or once knew it but then forgot. This may not prevent such episodes from happening, but it does a lot to keep them from escalating once they do, and makes apologies a lot easier afterwards.

Medications such as clonidine are of great help in that they subdue the tendency to spin rapidly into a hyperaroused and hyperreactive state by keeping the brain's noradrenaline from getting too high. If the child can stay out of the fight or flight state, he can more easily try to reason out where the communication went astray.

Brainstormers may display an emotional hyperreactivity that manifests as low frustration tolerance, touchiness, argumentativeness, stubbornness, and hypersensitivity to criticism. Oppositional defiant disorder is often misdiagnosed in brainstormers when the incorrect inference is made that such symptoms represent an organized and stable position of deliberate defiance to rules and authority.

Genetic studies by Comings (1995) and others claim to support that oppositional defiant disorder is, to a significant degree, a genetically acquired disorder. It appears likely that the dopamine D2 receptor gene when combined with the B1 allele of the dopamine B-hydroxylase gene may result in poor regulation of various neurotransmitters and in a syndrome of hyperarousal and hyperreactivity that would provide much of the biological underpinnings for oppositional and defiant behavior.

The primary neurophysiologic determinants of what is referred to as oppositional defiant disorder may have more to do with arousal and reactivity than with the child's attitudes about his or her behavior. The latter may be defensive reactions incorrectly misinterpreted by adults as malicious and premeditated: "You do these things deliberately to annoy me!" Or are adopted by the child to explain the symptoms: "I am not hot-tempered, and I am not out of control! The teachers are stupid, my parents are stupid, the rules are stupid and I choose not to cooperate! I am in control, because no one can make me do anything!"

There are many common faulty beliefs among mental health professionals regarding oppositional defiant disorder and conduct disorder. Such beliefs are also common to parents and teachers, and even to the child. In my experience, much of the most effective therapy of these disorders involves reframing such beliefs, shifting such paradigms, or rewriting the family mythology surrounding a patient, including the patient's personal mythology. This begins when the genetic and neurobiological origins are understood and accepted as the primary culprit.

About David: Responsibility versus Shame

Dear Dr. Horacek,

I am writing because I am concerned about David. I am Mrs. Summers, David's 1st and 3rd period teacher. I will try my best to make this as clear and understandable as possible. The purpose of this is to describe some of the behavioral problems that we have been having with David.

David has no respect for authority. When he is in our classroom, he has the feeling that he can pretty much do what he wants, when he wants to do it. He seems to have no idea of consequence. He has no real respect for other students or teachers for that matter. He seems to have no understanding of how things that he says may be hurting people's feelings.

The "Cushiony" Teacher's Chair

Following the 10:30 break one day, I walked down the hall to go into the class-room. It is a very small cubicle type of classroom, room enough for one table, one larger cushiony teacher's chair, and three regular student hard-back chairs. Well, I try to be lenient with him and the one other boy whom I have in there, because together they can get a little wild. This particular day, I walked in and, by lenient I mean sometimes David is allowed to sit in the teacher's chair and that's fine. The way I look at it is that its just a chair. This particular day the other student sat in that chair first. When I walked in there was a conflict going on. David was saying "Fine, I'll just grab this chair out of the other room across the hall." "No, David," I said. "We really need to get going. Just sit in another one." "No, I want this teacher's chair," said David. I said, "David, we really do need to get going. Why don't you let Brad sit in it today. Take your pick of whichever of the other three you want."

"No, I want THIS one," he said. David then continued across the hall with no regard for what I was saying. David grabbed a large, cumbersome, vinyl chair, dragged it through the hallway carrying it leg first right toward me. He appeared to be saying, "I'm bringing this chair in this room no matter what." I said "David, you need to stop right there and put the chair back."

"No, I just want to sit in this chair," he said. The whole time I'm saying this in a tone of voice that's as accommodating as I can imagine. The long and short of it is he brings the chair in without listening to me and I'm realizing quickly that its going to become a battle of wills. Either I give into him and let him think that he can have his way, which I cannot do, or I find a way to remove him. Well, he brings the chair in and he sits down. The other child has known David for a year and a half. He was very perceptive of the situation, and chose to totally withdraw from it. He seems to recognize the difference between one of David's unbending tantrums and normal little silliness episodes. The latter he will usually jump into. He and David will then wind up becoming silly and uncontrollable. And so the sign that this child was giving me showed me that this situation was only going to escalate. It came down to David sitting in the chair, refusing to obey me and thinking "Well, everything is fine now, I'm in this chair." I'm standing there saying, "David, you cannot leave it here." Finally I had to insist. "David, I am going to have to remove you if you have chosen not to leave. I cannot have you do this in my class-room."

"Fine, I'm staying." he said.

I tried to physically move the chair with him in it. At that point he got up, walked around to the other side of the chair, and we literally got in a tug of war over this chair. I knew if I let go of that chair he would fall hard against the wall. I just let it go. I had no choice at that point but to let it go because I had an important class to conduct.

I was then faced with the decision, do I go and call his parents and bother them at their places of work? This is what happens all the time. I know that Jim and Cindy have a hard time understanding, why they haven't heard about this before, why they haven't seen a detention here or there. This sort of incident happens every day with David, with different teachers at different times of the day. There doesn't seem to be a pattern and none of us really know what to do.

The Cheese and Crackers Incident

On another day David was walking toward the cubicles. A little package of cheese and crackers had fallen out of someone's cubby. David said "What is this stupid thing doing here?" He stepped on it and crushed the cheese and crackers. By asking the other children who witnessed it, I deduced it was him. I asked him why he did it. "It was in my way," he said. "David, do you think that's appropriate to just step on it just like that?" I asked. "Why not, I don't care. Karen leaves them here all the time. She always brings them and they're always falling out." I said, "David, don't you think it would be polite to just pick it up and put it back where it belongs?" "Uh-uh" he said. He never really has an adequate response. You can see that he doesn't really care.

Obviously, there has to be a consequence. "Now you have to clean it up," I said. "I'm not cleaning it up," he said. "David, you need to clean up the crackers," I told him. Even though I try very hard to keep a calm tone with him, it gets very frustrating. I finally got to the point where I had to raise my voice and say, "David, do it now!" He responded slightly, but very little. The whole time I was telling him this he was walking on top of the crumbs. It happened that he had on a pair of athletic shoes that have spikes. A chunk of the cheese became stuck to a spike and he saw it there and said "Oh, cool." He walked down the hall, leaving little cheese marks on the carpet, thinking, "That was really, really neat!"

Again, I'd like to emphasize that it is very frustrating to get into these situations with David, because its very obvious by his performance that he is a very bright, quick child. In a recent conference with Jim and Cindy, it became clear to me that that, in spite of the fact that he is involved in these disturbances practically every day, the child is still able to comprehend so much and perform so well at his academics that it is just amazing to think of what he would be able to accomplish if we were able to control this.

The Science Project: "Round Up the Usual Suspects"

Another recent incident involved the defacing of some science projects that were on display for all the children to see. There were some discrepancies in accounts as to who vandalized these projects. Without malicious intent, one of the usual suspects when something like this happens is David. He has a history of doing things like this at this school. It became clear to him that he was being singled out and he got a negative attitude about the whole thing. It came down to there being several children involved. David was finally asked by the director to write letters of apology to the respective students and to his parents saying that he understood that his behavior was not appropriate. He had the 10:00–10:30 break taken away from him. He was told to sit in a room and write the letters. When he was finished he was to take them to the science teacher, give them to her and go from there with whatever she instructed him to do. At one point he came out of the room and was wandering around the hall, looking for the science teacher. Ms. Boone, the director, intercepted him and asked him what he was doing. He said he was looking for Ms. Jensen to give her these letters. "David, you are supposed to be in that room, we'll come get you," she said. "She told me to bring them to her when I was finished," he said. "David, you don't just go walking around the hall. You were told to stay there so stay there," she said. It was apparent that he was already bitter about having to write the letters. You could see that this was escalating. I heard all of this from down the hall. I listened and took note of the situation. I could see what he was trying to do. He felt he was doing what he was told to do in taking the letters to the science teacher. He was also told by another teacher to stay in the room. That didn't go over well with David. He went back into the room and slammed the door. I could hear him kick a chair. He was downright unhappy.

Later, I tried to talk with David about why this had happened. 'All I wanted to do was give the letters to Ms. Jensen.' "David, do you understand that Ms. Boone had to step in because she didn't think that your wandering around was appropriate? Didn't she tell you she would find Ms. Jensen for you?" I asked. "Yeah, but I'm missing my break while she has to find her," he said. "Well, David, the fact is you were being punished for something that it was concluded that you did." I responded.

"But, I'm not," and he launched into this whole story about how other students were involved and another student admitted to him that he had done some of the damage. He denied everything. It had been concluded, however, that it was he who had done some of the destruction. This is where I don't know if I am trusting him too much. Is he looking to me to be an ally? I don't know but he was really looking for someone to talk to. We spoke about how he shouldn't accuse anyone else just because he is being accused. Did he see anyone do it with his own two eyes? I asked. No. "But Daniel admitted it to me." "Okay, do you think that is enough to go tell a teacher?" "Well, yeah." "Well, did you?" "No." "Do you understand how the situation had to then be discovered and how you became involved in it and had to be punished? If you would have gone through the appropriate channels you would have alleviated that potential for punishment by letting us know ahead of time that someone else had done this." We talked and at one point he said, "Well, I don't care, it doesn't matter, everyone is going to blame me all the time anyway."

I said, "David, I think that you just have some personality conflicts with the people in this school. Maybe you have some things that you need that we can't give you. We are trying but you have admitted to me that you can't control yourself. Well, how are we supposed to control you? Do you understand that?" "It doesn't matter. No one can help me anyway" he said.

David seemed very responsive to this discussion. About ten minutes later he was supposed to complete a test in my class from the period before. It was nearing lunch break. I said, "David, we have a situation now. I really enjoyed talking with you and I think we had a productive talk. I'd like you to remember some of the things that I told you about your going through the proper channels and whatnot. But right now we have a test. I really need to do this one oral section with you."

"Yeah, but its almost 12:00." "Well, David, what did we just talk about?" I asked. "I need to do this for you and you need to do this for me." "But, I don't WANT to do it," he said. "David, we need to do it now! I'm not going to be here later in the day and this is something that needs to be administered by me. You mentioned you wanted to finish it during computer class," I reminded him. "Yeah, I have that period at the end of the day. I can do it then." "Okay, here's the deal. We talked about your being flexible. If I let you take the rest of the test during computer class, then you need to go ahead and take this part for me now." I could see the situation was just escalating. I finally said, "David, this is just what we talked about. Do you see how you just need to compromise? Just take a couple of deep breaths. Like it or not, you have to do this."

"Fine, just read them!" he said and slammed his arm down on the desk. His answers were not as good as they could have been. He was merely filling in some blanks for me. But he did it and I tried my best to thank him and tell him that this was a very good step, that we had made a compromise. I would to do my part later because he did his part now. All the while he was saying, "Yeah, yeah" and walking out the door.

We can deal with students that get rowdy, have a moody day, or get cranky. Students will cuss occasionally. They know when they have done it and they know immediately that there are consequences. If you get firm with them and explain to them that there will be consequences, then they are immediately able to restrain themselves.

David is not. He flies off the handle. He will just assume he can get up and walk out of the room. He'll slam the door open and shut. He'll just leave. And that's if you're lucky. Most of the time, if we are having these incidents, I can tell him repeatedly that if he continues he is going to have to remove himself, but he won't. He will flat out refuse to leave. Now I am in a situation. I have five other students in my morning math class. He is back there not paying attention to my lesson at the board. Instead, he is disrupting other students, wasting my valuable time and completing hurting himself.

If I take the time to go back and try giving him one-on-one attention, he completely resists. I am then in a situation where I can't do my job. I have this child controlling the setting and not me. It's obvious to the other students that when he wants to do his own thing he will. Sometimes he does silly things that they laugh at. This causes him to escalate. He thinks its cute to throw things, to play with the blinds, slamming them up and down. If he wants the door open because its hot in the room, he will get up and open the door, right in the middle of class. If you stop and watch him and use the tactic of just isolating him and bringing him to the attention of the whole class, he starts smiling like, "Oh, boy, I'm the center of attention!"

We are not equipped to handle these situations. When he escalates, he will slam things and becomes verbally abusive toward other people. He will kick, throw, and break things without thinking. He rarely cries, unless he is very frustrated and feels that he is being unjustly held responsible for something. At such times he will insist that all he was trying to do was something that he should have been doing and trying to justify getting his way. Only time will fix the situation. I may step out of the room for a while. When I come back in and try to talk to him he just shrugs me off, insisting angrily that I leave him alone.

Afterwards he will work, but his outbursts are not conducive to conducting a normal classroom lesson. We are all very concerned for David's well-being. I am afraid that when puberty hits full force David is not going to be able to control himself.

David has hinted, at times, that he is depressed. He makes rather dark suggestions of not wanting to be around, and so forth.

"Does He Really Want to be A Terrorist?"

The first week of school, I tried to get to know each child. I talked with two boys in my class about their future. The first child said he loved to draw and mentioned agricultural interests. I then asked David what he thought he might be when he grew up. Both boys looked at each other and laughed. David said, "I'm going to be a terrorist." I thought this was a joke and played along. I asked what type of terrorism he would specialize in. "Car bombs and highjacking." We all laughed it off.

Several weeks later, I asked the boys again what they wanted to be. I reminded David that the last time he had joked around. There was a pause. This time the other student remained quiet and didn't become involved. This was the same boy that appears to be very perceptive of David's moods.

David's response this time was that he was going to be a serial killer. I thought that this might be cute, so I decided to play along again. I asked what type of serial killer he was going to be. He continued to list several ways to be a serial killer: putting bags over people's heads and beating them, stabbing them, hitting them over the head and throwing them to the dogs, and so forth.

I wasn't sure what all of this meant except that it didn't sound positive to me. It didn't sound very normal, whatever normal is. It just sounded to me like he felt this was all he could do.

David doesn't seem to have any self-confidence. He doesn't seem to have much pride in what he does. He does have a lot of potential. He can be so lively and funny and clever that it's just a shame to have to see these dark sides. Others have commented that he appears, at times, to be deeply depressed.

David tends to react to situations in an extreme way that we can't foresee and that we certainly cannot control. I do want to make it clear that David is okay by himself, if I can get him isolated and removed from a situation. He will often work wonderfully for me.

Sincerely,

Ms. Summers

OPPOSITIONAL DEFIANCE: FIGHTING THE SMOKESCREEN OR THE FIRE?

Oppositional defiant disorder can rapidly melt away in response to clonidine. This seems to me also to support the idea that oppositional defiant disorder does not result primarily from faulty values or beliefs, as it is unlikely a medication would have much impact on these so quickly. I have often found that when a child becomes neurologically competent in controlling his reactivity, he is often among the most relieved by this and appears eager to join the mainstream of his compliant peers and reap the praise of his parents and teachers. As the explosions of temper diminish, so do the rationalizations. This is seldom a conscious process. Most of the time if I ask a child why he has stopped being so irritable, touchy, argumentative, short-tempered, and so on since starting the medication, he will say simply that it is because everyone has stopped provoking him and there is no need for him to fight over anything. Often the best I can do for an explanation is to offer jokingly that many of my patients have noted that their medication seems to have no effect on them, but they are willing to take it because it makes everyone else behave better!

My impressions are derived, in large part, from my clinical experience and thus I'm sure are subject to a selection bias. There may be "pure" cases of oppositional defiant disorder that I have not had much experience with. Most of the cases I have had occasion to treat were brainstormers with "pseudo-oppositional defiant disorder." The form of defiance I see most often moves along like this: misunderstanding based on attention deficit, conflict over some resulting failure on the child's part, escalation into a temper outburst or withdrawal, cool-down period, retrospective interpretations of the episode as oppositionalism and defiance by the parent and as unfair treatment by the child.

The way I have come to understand oppositional and defiant behavior in the brainstormers I have worked with is that they often come into conflict with authority and rules innocently at first, as an oversight stemming from poor attention, or from overreacting emotionally to some frustration and losing their temper. This part seems heavily influenced by neurology. What then follows is an effort on the child's part to rationalize his or her behavior:

- I was right to act as I did.
- I was not out of control.
- No one can make me do anything.
- Everyone is stupid, the rules are stupid.

This is mirrored by the authority figure who interprets the behavior to the child:

- You have no respect for authority.
- You think rules don't apply to you.
- You think you only have to do what pleases you.
- You deliberately misbehave just to annoy others.

A neurophysiologic substratum of oppositional defiant behavior may involve the tendency to quickly get into hyperaroused and hyperreactive states. This is often a feature of certain types of ADHD. What follows is a misattribution of these symptoms to learned beliefs and values. Unfortunately, telling a child repeatedly over time that he is defiant may provide a self fulfilling prophecy, as the child adopts these interpretations as his own and makes them part of his self-concept.

It is sad to see such a child, accused of having declared war on the civilized world, more candidly admit in therapy the underlying fear and pain and perplexity that these symptoms and their naive mismanagement have caused him.

WORKING WITH COUPLES

The Case of the "Kitty Cat Chow"

"I just can't take it anymore!" Bob's wife exclaimed with that familiar look of exasperated futility that I so often see on faces in my office. "We've been married for twenty years now and he still does things just to annoy me. He likes to torture me. I don't know why anyone who claimed to love a person would intentionally do things for the express purpose of making the other person's life miserable!"

"Can you give us an example?" I asked.

Bob's wife was sitting on the couch. Bob was sitting next to her, reclining comfortably, as if he'd heard this litany a thousand times and had learned to endure it. "Well," she began, "I could give you countless examples." Suddenly one leapt into her mind. "Here's a perfect example: the Kitty Cat Chow!" Bob rolled his eyes. "He is leaving to go to the store. I say to him, "Honey, will you pick up some cat food?" "Sure," he says. Now, I tell him, "You can get any brand of cat food you want, it doesn't matter which, but the only one the cat will not eat is Kitty Cat Chow. So pick anyone you want, except for the Kitty Cat Chow." He goes to the store, he returns, and out of thirty brands of cat food there, what is the brand he shows up with? Right! Kitty Cat Chow! Now what other explanation could there be than that he did it deliberately just to make me angry. Why should I put up with that kind of abuse any longer?"

"Well," I said, "I suspect you know the answer to that one yourself. You can't tell me that you've been married for twenty years and you haven't figured out yet why he came back with the Kitty Cat Chow." She looked blankly. "Do you know?" I directed my question now to Bob.

"Huh?" he said with a start, "Oh, she's always harping on something. Is she complaining about that damned cat food again?"

I said, "Yes, did we lose you for a while there?"

"It's the same old thing, always upset about some little thing that doesn't matter."

"It does too matter," she started to heat up, "because if you loved me you would not do these things!"

I interrupted, "Well, now, let me see if I have the picture. He is leaving for the store, you tell him to pick up some cat food, and that he can come back with any brand except Kitty Cat Chow. He says something like, 'Yeah, yeah, OK' and heads off to the store. Later he returns with the Kitty Cat Chow, right? Now, you tell me what is going through his mind at the store. Come on, I can't believe you don't know!"

"Well," her eyes looked up and to the side as she visualized her husband in the grocery store in front of an isle of thirty brands of cat food. " If I know Bob, what is probably going through his mind is something like, "Now let me see, what is it she told me to get? That's right, Kitty Cat Chow!"

They both laughed, Bob nodding his head knowingly. "She thinks because I don't listen to her that I don't love her," he said.

"Well, isn't that what people who love each other do for each other? If you love someone aren't you interested in what they have to say? God knows I listen to you for hours—ranting and raving about this, that, and the other thing, but when I want to tell you about something that matters to me, you tune me out!"

"Why does he do that?" I asked. "Is that because of his ADD?" She already knew the answer. I nodded. We were all having fun now. She shook her head and said with a soft voice that was reminiscent of a young maiden of years ago: "I guess I'll keep him." The rekindled romance of the moment embarrassed her so, she added, "If I don't kill him first!"

The Case of Jack and His Wife

Jack Sprat could eat no fat,
His wife could eat no lean,
And so betwixt them both,
They licked the platter clean.
Mother Goose Tales

"What attracted you most about Jack when you first met?" I asked Jack's wife. She paused and stammered, as if she hadn't thought about these things in a long while. Then she smiled and I could see the memories in her eyes." He was fun! He had this adventurous spirit, and everything always seemed like we were on an adventure. The most ordinary things could sweep him up into a fury. . . . when things went bad, he always seemed deep and mysterious. His moods were intense and he was so passionate. He was very creative. He was a gourmet chef."

"Yes, I was. But who has time for that anymore?" said Jack.

"He was so charming, everybody liked him right off. He was known for his smile, and his off-the-wall sense of humor. I also liked the way he had a special soft spot in his heart for anyone who was suffering." But now I don't get to see that side of him much. He works all the time and comes home late and exhausted. Now I see more of his dark moods. He can get stuck on a negative track and you just can't get him off it. He is so disorganized I have to manage our bills and social calendar, pick up after him, make the bed . . . we never have any time to ourselves anymore."

"What did you like about her at first?" I asked Jack.

"I liked her stability and reliability. She always had both feet on the ground. The more time I spent with her, the less crazy my life was, and the more stable

I became. She was like an anchor for me. I could be lost in space but she always brought me back to earth. She had a sense of practicality that I never had. She could manage to pick out the main priority, think logically, and she had a certain insistence that meant that once she made up her mind, she would follow through to the bitter end. I guess nowadays I would call it nagging."

"How did it switch from insistence to nagging?" I inquired.

"I don't know. I used to like her pushing me on. You know, the woman behind the great man sort of thing. But I came to resent it after a while. I often don't think she understands me very well."

"What would you like for her to understand better?"

"Well, I don't know that I understand myself either sometimes. I guess the main thing is that I really don't mean to do things I do sometimes."

"What would be an example?"

"Well, I have a different sense of time than most people. I have always been late. It's not that I don't want to be on time, but I just lose track of time. I'm not making excuses, I just wish she understood that I'm not doing it on purpose."

"Well," she broke in, "why should I be the one who worries all the time for the two of us?" You're a grownup now. Why does he keep doing things the same way over and over again when it never works? Another thing he expects me to do is to read his mind. I feel like he is just another one of my children sometimes. I would like for him to pull his share of the weight."

"You sound pretty frustrated," I said.

"I am."

"When she gets that attitude, I just tune her out. I've heard that sort of thing all my life, from parents and teachers. I've just learned to tune it out. She's always complaining about the lawn. This week I decided that I was going to come home from work and mow the lawn no matter what. I was going to really surprise her. I thought about it all day. I was obsessed with mowing the lawn. I have to become obsessed with something to carry it through, otherwise I get easily sidetracked and never finish it. Well, I came home, bounded in the door, changed my clothes and was going to go right to it and not let anything stop me."

"The first thing I hear is, 'Honey, will you help me lift these boxes onto the closet shelf?' I figured, well, I'll just do this really fast and get on outside to the lawn. I was going to do the job in record time and be done by supper."

"The next thing she says is, 'Your old college buddy, Steve, is on the phone.'"

"I can't believe it! I haven't talked to this guy for over five years and here he is on the phone now! How can I not talk to him? I'm glad he called, but now is just a bad time. Well, I'll talk with him a while, and tell him I'll call him back later tonight."

"Get to the point! He takes forever to get to the point."

"I have to give you the background so you'll understand the point! Jack said.

"Well, we'll all die of old age before you get to the point," said his wife.

"The point is this: After I got off the phone and was headed for the back door to start mowing the lawn, she starts nagging about how I never mow the lawn and that if I don't mow it today it will be too high and impossible to get the mower through."

"That's your point?" his wife said.

"No, the point is that when you said that, suddenly the wind went right out of my sails. One second I was going to mow the lawn or die trying and the next second I had lost all of my motivation. Once you told me to do it, I didn't want to do it anymore."

"Is that infantile or what?"

"It's just that I wanted to be able to show you that I could do it without your telling me. Once you told me to do it the victory was gone."

"I just want to get the lawn mowed. How am I supposed to read your mind? Why do you have to be inspired all the time to do anything? In life we all have to do things just because they are our responsibility!"

"When she starts lecturing me like I am a child, I just can't help pulling away and tuning her out."

"Are you saying she's just like your mother?"

He laughed, "No, she's not like my mother. She's more like my third-grade teacher, Mrs. Smith, who used to hound me all the time about my handwriting. I got an F in handwriting in the third grade. For a while I learned that if I wrote very small I could write pretty neatly, but Mrs. Smith said she would need a microscope to read it."

"There he goes, always getting off again on a tangent. He can never stick to an issue."

"What was the issue?"

"I don't even know anymore."

"Well, it sounded like the issue was shame."

Silence for awhile.

"Well, I don't mean to shame him. I often think he takes it that way though."

"I guess I'm back there sometimes instead of here. All my life people around me have had their complaints. I remember as a child asking my mother at bedtime once why I was different from everyone else. She said I was special in my way and she loved me just the way I was."

"Well, I'm not your mother, and I can't love you just the way you are if its going to lead me to a nervous breakdown."

"What is it about these problems that is going to lead you to a nervous breakdown?"

"Well, I always feel that if anything goes wrong it's my fault. I have to keep everything in order. But with this crew it's impossible. I go over to other people's houses and they look like model homes. I'm ashamed to have anyone over to our house. It always looks like a disaster area."

"You might have to accept that your house will never look like a model home."

"Actually, I wouldn't want my kids to be like theirs either."

"What do you mean?"

"Well, they are so conventional and compliant. I like the artistic bohemian nature of my kids. Did you know that Timothy won an art contest? I was never good at art. I guess I live vicariously through my kids."

"And through your husband too."

"Yes, I guess if we could just manage to have some time to ourselves we could rekindle the old flame."

"That will take some planning and organization. Let's see what we can come up with."

REVISING PERSONAL AND COLLECTIVE MYTHOLOGIES: USING BRAINSTORMERS FROM HISTORY

myth n [Gk *mythos*] (1830) 1a: a usu. traditional story of ostensibly historical events that serves to unfold part of the world view of a people or explain a practice, belief, or natural phenomenon.

Webster's Ninth New Collegiate Dictionary (1990), p. 784.

An important part of the process of healing is the revision of faulty beliefs and expectations, or "personal myths," about the self. Identifying successful brainstormers from history is an important means of illustrating to brainstormers of today that the difference between famous and infamous may lie in how the raw material of a brainstormer is cultivated. A vision of a child projected into the future by significant attachment figures (i.e. parents, teachers, coaches, and other mentors) creates a personal mythology for the child, a hypothetical future self.

Thomas Alva Edison: The Second Grade "Dropout" Who Changed the 20th Century

The minister, of course, taught by rote, a method from which Alva was inclined to dissociate himself. He alternated between letting his mind travel to distant places and putting his body in perpetual motion in his seat. The Reverend Engle, finding him inattentive and unruly, swished his cane.

Robert Conot (1979)

Edison worked on many projects at the same time. For example, in 1917 he had more than forty inventions in process. Edison credited his inability to stick to one task as being the power of his creative efforts:

> "Look, I start here with the intention of going there [drawing an imaginary line] in an experiment, say, to increase the speed of the Atlantic cable; but when I have arrived part way in my straight line, I meet with a phenomenon and it leads me off in another direction—to something totally unexpected." [Miller 1931, p. 48–54]

When it came to perception of time, Edison was lost. Experiments were timeless. In Edison's mind events blended and telescoped into each other and he misplaced even fairly recent events by as much as three months. "I have got no memory at all for dates," he confessed.

Edison's hours were so erratic that he was nearly useless as a manager—some days he showed up at ten or eleven in the morning; on others he went home when everybody else came in.

He kept no books, but jabbed all his records on tow hooks. When he finally agreed to retain a bookkeeper, it took three months to determine whether Edison was in the red or black.

Thomas Edison transformed the 20th century with his invention of the electric light bulb, the central power generating station, the phonograph, the flexible celluloid film and movie projector, the alkaline storage battery, and the microphone. "Little Al" registered more than 1,300 major patents, valued at over $25,000,000,000, before his death in 1931.

A Tribute to "Little Al's" Mother

"I discovered early in life," Thomas Edison once told a friend, "what a good thing a mother was. When she came out as my strong defender, when the schoolteacher called me 'addled,' I determined right then that I would be worthy of her and show her that her confidence was not misplaced. She was so true, someone I must not disappoint. She was always kind and sympathetic and never seemed to misunderstand or misjudge me."

"The effects of her early training I can never lose," he continued. "If it had not been for her appreciation and her faith in me at a critical time in my experience, I should very likely never have become an inventor. You see, she believed that many of the boys who turned out badly by the time they grew to manhood would have become valuable citizens if they had been handled in the right way when they were young. Her years of experience as a school teacher taught her many things about human nature and especially about boys. I was always a careless boy, and with a mother of different character I should have probably turned out badly. But her firmness, her sweetness, her goodness, were potent powers to keep me in the right path. The memory of her will always be a blessing to me." (Miller 1931, p. 48–54)

Benjamin Franklin: The Late Bloomer in Math

Sally looked sad. "Why the hounddog face?" I asked.

I could have guessed. I knew she had gotten a D in math on her report card. I was Sally's doctor and had been helping her with her attention and learning problems. Sally was a very good reader, and very smart. For some reason, math had always been difficult for her.

"I'm just no good at math. My teacher says I make careless mistakes. She says I am good at math when I choose to be. I don't know what she means. I do care, and I try very hard. My math problems just keep coming out with the wrong answers. I keep making stupid mistakes. People who can't do math are always failures in life. I guess I'm going to be one big loser."

"That's not necessarily true, Sally. History is full of examples of very successful people who had problems in math when they were your age. That didn't stop them from going on to great things."

"Yeah, name one!"

"Well, Ben Franklin would be one example."

"Ben Franklin? That funny old man that flew the kite in the lightning storm?"

"How did you know about Ben Franklin? Did you study about him in school?"

"I read about him on the back of a cereal box. It said he proved lightning was really electricity. Did you know a guy in France got killed trying to fly a kite in a storm like Ben Franklin? It said on the cereal box for kids not to try it. Ben Franklin was sad that people got killed by lightning so he invented the lightning rod."

"You're quite a knowledgeable historian."

"I'm always reading stuff like that. My dad says I taught myself how to read before I even went to school."

"He told me that too. That's what reminded me of Ben Franklin. Ben loved to read, taught himself to read before he ever went to school, just like you."

"I'll bet he never got a D in math."

"No, he always got F's in math when he was your age."

"Ben Franklin got F's in math?"

Little Ben could never learn arithmetic as a child. He dropped out when he was 10 years old, after only two years of school."

"Didn't his parents make him go?"

"Ben Franklin was born in 1706. In those days only wealthy families could afford to send their children to school. Ben had sixteen brothers and sisters and his father barely made enough to support his family as a soap and candlemaker in his small shop. Ben's father told him he could no longer afford to send him to school. He needed him to work in the soap and candle shop."

"Was that because Ben got F's in math?"

"I'm not sure I know the whole story. I do know that Ben went on to educate himself by reading everything he could get his hands on."

"Like cereal boxes?"

"Well, there wasn't much like that to read in those days. Even a book was hard to come by back then."

"How did he read, then?"

"Ben went to work in his brother's print shop. There was always a lot to read there. Ben saved his lunch money by eating only vegetables. Whenever he had saved enough he would buy books."

"Did Ben hate math?"

"If Ben hated math as a child, he must have learned to like it as an adult. When he grew up he taught himself math, too. He used to like to make up math games in his head. Ben Franklin was considered by many to be one of the most educated persons of his time. They called him 'The First Citizen of the 18th Century.'"

"Is that like Student of the Week, only for a whole century?"

"I guess you could say its something like that. Ben did get awards for his achievements. Even though he completed only two years of elementary school he was given an honorary degree from Oxford University."

"I know more stuff about Ben Franklin." Sally's memory opened like an encyclopedia. Suddenly Ben Franklin was more than just a funny little man flying a kite in the rain. He was a kindred spirit, a child who had suffered, as Sally had, with the shame of failure in school."

"Like what?" I asked.

"I know that he helped write the Declaration of Independence and the United States Constitution. He invented hundreds of neat things, like the Franklin stove that my grandma has in her living room, and the bifocal glasses that she wears. I told her all about Ben Franklin once. Grandma told me that every $100 bill has a picture of Ben Franklin on it. I'll bet she never knew he flunked arithmetic, though."

"I wonder what your grandma would say about that?"

"Grandma says some people are late bloomers. She'd probably say Ben Franklin was a late bloomer in math."

"Maybe one day you will become good at math like ol' Ben did. Maybe you'll even give some wonderful things to the world yourself."

"I don't know about that. Great people are always boys. You don't hear about girls doing stuff like that."

"That's not true, Sally. History is full of very accomplished women in history who had problems similar to yours when they were your age."

"Yeah, name one."

"That's a story for another time."

"O.K. I might find a good story about a girl myself."

"Maybe you could find a biography of an accomplished woman and read about her childhood."

"I might do that. But I might spend some extra time on my math first, just in case I'm a late bloomer."

Amelia Earhart: No Fear of Flight

Emily picked up the little toy guitar and smelled it. "It smells good, like wood!" she said. She then held it up to her ear like a sea shell. "Did you know you can hear the sea in here?" she asked. Then, without waiting for an answer, she hummed and then hooted like an owl into the guitar. "Hey, there's an echo in here! Yodeladehooo!" She knocked on the flat wooden top, "Hello, anybody home in there?" She then plucked a single string and stopped, as if in a trance, to listen to the single note, sounding all by itself, vibrating from the string into the air. She listened as it slowly faded into silence. "That's pretty," she said wistfully.

Emily was a young brainstormer I had been treating for attention deficit disorder. She was different from many girls with ADD in that she also had the "H" part that stands for "hyperactivity," making the diagnosis ADHD. The "H" for Emily meant that she was in constant motion. She had great difficulty sitting still for long periods of time, such as in school. Her body seemed always to want to be moving. In class she wiggled constantly in her seat, and she found any excuse to get up and walk around. Her mother frequently had to buy her new blue jeans as she wiggled so much in her chair that she wore holes in the seat of her pants.

Emily was considered a tomboy by others because she preferred the activity of team sports, often playing baseball, basketball, or other sports with the boys. She was less comfortable with her girl classmates, who liked to sit and talk with each other for long periods of time. Emily would get restless and bored and have trouble following the conversations. She never felt she fit in with either the boys' groups or the girls' groups. Often she played alone when she wasn't able to talk the boys into letting her join in as "one of the guys" on a team.

"What grade did you get on your smelling test this week?" I asked.

"You mean my *spelling* test?" She attempted to correct me.

"No, you know, your smelling test," I repeated.

"We don't have smelling tests," she said, a little annoyed.

"That's too bad," I said. "You seem to have a very good nose for that guitar. If you did have smelling class you would probably get good grades."

"Nobody has smelling tests," she insisted.

"They do in chef's school," I teased.

"How about music class? You can make a lot of music on that little toy guitar. Are you a musician?"

Emily did not answer. Instead she leapt up and pretended to play a hot lick on an imaginary electric guitar. "Look, Ma, I'm on MTV!" Emily poured her soul into her little pantomime.

"Do I spy an aspiring guitarist?" I speculated, half asking myself.

"I do want to play the electric guitar. I think it would be fun to play lead guitar in a band. But girls don't get to do that," she said disappointedly.

"What ever gave you that idea?" I objected. "There are many women musicians who play the guitar."

"Not the lead guitar," she insisted. Girls usually sing and strum and look pretty. Have you ever seen a lead guitarist that was a girl?"

"Well, I'm not sure I'm the expert on that subject," I said, but I don't see why you couldn't play the lead guitar if you really wanted to."

"My parents bought my brother a drum set but he never plays it. When I asked if I could take electric guitar lessons they said that I should play the flute or something more ladylike."

"You could play the flute in a band," I offered.

"But I don't want to play a flute. I want to play the lead guitar. I like rock and roll music. I like to listen to the lead guitar parts the best. My brother says only boys play lead guitar."

"Well, maybe someday you might help change those old-fashioned ideas about what girls can and cannot do," I said.

"How can one person change the way people think?" she asked.

"Well, its been done many times before. In fact, you remind me of a little girl who once changed the way the whole world thought about what girls were capable of. She proved that girls could do many things as good as or sometimes even better than boys."

"How did she? Did she play lead guitar in a rock and roll band?" Emily asked with sudden interest.

"No, she wasn't a guitarist. She flew airplanes," I answered.

"So, my Aunt Betsy is an airline pilot. What's so different about that? I don't want to be a pilot, I want to play the guitar." Emily sounded disappointed.

"It's true that its not so unusual these days for a woman to be a pilot. But it wasn't always like that, especially in the earliest days of aviation," I offered, hoping I could recapture her interest.

Emily thought to herself for a while. She had a distant look in her eyes, as if her thoughts had carried her someplace far away. Suddenly she looked at me and said, "What's *aviation* mean?"

"Well, it means 'having to do with airplanes,'" I answered.

"Have you been to Kitty Hawk?" she asked. "I went there with my family on vacation. I saw where the first airplane flew. These two brothers made it. It looked like a huge box kite. They flew it off of a big sand dune. It was kind of silly because it only flew for twelve seconds or something like that. I guess that was pretty long for being the first airplane," she said.

"Well, the little girl that you remind me of grew up during the times that just followed that day at Kitty Hawk. Those were the earliest days of the first airplanes. She loved airplanes and grew up to be one of the world's greatest pilots. A lot of people back then believed that flying airplanes could only be done by men. She wanted to prove that women could do about anything a man could do, including flying airplanes. She set a lot of early world records for flying. She was the first person, for example, to fly all by herself across the Atlantic Ocean. She proved to the whole world that women could become good pilots. She helped make opportunities in aviation open to women like your Aunt Betsy, and forever changed the world's attitudes about what women were capable of."

"What was the little girl's name?" Emily asked.

"Her name was Amelia Earhart," I answered.

"Did she have ADD like me?" she asked.

"I don't know," I admitted. "That was before people knew about ADD."

"Why do I remind you of her, then?" Emily asked.

"Well, you look a little alike, for one thing. You are both slender, have curly short brown hair, and smile with your mouth closed," I observed.

"That's because I have this gap between my front teeth. My brother says it makes me look like a hillbilly," she said, a little embarrassed.

"That's the same reason Amelia smiled with her mouth closed," I said.

"Did people say she was a tomboy?" she asked.

"Yes, they did. Amelia was always very active. She craved activity, excitement, and adventure. Do you know what her greatest fear was?" I asked.

"Being bored?" Emily guessed.

"Yes, I wonder how you knew that," I pondered in mock bewilderment.

"Amelia was also a bit lonely and shy. She just couldn't seem to fit in. The caption under her picture in her school yearbook read: 'The Girl In Brown Who Walks Alone.'"

"I wish I had more friends," Emily said sadly, "I think people think I'm kinda weird. If I played lead guitar in a rock band I could be as hyper as I wanted and it would be cool instead of weird!"

"Well, you may have something there," I agreed. "I don't think I know of a rock and roll band that was ever criticized for being too hyperactive . . ."

"What happened to Amelia?" Emily interrupted, still back on the previous subject. Did she keep on flying until she was a wrinkly old lady pilot?"

"No, she got lost at sea trying to be the first person to fly around the world. No one ever found her or knew what became of her," I answered.

"Oh, great! Don't tell my mother that I remind you of someone that disappeared like that! I make her too nervous already!" she exclaimed, then became suddenly quiet. "It's sad, though, that she got lost. . . ."

"Well, Amelia knew the risks involved in what she was doing and accepted them. Amelia always said she would prefer to live a short and adventurous life than a long and boring one," I offered.

"I'd rather live a long and adventurous life," Emily responded. "I still don't want to be a pilot. But if Amelia could prove that a girl could be one, then maybe I can prove that a girl can play the lead guitar in a band," Emily said decisively.

She fell silent. Again that wistful smile crossed her face, as if she were far away, perhaps imagining it.

Wolfgang Amadeus Mozart: The Case of "Little Wolfey"

That was Mozart! That giggling dirty minded creature I'd just seen crawling on the floor!

(Shaffer 1984)

It occurred to me as I watched Peter Shaffer's *Amadeus* that Shaffer's portrayal of the child Mozart as the "impetuous brat" could have been modeled after many of the patients I saw routinely in my daily practice. In one scene, for example, Mozart's father is apologizing for his son to the Kaiser, "It's all my fault, I have spoiled him, indulged him too much!" For a moment I was not sure if I was in Vienna in the 18th century or back at work in my office!" In another scene poor Salieri, who had been so looking forward to meeting Mozart, the great composer, dropped his jaw in shock as he perceived Mozart to be reckless, irreverent, tactless, arrogant, hyperactive, impulsive, and so on. Yet Mozart's spontaneous and imaginative compositions, his passionate "brainstorms" that seemed to pour endlessly from his mind, will move us for all time.

On the page it looked like nothing. The beginning simple almost comic. Just a pulse—bassoons; basset horns; like a rusty squeeze box. Then suddenly, high above it an oboe. A single note hanging there unwavering until a clarinet took it over; sweetened it into a phrase of such delight! This was no composition by a performing monkey. This was a music I'd never heard, filled with such longing, such unfulfillable longing, it seemed to me that I was hearing the voice of God. [Shaffer 1984]

In their book, *Driven to Distraction*, Hallowell and Ratey (1994) briefly refer to Mozart:

Throughout history there have been many great men and women who have had various learning disabilities that they managed to overcome. Although it can't be proved that he had it, Mozart would be a good example of a person with ADD: impatient, impulsive, distractible, energetic, emotionally needy, creative, innovative, irreverent, and a maverick. [p. 43]

Solomon (1995) reported that, as a small child, Mozart was said to have

a lively disposition for every childish pastime and prank, pursuing these with such absorption that he would forget everything else, including his meals . . . whatever he was given to learn occupied him so completely that he put all else, even music, on one side; e.g., when he was doing sums, the tables, chairs, walls, even the floor was covered with chalked figures. [p. 39]

Mozart was also described by Auguste Tissot in 1776 as becoming hyper-focused when he became involved in a pursuit:

[H]is imagination is as musical as his ear: it always hears many sounds together; one sound heard recalls instantaneously all those that may form a melodious sequence and a complete symphony. . . . He was sometimes involuntarily attracted to his harpsichord as by a secret force, and drew from it sounds that were the lively expression of the idea with which he had just been occupied. One might say at these moments he is himself the instrument in the hands of music. [p. 49]

Monet: "Painting and Fidgeting"

There are only two things I have ever done well: paint and fidget!

Monet

Monet is thought, by some historians, to have had Tourette's syndrome. Apparently his multiple motor tics are well documented. Fortunately for Monet, and for the rest of us, he found the opportunity to do the things he did well. If we could similarly find each child's talents and exploit them to the fullest rather than consume the better part of a childhood trying to remediate disabilities, we might have more people like Monet.

Albert Einstein

Details of Albert Einstein's early school days were first documented by his sister, Maja Winteler-Einstein (1987), which was later cited in a biography by White and Gribbin (1994). She remembers that Albert was not especially happy at the elementary school (Volksschule) he attended. His father once asked the school's headmaster for advice on selecting the best future career for Albert. The headmaster's reply was that it didn't matter because Albert would never make a success of anything. He showed no particular aptitude for mathematics although, according to his sister, what he lacked in speed and accuracy he made good by being reliable and persevering in his work.

Maja's recollection was that, as a young child, her brother had a bad temper which she believed he must have inherited from his maternal grandfather. She remembered that when Albert would throw a temper tantrum, "his face would turn completely yellow, the tip of his nose snow white, and he was no longer in control of himself." This description of a stormy Little Albert is in marked contrast to the gentleness for which Einstein became famous later in his life.

Albert transferred to the Luitpold Gymnasium at the age of ten. This was a very rigid and formal school. Albert soon began to clash with this system. The teachers there did not appear to understand or have any sympathy for the way Albert's mind worked. They soon came to the conclusion that he was a wastrel. His Greek master declared, again, that he would never be successful in anything. He was to be proved wrong. Years later, after the Luitpold Gymnasium was destroyed in a World War II bombing raid, it would be rebuilt under a new name, The Albert Einstein Gymnasium.

At age fifteen Einstein transferred to a boarding school in Munich. Six months later he was expelled. One of his teachers had declared in front of the other students that he would have preferred it if Einstein had not been in the class. When Einstein then asked why, since he had done nothing wrong, the teacher replied: "Yes, that's true. But you sit in the back row and smile, and that violates the feeling of respect which a teacher needs from a class."

Einstein attempted to enroll in the Federal Institute of Technology in Zurich, but failed the entrance exam. He waited a year and reapplied, this time gaining entry. He blossomed in the flexible, tolerant intellectual ambiance of this Swiss college. Albert Einstein went on to be a Nobel laureate and peace campaigner. He gave the 20th century post-Newtonian physics. Today his name is synonymous with genius. Like many brainstormers who floundered in the regimented learning programs of elementary school, he excelled in college when he was able to apply his own style of thinking and learning.

JFK: The Case of the Perpetual Motion Machine

He was forever pulling up his socks, toying absently with his telephone, arranging papers on his desk and then rearranging them. . . ."

James A. Reed,
Assistant Secretary of the Navy

Perpetual motion has become the Kennedy signature.

William Manchester 1962

In 1962, before president Kennedy was assassinated, William Manchester wrote *Portrait of a President*, a biography of John F. Kennedy. Such well documented descriptions of Kennedy by his contemporaries raises the question of whether his tremendous drive and talents had some origins in a hyperactive temperament. If so, Kennedy would be an example of how such energy could be successfully harnessed and channeled into a highly productive life. Was JFK a brainstormer?

As a young man in school at Choate, prior to his days at Cambridge, Kennedy is remembered by a classmate: "The biggest complaints about him were that his room was never neat and he was always late to classes" (p. 97).

Reed, then Assistant Secretary of the Navy, was a longtime friend of Kennedy's. Their relationship dated back to World War II when they served together on the same PT boat. Reed described Kennedy from this vantage point: "He had less time for trivia, and he was more restless. He will never be methodical. Every week or so he misplaces his reading spectacles—he's slightly farsighted—and has to acquire new ones" (p. 37).

While on a patrol, Kennedy's PT boat was rammed and sunk. Eleven seamen survived but were stranded in enemy waters that were known to be shark-infested. One of the crew was badly burned. Kennedy had injured his back when he was thrown against the cockpit, an injury that would follow him the rest of his life. He later recalled thinking, "This is what it feels like to be killed." Kennedy towed the injured sailor for four hours, using the man's life jacket strap and leading the crew to an island over three miles away. Because he used his teeth to tow the sailor, he swallowed a great deal of salt water. Upon landing on the beach, he promptly threw up. The next evening he swam out into the ocean with a pistol and lantern and treaded water through the night looking for a rescue boat, but there were no American patrols in the area (p. 154).

As a naval officer in World War II, Kennedy had received a low rating in military bearing and neatness. When he left with his PT boat, he did not turn in the paper work concerning where he was going, who was on board, and so forth (p. 48). There would be no rescue coming for PT-109. Unaware that they had been written off, the crew thought a Navy rescue boat must be scouting the area and wanted to sit tight and wait to be rescued. They had seen a Japanese barge pass within a few hundred yards and they were concerned that they would be discovered unless they laid low. Much to their dismay, Kennedy insisted on moving on. In the end, when the crew found out that they had been given up for lost, they realized that Kennedy's hyperactive and restless drive had been what brought them all to safety (p. 163).

One of the survivors, Barney Ross, later recalled Kennedy's response to the entire incident. "The big thing that came out in Kennedy that week was his drive." I knew it was useless for him to swim out in the water that first night. You couldn't stop him, though. He didn't make a federal case out of it, but there it was. He just had to find a way back. And then when we were picked up, he couldn't wait to get command of another boat. Everything was go, go, go with him. If it had been up to the rest of us, we would've been content to sit there and wait to the be rescued" (p. 163).

Kennedy was later decorated as a celebrated war hero and the story of PT-109 became well known. Like many war heroes, however, Kennedy did not seem impressed by his valor. A young boy once asked Kennedy how he happened to become a war hero. "It was involuntary," he replied. "They sank my boat."

As the nation's president, Kennedy was to be known for his style and pageantry. The organizing of "Camelot," however, was mostly Jackie's contribution. As a young bachelor senator, Kennedy preferred to wear rumpled khaki trousers. His socks were often mismatched. During the presidential campaign, he was forever borrowing pencils and even combs from the press. He was impatient about stopping to eat, often preferring to eat on the go, carrying candy in his pockets to munch on. James Reed remembered the shocked look on the face of a hostess when Kennedy, overfocused on a dinner conversation and ignoring his meal, pulled caramel candies out of his pocket and began eating them (p. 97).

Kennedy may have had tactile defensiveness. This is a common brainstormer trait in my experience. This symptom is characterized by a hypersensitivity and aversion to light touching by other people, clothes, and so forth. Persons with tactile defensiveness often pull at their socks and other clothes. They are irritated by the tags in their shirts, the seams in their socks, or the bed covers on their feet. They often prefer to wear light clothes (Richards 1977). Kennedy hated to wear heavy clothing. He did not even own an overcoat and avoided the hats and vests that were the proper uniform of the presidency. To compromise, the President's tailor made him clothes that looked presidential from afar or on TV but were of very light weight. "The President," his tailor explained, "has steam heat instead of blood." Kennedy explained, "I can't hold back the stops. I have to go flat out, all out."

Kennedy was known for his motor hyperactivity. When sitting he was constantly moving and seemed preoccupied with moving on to whatever was next. A news reporter commented that Kennedy "never sits in a chair; he bivouacs in it." Kennedy's fidgeting was hard on the White House chairs. Two of his chairs fell apart. On one occasion Kennedy was sitting in a swivel chair at a conference with congressional leaders. Kennedy wriggled and fidgeted in the chair until it suddenly collapsed and the President was dumped on the floor (p. 181).

It is interesting to note that, like so many brainstormers that I have treated, Kennedy had a history of encountering a psychostimulant and liking its effects. He was prescribed amphetamines during his presidency by Dr. Max Jacobsen, as documented in *A Woman Named Jackie* (Heymann 1990). If Kennedy was truly hyperactive, he may have experienced paradoxical effects of amphetamine and actually been calmed down. This was in the early days of amphetamines before much was known about them and before they were regulated. When his brother Robert expressed concern about the President taking medications, the effects of which were incompletely understood, the President replied, "I don't care if it's horse piss. It works."

Following is a partial list of patients Dr. Jacobson treated with amphetamine during that time period. How many of these well-known people may have been brainstormers: Winston Churchill, Cecil B. DeMille, Judy Garland, Marlene Dietrich, Peter Lorre, Tennessee Williams, Truman Capote, Eddie Fisher, Anais Nin, Henry Miller, Anthony Quinn, Yul Brenner, Hedy Lamarr, Andy Williams, Eddie Albert, Mickey Mantle?

Winston Churchill

Winston Churchill's early school days are well documented by Martin Gilbert (1991) in his book, *Churchill: A Life*. Abundant records from the various boarding schools he attended and his correspondence with his parents paint a vivid picture of young "Whinny." His parents first sent him to attend boarding school at St. George's when he was just turning eight years old. Winston's first report card from St. George's listed him as last in his class. Under Grammar it read, "He has made a start," and under Diligence, "He will do well, but must treat his work in general, more seriously next term." The headmaster's comment was, "Very truthful, but a regular 'pickle' in many ways." By the end of the school year Winston's academic grades were good, especially in history and geography. His conduct grades, however were still exceedingly bad. His teacher commented, "He is not to be trusted to do any one thing, and his lateness for morning school, twenty times in the forty day term, is very disgraceful. He is a constant trouble to everybody and is always in some scrape or other. He cannot be trusted to behave himself anywhere. The headmaster did acknowledge that Winston had "very good abilities" (p. 6).

At age ten Winston transferred to Brighton, where he did not do well. At the end of the first term he was at the bottom of his class in French, English, and Mathematics. His teacher commented that there was a decided improvement in attention to work toward the latter part of the term. At the end of the school year Winston was still at the bottom of his class in conduct, being thirtieth out of thirty. In spite of his poor conduct his academic grades were high. He was first in his class in the classics and third in French. His teacher, Charlotte Thomson, wrote, "If he continues to improve in steadiness and application, as during this term, he will do very well indeed."

At 14 years of age Winston attended school at Harrow. The assistant master there wrote his parents and encouraged them to "speak very gravely" with him about his "forgetfulness, carelessness, unpunctuality, and irregularity in every way." He was described as "constantly late for school, losing his books and papers and various other things into which I need not enter—he is so regular in his irregularity that I really don't know what to do; and sometimes I think he cannot help it" (p. 20).

During the summer, when Winston was sixteen, he received an letter from his mother. "You work in such a fitful inharmonious way that you are bound to come out last—look at your place in the form! Dearest Winston you make me very unhappy—I had built up such hopes for you and felt so proud of you and now all is gone. My only consolation is that your conduct is good and that you are an affectionate son—but your work is an insult to your intelligence. If you would only trace out a plan of action for yourself and carry it out and be determined to do so, I am sure you could accomplish anything you wished." In the fall his mother was again upset with him when she learned that he had started smoking. "Darling Winston, I hope you will try and not smoke. If only you knew how silly you look doing it you would give it up, at least for a few years" (p. 25).

Winston did give up smoking for awhile, but as the reader is well aware, the Prime Minister of Great Britain was rarely seen without his cigar. Was he a brainstormer medicating himself with the cortical stimulant nicotine? One wonders what type of response he had to Dr. Jacobson's medications.

FINDING AND CULTIVATING
THE BRAINSTORMER'S CREATIVITY

Madness, provided it comes as the gift of heaven, is the channel by which we receive the greatest blessings.

Socrates (In *Plato, Phaedrus and the Seventh and Eighth Letters*, trans.
Walter Hamilton. Middlesex, England: Penguin, p. 46.)

Why is it that all men who are outstanding in philosophy, poetry or the arts are melancholic?

> Aristotle (In *Aristotle, Problems II: Books XXII–XXXVIII*, trans.
> W. S. Hett. Cambridge: Harvard University Press 1936, p. 155–157.)

Still crazy after all these years . . .

> Paul Simon

Madness, as used by Plato and Socrates, encompassed a wide range of states of thought and emotion, not just psychosis, but the emphasis was on a profoundly altered state of consciousness and feeling (Jamison 1993).

I have always been struck by the tendency that brainstormers have toward creative talent. This often takes the form of art and musical talent. How often has the juvenile delinquent won art awards for drawings, how often has the parent's worst threat of punishment been to take the wayward child's music away. Brainstormers often have a long history of success deprivation. An important part of treatment is to help them identify and cultivate their talents. Often these are expressed in unconventional ways.

Talent refers to the possession of a high degree of technical skill in a specialized area. Thus an artist may have wonderful technical skills but may not succeed in evoking the emotional response that makes the viewer feel that a painting, for example, is unique. Creativity is evidenced not only in music, art, or writing, but throughout the curricula, in science, social studies, and other areas.

Problems associated with convergent thought often have one correct solution. But problems associated with divergent thought require the problem solver to generate many solutions, a few of which will be novel, of high quality, and workable—hence creative.

Intelligence and creativity do not appear to be the same thing and a highly creative child may or may not be highly intelligent.

Torrance (1974) defined the elements of creativity as fluency, flexibility, originality, and elaboration. Ideational fluency tasks require children to generate as many responses as they can to a particular stimulus, as is done in brainstorming.

Brainstormers seem to have in common the ability to think innovatively. This may be intrinsically tied to the ability to fall into an open (and therefore distractible) state of consciousness. This is associated with highly developed abilities in divergent and expressive skills. They have an uncanny capacity to elaborate, to discover unusual similarities or analogies, to link ideas or objects that are not ordinarily associated with each other and, in so doing, to fuse new meaningful relationships.

Levine (1987) noted that it was not unusual for persons with such deficits to also have unusual strengths in higher order cognitive processes such as divergent thinking. They may be especially talented at forming concepts, dealing with abstractions, and employing rules. Some discover strategies, without consciously realizing it, that make use of higher order cognitive manipulations that enable them to partially bypass their cognitive deficits.

Brainstormers are often gifted underachievers who may have rich and rapid ideational fluency with poor concentration due to an apparent inability to harness and channel thought processes in a productive way. They may have difficulty slowing down their thoughts, controlling the free flight of their ideas, and attending to details. In order to bring their concepts into fruition, they must be able to harness a compensating burst of focused energy.

Chris: The Guitarist Who Couldn't Read Music

Chris was a virtuoso on the guitar. He played all styles of music by ear. He often sat for hours working out original compositions while sitting on his bed. His mother would come in regularly and chide him to put his guitar away and spend more effort on his homework. Chris tried to play in the high school jazz band. He was good at jazz. In fact, Chris was intimately connected to the very soul of jazz. He would take a simple tune and spin out endless jazz variations on the theme.

Chris failed his band class. While playing with the band, the band teacher would suddenly look perplexed and his eyebrows would knit together. He would first be confused, then angry. He would stop the band and say, "Chris, what are you doing? That was not what was written on the page." Chris didn't have much to say for himself except, "Well, it sounds good, doesn't it?" "Chris," the teacher would say, "the purpose of the class is to learn to read music and to play it like the composer intended for it to sound. This is not a class in composition."

Chris would play his own version of the music. He played from his heart, but never seemed able to play a tune the same way twice. The music was fluid to him, and it changed with endless variations. He was a kindred spirit to the original jazz composer who spun out the original variation in much the same way.

Chris would often skip school and go downtown to the music shop and hang around the guitar section talking with the salespeople. Chris was always welcome there. They sold guitars when Chris was around. He would try out different instruments and customers would gather around to listen and enjoy his music. The customers wished they had the gift to play guitar like Chris. He inspired them to want to acquire a guitar and sign up for guitar lessons.

Why did Chris fail band class? He was too slow when it came to reading music. He often missed the teacher's instructions. When he got lost, instead of playing what was on the page he just made up the music out of his head. Jazz passed out of his soul with the sweet fluid spontaneity and originality that must have inspired the original composers.

One Percent Inspiration, 99 Percent Perspiration

Brainstorms often appear to be preceded by brief and intense states of high spontaneity, low inhibition, and freedom from the constraints of conventional ways of thinking. As with Mozart, who was characterized as "the instrument in the hands of music," novel ideas are experienced and discovered rather than created. Harvesting the raw material that springs forth, however, requires a mind that can also sustain a focused effort over time, disregard intrusions, and retain a task-oriented commitment and discipline. It is perhaps the ability to move between, or simultaneously sustain, these two seemingly opposite states of mind that is the defining characteristic of the prolific artist or inventor—the ones who welcome the unpredictable and sometimes dangerous storm, knowing that to harvest its fury is to tap into the raw essence from which creativity is won.

Edison has often been quoted as saying, "Invention is one percent inspiration and 99 percent perspiration." In other words, it takes only one good idea to invent something. The rest is perseverance. Brainstormers, on the other hand, seem to get stuck in the "good idea" mode. If they are asked to come up with a project, they come up with six great ideas. Before they get half-started on one, they come up with six more. They often have a spectacular ability to find novel solutions, new ways of thinking and seeing things. In this way they share a crucial characteristic of the people who contribute new things to our world.

The difference appears when it comes to following through and bringing an idea to final fruition. Persons with attentional problems are well known to have a host of projects started, but few ever finished. They cannot seem to sustain focused mental effort for long. On the other hand, there are those who are very capable of stoically plodding along methodically until the last "t" is crossed and the last "i" is dotted. They often lack the ability to come up with novel ideas. It is interesting to see what happens when these two opposites team up. One then becomes the spark plug, the brainstormer, and the other sees to it that a plan is organized and carried out. In industry, such use of teamwork can be very productive and task oriented. Individuals who can move flexibly between these two poles are fortunate indeed. Such creative and also highly productive people can open their minds to novel ways of thinking, come up with Edison's one percent of inspiration, and then zoom in to persistent task-oriented effort and hang in there through the 99 percent phase of the project—or, as Edison did, hire a staff to help carry out his ideas while he went on to his next brainstorm.

Brainstormers often tend to think many thoughts simultaneously. It's as if they are watching multiple TV screens at the same time. Trains of thought proceed on parallel tracks. Non-brainstormers tend more to think sequentially. They often follow one train of thought until it is completed, then start another. Creative moments for brainstormers might come when their independent parallel trains of thought find connections. To illustrate how this might happen, let's imagine the invention of Life Saver Holes candy.

The "Invention" of Life Saver® Holes?

The first time I saw a pack of Life Saver holes I said to myself, "That looks like the kind of idea a brainstormer would come up with." I amused myself with the following fantasy as I chomped away on them:

> I imagined a team of marketing executives from an advertising agency sitting around the conference table staring at a Life Saver lying in the middle of the table. This team had been assigned the task of coming up with a new marketing campaign for Life Saver candies. They are stymied. "My grandfather ate Life Savers when he was a boy," exclaimed one executive in exasperation. "They are what they are, how can they be seen in any other way? There's no other way to think about Life Savers other than the way everyone always has. It's like a Coke, it's classic. You can't change it—it would not be a Life Saver if you changed it in any way. What can we do?" The brainstorming team continues to stare at the Life Saver lying there on the table for another hour, and still it looks like the same Life Saver.
>
> Meanwhile, the janitor comes in to take out the trash. The janitor, who never made it through school due to an as-yet-undiagnosed brainstorm syndrome, is thinking about how much he could use a cup of coffee and perhaps a bag of nice fresh donut holes from the corner bakery. As he empties the trash, he becomes distracted by the conversation at the table and peers over the executive shoulders at the Life Saver. Suddenly the Life Saver and donuts link and he im-

pulsively interrupts, "Why don't you make Life Saver Holes?" He is answered with a sharp retort, "Why don't you just do your job and stop interrupting us? We are engaged in some very important work here and we don't have time for fooling around!"

After the janitor leaves, someone says, "You know, he's right. It's a great idea. Let's do it!"

Of course, I have no idea how the idea for Life Saver Holes really came about. The point in telling the story, however, is that the ability to look at the Life Saver and then immediately have the idea for Life Saver Holes is a perfect example of the kind of creative thoughts that distract brainstormers in school— or from completing a task. These distracting thoughts can also be an asset given the right time and in the right situation. How this is managed by highly creative and productive people still remains a mystery. It is a mystery worth looking into.

12
Dysgraphia and the
Brainstorm Syndrome

Dysgraphia: inability to write properly; it may be part of a language disorder caused by a disturbance of the parietal lobe or of the motor system. Also called status dysgraphicus.

Dorland's Illustrated Medical Dictionary 27th Edition (1985), p. 517

WHAT IS DYSGRAPHIA?

Mary took a test on the state capitals. She got every one right, but got everyone wrong. She could say the capitals, but when she wrote them down she misspelled every one. She got an "F" on her test.

David loved to make up stories. He would talk your ear off about the adventures of his imaginary characters or about his real experiences at the circus or the zoo or about the man who owned the Italian restaurant who always gave him a free slice of provolone cheese. When asked to write a page about his summer vacation, however, he turned in only a few simple sentences.

Tom was in big trouble. For punishment he had to neatly write "I will not turn in messy work" a hundred times. He was refusing to do it, and would not be allowed to play Nintendo until he did.

Julie's parents were worried because she reversed her letters when she wrote. Does she have dyslexia, they asked?

COMMENTS FROM TEACHERS

"Does not use time wisely"
"Not working to ability"
"Homework incomplete"
"Does not follow directions"

179

"Minus five points for lack of neatness"

"This is unacceptable, do it over"

"You can go back to printing next year, but for this year you need to learn cursive"

"You need to take responsibility for your homework journal"

"Frowny faces."

COMMENTS FROM PARENTS

"I don't understand. Last night I drilled him on his spelling list and he knew every one. This morning at school he failed his spelling test. Does he have a memory problem?"

"You have to learn how to take notes in class. How are you going to study for the tests without notes?"

"I know you can write very neatly when you want to."

"I said neat, not microscopic! I would need a microscope to read this!"

"He's just lazy."

"This is messy work. It shows a basic lack of respect for the teacher."

"He spends more effort avoiding his homework than it would take to do it!"

COMMENTS FROM STUDENTS

"This is stupid!"

"I hate to write!"

"I hate school!"

"I hate you!"

These school children suffer from a common but rarely recognized learning disability: dysgraphia. About 80 percent of the brainstormers that I treat have a significant degree of dysgraphia. Although it often appears to be a part of the neurological complex of symptoms of ADHD, it is not listed as a diagnostic criterion and is seldom discussed. Yet I have found that this disability, though as plain to see as the nose on one's face, remains invisible and undetected far too often. I have found that my ADHD patients with dysgraphia are often more impaired by the dysgraphia than by their attention problems.

Johnny brought in his schoolwork to show me. It was written in pencil, and you could see how much weight he had put on the pencil tip because you could see and feel it, almost like Braille, from the other side of the paper. There were numerous smudge marks on every line from corrections and in places the erasure had worn little holes through the paper. Written at the top in red ink was, "This is sloppy! Do over!"

Looking closely at Johnny's handwriting revealed that it was not sloppy at all. On the contrary, each letter had been crafted with the utmost care. There was a tremor in the lines and each letter was a different size. Every letter leaned in a different direction from its neighbors on either side. Some letters were reversed or were missing entirely.

It was clear from looking at this portrait of a disability that Johnny had to focus so hard to control the tip of his pencil that he wrote only one letter at a time, hyperfocusing on it alone rather than on the whole word or sentence. This was not careless, sloppy work, but meticulous and painstaking. It was also entirely legible.

As if to apologize for his poor penmanship, Johnny had drawn numerous little ornaments on his letters to dress them up. There were little curlicues attached here and there, and a Halloween pumpkin inserted between two words.

"It took him forever to write that, and its still messy!" his mother said in exasperation. "I don't know why he spells the easiest words wrong. I know he can spell them because if I ask him he can spell them out loud with no problem. He just doesn't seem to care about the quality of his written work. When the teacher tells him he has to do it over, he refuses. He says he hates to write! How is he supposed to get through school without writing?"

"What can we do about Matt's lying? When we ask him about his assignments he says he doesn't have any. Later we find out that he was lying. We tried the 'homework journal,' but that was a miserable failure! When he didn't lose it, he just carried it home with blank pages. The teacher was supposed to sign it each day but she said it was his responsibility to copy down the assignments from the board and then ask her to sign it for him. She insists that he needs to learn to take more responsibility. We've tried every kind of punishment and nothing works. Now he is lying to us. Last week he got caught forging the teacher's signature. We just don't know what to do."

Billy sat in the front row because of his high distractibility. His teacher had placed him there as part of an accommodation plan to help him pay attention. This seemed to work pretty well in terms of his paying better attention to her when she was speaking.

"Oh, class! This is the homework assignment. Be sure to write it down!" the teacher said as the chalk tapped it onto the blackboard's upper right hand corner: "Math—Chapter 11 problems 3, 7, 9, 10, and 13. Due on Thursday!" The bell rang and everyone quickly finished scribbling in their homework journals and in a flash the room was empty, except for the teacher and Billy. Billy was on "r" in the word *problems*. He looked up at the board and then back to his paper . . . "o" . . . looked up at the board and again back to the paper . . . "b" . . . again back to the board. "Johnny, are you going to be late for your next class?" "No, ma'am," Johnny said as he quickly slipped his homework journal into his book bag, hoping the teacher would not remember to check it. "Bye," he said and scurried out of the room. The teacher shook her head. "Always a dollar short and a day late," she sighed.

I often first suspect dysgraphia from samples of my patient's handwriting at the time of the initial visit. When the patient is asked to fill in answers on various forms, the distinctive signature of dysgraphia leaps from the page. While I use no formal method of assessing handwriting, the daily inspection of samples of handwriting of all ages and abilities has given me an extensive normative base. Elementary school-age children often have problems with letter reversals, spelling, punctuation, and so on, but there is a particular meticulous and tedious quality that is readily recognizable, an intense but only modestly successful effort at writing neatly. Interestingly, there is almost always a similar dysgraphic flavor to the handwriting of at least one of the parent's. This is almost always borne out by the parent's history of problems similar to those of the child in school and in life.

Children with dysgraphia may or may not have gross motor problems. Many of my dysgraphic patients are good athletes. Often dysgraphic children love to draw and may be unusually good at it. In fact, they are often reprimanded for drawing "too much" in class. Many older children and adults have found that they can learn to type and that typing is faster and easier for them than writing.

A BRIEF HISTORY OF DYSGRAPHIA

An Austrian neurologist, Dr. Josef Gerstmann (1940), first described "agraphia" fifty years ago in adults who had suffered brain injury. In this disorder the patient totally lost the ability to write. Later it was found that children with no history of brain injury could exhibit similar symptoms with partial impairment in writing, or "dysgraphia." While some cases of dysgraphia are associated with a history of brain injury, in the majority of cases the causes are not known. Dysgraphia does appear to have a large contribution from heredity, frequently tending to run in the family. It rarely occurs alone, but is usually associated with various other neurobiological symptoms.

Dysgraphia appears to be caused by problems in the fine motor planning area of the brain. Normally, children quickly develop fine motor programs, stored in the brain like little computer files, that make writing a letter, or even a whole word, an unconscious process. They can concentrate on the content of their writing rather than on the task of moving the pencil. People with dysgraphia consciously have to attend to forming and carrying out the complex sequences of fine motor movements used to form letters. Because they have to concentrate so hard on controlling the pencil, they often forget what they are writing about. They also cannot attend to rules of punctuation, spelling, and so on. If the child with dysgraphia could express his frustration, he might put it like this: "I can think, or I can write, but I can't think and write at the same time," or "You can have it correct and sloppy or incorrect and neat, but you can't have it both ways." A dysgraphic child is often criticized for sloppy writing. As the child slows to a snail's pace he is praised for his neatness ("See, I knew you could write neatly when you want to"), but penalized for not completing the work.

Writing is a complex process and problems with writing can result from dysfunction in a number of integrated neurological systems. Problems with visual-motor scanning, for example, make it difficult to copy from a book or the board. This difficulty is often evident in a low "coding" subscale of the WISC–R test, commonly given to school-age children. In spite of this low subscale on the WISC–R, dysgraphia is often missed due to the scoring conventions used. It is common in my experience with such children to see subscale scores on the WISC-R in the 14 to 16 range, reflecting an overall high IQ, but have a coding subscale in the 2 to 4 range. This is often not considered diagnostic of anything when conventional test interpretation protocols are used.

Dysgraphia is more often picked up by such instruments as the Woodcock–Johnson achievement tests. This battery of tests is fairly sensitive to what is termed "a disability in written expression." Perhaps the most sensitive diagnostic test for diagnosing dysgraphia is still visual inspection of the handwriting and a thorough history, including input from the child's teachers.

DYSGRAPHIA, THE *DSM* AND THE *ICD*

The term dysgraphia cannot be found in the *DSM-IV*. The closest diagnostic term listed in the *DSM-IV* (1994, p. 51–53) is disorder of written expression (315.2), included in the section on "Learning Disorders" (formerly "Academic Skills Disorders"). The essential feature of disorder of written expression, as defined here, is:

   A. Written skills, as measured by individually administered standardized tests (or functional assessments of writing skills), are substantially below those expected, given the person's chronological age, measured intelligence, and age-appropriate education.

B. . . . significantly interferes with academic achievement or activities of daily living that require the composition of written texts.

Dysgraphia is listed in the ICD-9-CM section of *Disorders of the Nervous System and Sense Organs* (781.3). It is considered to be a specific type of dyspraxia (motor coordination problem). The diagnostician can thus choose between listing dysgraphia as a mental disorder or a neurological disorder.

EMOTIONAL PROBLEMS ASSOCIATED WITH DYSGRAPHIA

Dysgraphia is associated with emotional difficulties. These appear to develop, in part, as a result of missing the diagnosis and failing to accommodate the disability effectively. Dysgraphia often does not cause significant impairment in a child's school career until about the third grade when the demands for writing increase rapidly. As students with dysgraphia encounter more and more difficulty, they often begin to show signs of anxiety, stress, depression, frustration and anger, avoidance of schoolwork, and rebellious behavior. They appear unmotivated and unresponsive even to the most severely punitive measures. In fact, as the child is increasingly shamed and humiliated by repetitive failures, especially in view of his peers, or punished at home by well-meaning parents, it is not at all rare for them to begin lying about their schoolwork rather than admit to having failed to complete it. Rather than reflecting a lack of motivation, such lying behavior often reflects a highly motivated child who is frustrated and humiliated, who desperately wants to avoid disappointing his parents and is becoming increasingly sensitive and intolerant to criticism.

In time this may result in demoralization, low self-esteem, deficits in social skills, and dropping out of school. Adults may have significant difficulties in employment or social adjustment. Many individuals with conduct disorder, oppositional defiant disorder, ADHD, major depressive disorder, or dysthymic disorder also have dysgraphia. There may be underlying brain dysfunctions impairing cognitive processing (visual perception, linguistic processes, attention, or memory). There may be found in the history potentially contributing factors such as a genetic predisposition, history of perinatal injury, and/or various neurological or other medical conditions. A significant degree of dysgraphia almost always comprises part of the symptom cluster of a static encephalopathy.

It is a tragedy every time a child fails out of school and becomes a dropout because of an undiagnosed learning impairment due to a medically treatable disorder. The prisons are full of people who never made it in life because such handicaps were not recognized and medically treated before a damaged self-esteem and disillusionment led them to an alternative lifestyle on the street. Dysgraphia is but one of many such disorders that are not difficult to understand and treat but can lead to disaster when overlooked or ignored.

An analogy might be that of fueling an airplane before a long trip. It is not difficult to understand the need for enough fuel. It is not technically difficult to fill the tanks. In some ways it is almost a trivial issue, except when neglected. When fueling is properly attended to, the flight can proceed normally. Similarly, with a few simple accommodations, the dysgraphic child who hates to write may find that the writing that goes on in the mind is the important part, rather than the writing that spills from the tip of the pencil onto the paper. If the child's thoughts can be harvested in spite of this disability, a dysgraphic child can become a poet, a novelist, a journalist, or any kind of writer he wishes. In fact, a gifted young patient of mine revealed to me how his fondness for writing poems stemmed from his dislike of handwriting. "I like poetry," he explained, "because its short and I don't have to write much."

ACCOMMODATIONS FOR DYSGRAPHIA

Perhaps the most central problem with the traditional approaches to such learning disabilities as dysgraphia is that the focus has tended to be on remediation rather than accommodation. Dysgraphia usually does not respond well to remediation. There are exceptions to this, however. Copying from the board can be a problem if a child has visual motor problems that make it difficult to scan back and forth from paper to board. Such children can be helped by making sure they face the board and don't have to keep turning around to look at it. Even sitting at right angles to the board makes things difficult.

Having enough time to copy is also important. Some teachers report that they do not want to put the assignment on the board until the end of class because they don't want students to try to start working on it during class time. By waiting until the last minute, the student with problems copying from the board will not have enough time to finish.

Dysgraphia often does improve with maturity. In the meantime, efforts would be better rewarded if aimed at circumventing dysgraphia rather than getting rid of it. Following is a list of potential accommodations to help students with dysgraphia.

ELEMENTARY SCHOOL
1. Spelling: oral drill, multiple choice.
2. Neatness: grade separately from content grades.

3. Homework journals: teacher or study buddy helps with writing.

4. Dictaphones: have the child learn to think out loud into a tape recorder when formulating an answer. Then he or she can concentrate on writing it down from the tape without having to create the answer at the same time.

5. Typing: learn to type. Many children can type more easily than write once they get the hang of it. Learn with video games that require typing.

6. Have the child dictate answers to the parent, tutor, or teacher, who writes them down.

7. Do not require the child to copy the assignment from the board. Let him have a copy of another student's or give the student a copy made by the teacher.

8. Write the assignment on the board early in the period, allowing enough time for everyone to finish copying it.

9. Check the student's copy for errors.

10. Have a phone number of a classmate who is willing to give the assignment over the phone in the evening if it is not successfully copied.

11. Dictate on tape instead of writing.

12. Accept the disability and do not spend too much time remediating it at the expense of other important skills that can be developed more successfully.

13. If the handwriting is legible, then it is "good enough."

14. Accept any good and honest effort without penalty.

15. A child should spend about the same amount of time and effort writing as most peers. This may mean accepting less volume of written work.

16. Modest time extensions, when appropriate, should be allowed to finish writing, but avoid expending too much of the child's learning time and effort on dysgraphic handwriting.

17. Learning to type is often not fun. Even dysgraphic children, however, will spend hours playing video games that depend on typing commands. With a little guidance on how to maintain correct hand position, typing skills are acquired through play.

18. Heavy demands on writing can be timed with maximum medication effects. Cortical stimulants can have a profound though sometimes brief (lasting only several hours per day) effect on improving handwriting.

19. Don't penalize for neatness, spelling, or punctuation. Grades for these areas of learning should be given only when that is the specific content area being evaluated (e.g., a spelling test or grammar test).
20. Do not emphasize cursive writing. While the rare dysgraphic child prefers it, my experience is that virtually all discard cursive, or end up mixing cursive and printing.

The child's best effort should be accepted. Mild problems can often be partially remediated but too often remediation of dysgraphia becomes the central preoccupation of a child's academic life, contributing much more to academic failure in the end than success.

HIGH SCHOOL AND COLLEGE
Class Lecture Notes:

1. Photocopy the notes of another student in class.
2. Tape-record lectures.
3. Obtain a copy of the teacher's lecture notes.

Written Assignments

1. Allow extra time to complete writing assignments.
2. Use a word processor.
3. Use a human and/or computerized editor (spell check, grammar check, "text-to-sound," and so forth).
4. Write and turn in paper in stages.

Exams
It would help if teachers or others who prepare the exams would adopt the following suggestions:

1. Extend time.
2. Provide environment free of distraction.
3. Alter response format of test.
4. Give take-home exam.
5. Break exam into several smaller exams.
6. Give oral exams.

7. Test the student by dialogue rather than written tests. Many kids with dysgraphia can produce more complete answers by oral examination than by written expression.
8. Have the student tape lengthy essay responses and hand in a tape supplemented by a brief written synopsis.

The list of potentially helpful accommodations for dysgraphia is endless. The main problems do not stem from a lack of practical solutions, but from those who see this neurological problem as a sign of moral weakness or indulgent parents and feel it is imperative to make it go away. Many gifted people have dysgraphia. Don't let anyone convince the child or adult that he or she is lazy or uncooperative.

13
Disability and Responsibility: "Excuses" or "Reasons"?

If a raw egg meets with a hard floor, neither the egg nor the floor considers good intentions. One of the most common questions that I am asked by parents, teachers, and even legal authorities is whether a neurobiological disability is an excuse for misbehavior. Will the old excuse of "the devil made me do it" be replaced with "the neurotransmitters made me do it"?

THE CASE OF BOB AND THE $100 COCA-COLA®

Bob was traveling home from visiting his parents in the San Francisco area and was sitting in a concession area in the San Francisco airport. He ordered a Coke and sat waiting for his flight and reading a book. After a while, the waitress came by with the tab, which was for $1. Bob reached in his wallet and realized that the only money he had was a $100 bill that he had gotten from cashing his traveler's checks at the bank that morning. He had thought at the time it would be easier to fly six hours sitting on one thin bank note than a wad of small notes. Now he had to break it anyway, and he handed it over to the waitress. He went back to reading his book, until he heard the final boarding call for the flight. He leapt up from his seat and hurried on the plane just in time. As the plane was leaving the ground, he realized that he had not gotten his change back for the Coke. He had just paid $100 for a Coke! When he arrived in North Carolina he called and tried to track down his change. He didn't have much luck.

Now let's look at some potential excuses Bob might offer:

It is the responsibility of the waitress to bring me my change. I waited a
    fair length of time and she didn't bring it back!
I was distracted by the book I was reading and lost track of the time and
    forgot the change!
I would have missed the plane if I had stopped to get my change!
The airport was noisy and the boarding announcements were not clear. I
    didn't realize the plane was ready to leave!

Now if we accept that Bob did not deliberately pay $100 for a Coke, and
that his oversight was entirely innocent, is he to be held responsible for his mistake? The argument is moot either way, as he never saw his $100 again. The
point is that reality holds us responsible. The practicalities of everyday life make
us suffer for our mistakes.

What was the reason he lost $99 in change? He simply forgot. Is that an
excuse? Well, it wouldn't get his money back, but it would be the most accurate explanation of what happened. Perhaps the most important issue is that a
reason makes him responsible, but does not excuse him from the consequences.
It's easier to hold someone responsible for his or her behavior while still forgiv-
ing them if we understand that the reasons for the behavior were innocent of
any dark motives.

THE CASE OF SUZY: "DADDY, I TOTALED THE CAR!"

A 16-year-old female patient of mine was driving down the road one day
while trying to tune in a station on the car radio. She became overfocused on
the radio dial and when she looked up all she could see were tree leaves and
branches as she crashed through the woods at the side of the road. Fortunately
she was not injured, but her car was totaled. What role did over focusing play
in her auto accident? Researchers in the U.S. (Barkley et al. 1993) and more
recently in New Zealand (Nada-Raja et al. 1997) found that adolescents with
ADHD were more likely than their peers to commit driving offenses. Female
adolescents, in addition, were more likely to be in crashes. Does the fact that
Suzy has been diagnosed with ADHD offer a reason or an excuse? Perhaps the
reason she crashed was that her attention to her driving failed her. Is that an
excuse? Well, it didn't fix her car, and had she been seriously hurt it wouldn't
have made the blood any less red. Trees are just as hard for persons with disabilities as for persons without them.

What is the point? If we accept a neurologically based symptom as the reason she crashed her car, we will readily forgive her. We then focus our attention on how to make her (and everybody else) safer in the future. For example, perhaps she should take her medication when she drives. If we limit ourselves to theories of irresponsibility and other forms of moral blaming, we don't improve the odds against future crashes.

If excuses remove responsibility, then they are often irrelevant, as responsibility eventually comes automatically. If reasons remove moral blame from an innocent mistake and focus attention instead on real opportunities for problem solving, then reasons are a good thing.

THE CASE OF REBECCA: "I DID TOO DO MY HOMEWORK! I JUST FORGOT WHERE I PUT IT!"

Rebecca has gotten zeros on every math homework assignment this year. While her test grades have been quite good, her overall grade average for the class is low. Rebecca has problems with attention. Is this an excuse? Should we just ignore the zeros and tell her she does not have to be responsible for her math homework?

Let's look for reasons instead. We find after doing a little detective work that Rebecca completes her math homework every night. When she comes to school the next morning it is tucked away neatly in her book bag. On the wall is a box for the students to put their math homework in at their leisure. Rebecca comes home every day with her math homework still in her book bag. The reason she does not turn it in is that she forgets to put it in the box.

How does recognizing the reason help? All year the teacher and parents have been scolding Rebecca for her low math grades and for refusing to take responsibility for her homework. This has served only to undermine Rebecca's self-confidence, motivation for math, and trust that the teacher and the larger adult world will understand and support her. Now that we know the reason we can come up with a solution. The teacher will remind Rebecca to turn in her math homework and will make sure she does. Is this fair? Yes.

But how will she ever learn responsibility? Certainly not by failing math. Perhaps if Rebecca is encouraged to remember, given a few extra points when she does, and backup when she doesn't, we can help her try to take on this responsibility over time. With this approach Rebecca was soon turning in her homework four out of the five days. But when she forgot, her teacher still reminded her and made sure she got the homework. Why? Because this is the fair way to deal with a disability.

In my experience, the fear that such individuals will exploit their diagnosis by inappropriately using it as an excuse for any shortcoming is ill-founded. In many cases it is nearly impossible to stop the patient from morally condemning him- or herself for shortcomings attributable to their biological limitations. Most patients would more readily accept a moral condemnation over the explanation that frightens them more: something is wrong with their brain.

14
Four Brainstormers Revisited

In this chapter we revisit our four brainstormers from Chapter 2 with the perspectives we have explored in this book. We are now better prepared to appreciate how their situations unfolded.

EMILY

"That's all we need, another cook in the kitchen!" Dad paused, looked over the letter in his hand and sighed. "Sure," he said finally, "whatever it takes to help Emily, you know I'll do it. I just hope this doc isn't a quack!"

When I first met Emily she was a quiet, shy, thin wisp of a girl with a soft voice and somber expression. It was hard to imagine her being rude to anyone, or having a temper for that matter. I had asked Emily to fill out an "incomplete sentences" form as part of her initial evaluation. Her parents reported that "This was hell! It took her about twenty-five minutes and it was not fully completed." An inspection of her handwriting revealed an obvious dysgraphia. Some noteworthy responses were:

I am ashamed that I: *am not able to play*.
I worry about: *my work*.
I love: *art*.
It isn't nice to be: *in school*.
There are times when I get: *bored*.

I hate: *work.*

It makes me sad to: *see my friends play without me.*

If I only knew: *what is happening to me.*

I would like most to: *play.*

Despite her teacher's observation that she avoided her peers, it appeared that Emily was very lonely. She seemed to want very much to play with the other children. I asked Emily what she thought about when she was off by herself at recess. "Oh, nothing, just doodling in my mind." Emily looked nervous, her eyes casting first down to the floor, then darting about the office room, scanning every nook and cranny, and finally settling on the little toy piano.

"Do you play the piano?" Emily asked. Then, not waiting for an answer or permission, went over and sat down at the keyboard.

"Only a little," I said.

"Do kids that come here play it?" Emily asked.

"Some of them do, if they want to," I said.

I used to take piano lessons," she said proudly, "but I didn't like to practice the lessons. I prefer to make up my own music." Emily relaxed more as she pecked away at the little keyboard. Here was a haven, a safe harbor for her to hide from my questions for a while. As she played she began to talk more. It immediately became apparent that Emily had a very quick mind. I had the impression she might make a good musician one day. It was a shame that so much of her energy was dispersed by her stormy temperament.

As I got to know Emily I learned that she was ashamed of her lack of discipline and the short fuse on her temper. She withdrew from her classmates because she was trying to avoid conflicts that she could not trust herself to handle without overreacting. So much of her energy had been spent hiding.

It was first necessary to complete my independent evaluation of Emily's difficulties. I had long before learned not to accept previous diagnoses on blind faith without obtaining as much information as possible from old records and evaluations and completing my clinical evaluation.

After evaluating Emily, I met with her parents to further discuss their concerns and my initial impressions. Emily's symptoms did meet the *DSM* diagnostic criteria for ADD. This diagnosis, however, captured only a thin slice of a broader complex array of symptoms: anxiety, social avoidance, volatile temper, moodiness, fine motor coordination problems, a reading disability, meticulous perfectionism, sleep problems, and so on. These would not fit into any single diagnostic category. A medical workup revealed no endocrine, metabolic, or other sources of problems that could be contributing to her symptoms. At a loss, I agreed with the diagnosis of ADD, but secretly, to myself, her diagnosis was "brainstormer."

I worked with Emily and her parents for two years. The following is a brief abstract of her treatment.

Medical Counseling and Education

In the treatment of any neurophysiological disorder, education of the parents as well as the child is a key part of the therapy. Detailed discussions of what the symptoms are and what they are not are important to set the groundwork for implementing any effective management. Most of the damage to a child's developing self-concept appears not to be from their neurological deficits. It appears, instead, to accumulate slowly over time as the result of being misunderstood and mismanaged. The adults and peers in the developing child's life are most often well-meaning but uninformed. Emily's parents were eager for information and devoured any articles, video tapes, books, or other reference materials recommended to them. They were referred to the local chapter of the support network Children and Adults with Attention Deficit Disorder (CHADD), and became very involved.

An important part of the educational aspect of treatment was discussing the risks versus the benefits of various medications. Some, like the stimulants, have a long, well-established track record. Others are newer, and some could even be considered still experimental. Emily's parents needed enough information to be able to participate actively in the decision-making process and be able to give informed consent for medical treatment.

Behavior Management

Emily's parents needed a system for managing her difficult behavior. They were referred to a book by Thomas Phelan (1984) called *1-2-3 Magic* and a videotape version by the same title and author (1990). This is a method that I have recommended to many parents over the years. Virtually all parents reported very positive results. Emily's parents were no exception. They found Dr. Phelan's methods to be very practical and effective. Fine-tuning of this behavioral management system was possible by a review of particular incidents as they arose and troubleshooting during consultative visits with Emily's parents.

Treatment with Medication: Smoothing The Roller Coaster

We discussed that sometimes high doses of a stimulant have been associated with social withdrawal and that this could be a contributing factor in Emily's case. The up-and-down, peak-and-trough side effects were common problems with stimulants, referred to informally as "roller coaster" effects. They often resulted in symptoms such as intense emotional outbursts that occurred with the regularity of a train schedule, usually at about 11:00 A.M. and 4:00 P.M.

We decided to modify her medication to a lower dose of the controlled-release stimulant Adderall.

We also discussed additional options for medications in the future. Emily's problem of initial insomnia could have been made worse by using stimulant therapy. We reviewed research and clinical experience that supported the safe and effective use of clonidine to treat sleep problems like Emily's and in controlling the kinds of symptoms Emily had been displaying during the day that were not controlled by the stimulant alone. We discussed literature that showed clonidine, used in combination with a cortical stimulant, might provide very good results.

Switching Emily to a low-dose of Adderall avoided the peak-and-trough side effects and decreased her rebound symptoms after school. However, she continued to have problems with anxiety, social isolation, moodiness, poor appetite, and poor weight gain.

Attempts at using clonidine were at first problematic. The oral tablets peaked within an hour, caused sedation, lasted only two or three hours, and had a rapid fall off with rebound hyperarousal. A low dose of clonidine at bedtime was effective in getting Emily to sleep, but her problem of waking in the middle of the night with nightmares got worse. The nightmares were caused by the clonidine after it wore off in the middle of the night. A trial with a transdermal patch proved effective, achieving the desired "smooth" effects, but Emily unfortunately developed a contact dermatitis that got steadily worse over time and the medication had to be discontinued.

A trial of the antidepressant desipramine appeared to have some mild positive effects on her mood and appetite. She still had a way to go, however, so we decided to try a new treatment I had recently developed. This was a compounded form of clonidine that could be taken as an extended-release oral capsule. This was added to the stimulant and antidepressant. Emily finally stabilized nicely. This regimen was maintained with little difficulty from that point on.

Individual Counseling with Emily

Time spent in medical counseling with Emily was mostly educational and supportive. She seemed always to need to do something while we talked. We played "Math Blaster," "SimAnt," and other computer games, or she would peck at the piano. During her visits she learned about her problems, what caused them, and how the medication worked. She seemed to enjoy talking about her concerns in her time and in her way.

Emily appeared to have a lot of interpersonal vulnerability. She desperately desired to have good relationships with others, which created a lot of anxiety for her. She had experienced a lot of past disappointments and hurt and interpreted these conflicts as others mistreating her in harsh and unfair ways. She had felt lonely, sad, and inadequate. Her defensive style—quickly turning her misunderstandings into feelings of hostility—had only made things worse. She often ended up having hostile feelings and critical thoughts toward her peers, and the rude or otherwise distancing comments created by her own sensitivity caused them to avoid her, or at least to be somewhat uncomfortable around her.

Over time, as Emily became more neurologically competent with the aid of her medication, and able to control her quick temper, she began to settle down. As this happened, she was able to experience more success socially and started to let go of the defensiveness and blaming that had complicated her problems.

Liaison with the School

I referred Emily's parents to a private educational specialist whom I had found very effective in assisting in schools where specific accommodations were needed. She observed Emily in the classroom and noted that on higher doses of stimulant Emily appeared to become more compulsive and perseverative. This was helpful in adjusting her medication to the optimal dose.

The consultant communicated with the school psychologist who had done the testing that had certified Emily as learning disabled in reading and written expression. The psychologist was thus familiar with Emily, though she was not actively involved with her at that point. Some discussions were held on how an individualized education plan could be drafted that would include more specific accommodations.

After several years Emily's family moved away due to her father's job transfer. She continued on her same medication, obtaining the compounded clonidine by mail from the pharmacist that had been filling my prescriptions for her. The last report on Emily was that she was making new friends and doing quite well. Her report card continued to reflect all A's and B's, and she was in the academically gifted program at her school.

In Emily's case treatment went very well. By the time we parted company, she was making good use of the creative talents she had always possessed. She was now better able to make friends and to tolerate the frustrations and conflicts of life in elementary school. Some residual symptoms remained and possibly always would. But now Emily, her parents and her teachers could better understand her symptoms as part of a neurobiological syndrome. Though her resulting disabilities might never be totally cured, they could be controlled and even, at times, turned to her advantage as talents.

JULIE

When I first met Julie's parents they were burdened with guilt. Her mother was worried that she had done something wrong, or that something had happened during the pregnancy. Julie had had a case of german measles in infancy and there was always the question, "Did this cause her to be brain-damaged?" Her father blamed himself, feeling that he was just not a good disciplinarian.

Julie seemed to enjoy coming to the office. She would never say a word to me but instead remained silent in her mother's lap. She clung to her mother and hid behind her coat as she studied me with keen interest in a onesided "peek a boo" game. I downplayed her behavior and discussed her problems with her parents, knowing she was listening to every word.

We decided to try Julie on a very low dose of clonidine and worked up in gradual steps to higher doses. The clonidine appeared to produce clear and immediate results. Not only did it calm the tantrums, but Julie was soon talking comfortably to the preschool teachers and others with whom she had been previously mute. The only problem was that she would become briefly sleepy about an hour after the dose. Giving the next dose more than four hours later usually resulted in a rebounding into one of Julie's overaroused furies.

Julie also had a history of difficulty getting to sleep and staying asleep. The clonidine had quite a dramatic effect on getting her to sleep without fail. She continued to have problems waking in the middle of the night, however, and most nights ended up in her parents' bed by about 2:00 A.M.

Friends and family had admonished the parents to "get tough with her or she will never learn to sleep through the night." When she showed up so frightened with a nightmare, however, they could not resist their parental instincts to comfort her, or their fatigue and need to get a good night's sleep. The clonidine, which had worn off four hours after the bedtime dose, was of no help in the middle of the night. Another clonidine dose in the middle of the night would take an hour to take effect.

In Julie's case the sustained oral clonidine, Clonicel®[1] quickly stabilized her symptoms and regulated her sleep.

Four years later, I was attending a circus with my family. At the end of the first half of the show and just before the intermission, the ringmaster announced a drawing for a new bicycle. He stood in the middle of the ring and held the box high while a clown picked out a ticket. "The winner is Julie, number 100692!" he announced with a ringmaster's flourish. Yes, it was our little Julie, the selectively mute preschooler. "Come here, little girl, and get your bicycle." Julie hesitated. She whispered to her father, "I don't want the bicycle!"

There was a long, uncomfortable silence as the ringmaster stood with the shiny new bicycle while Julie sat frozen in her seat. Her father stood up and took her hand and gently led her to the center of the ring. The ringmaster bent down to her with his microphone. "Now, what's your name, little girl?" I wondered if Julie would speak. "Julie," she confessed. "And what school do you go to?" Silence. "Well, how old are you?" "Six and a half," she answered meekly to the hundreds of onlookers. The crowd giggled nervously. "Well, congratulations, Julie, here is your new bicycle." There was an explosion of applause as Julie and her father rolled her new bicycle from the ring.

"Yes," I thought to myself. "Congratulations, Julie!"

After the circus I said hello to Julie's proud parents. They reported that she was making all A's in the second grade. She especially loved math and appeared to do it "effortlessly." She was socially poised and engaging. Her teacher pronounced Julie "the best student I've ever had!" When it became difficult for Julie's parents to afford the tuition for her private school, Julie was given a full scholarship. The investments made in addressing Julie's problems as a preschooler now appeared to be paying big dividends!

---

1. Clonicel® is the trademark for the patented formulation of extended-release oral clonidine. A license to prepare Clonicel® may be obtained free of charge from the author by any qualified pharmacist skilled in the process of compounding and agreeing to comply with all applicable laws and regulations pertaining to the practice of compounding. Clonicel® can be compounded only for individual patients as prescribed by the treating physician. Clonicel® may not be manufactured, stored in bulk, or in any way distributed without Food and Drug Administration approval.

JESSE

When I began seeing Jesse, he had not been in treatment for some time and was having a lot of difficulty in school and with his behavior. He had been treated with Ritalin in the past but had not been on medication since the previous school year.

I started Jesse on Adderall. With some adjustments, using the controlled-release Adderall and a shorter-acting afternoon tapering dose of Dexedrine, this was well tolerated without significant rebound problems. Jesse immediately showed steady improvement in his behavior and report card. He ended the year with A's and B's. Teacher feedback to me reported an immediate, dramatic, and even "striking" improvement.

Jesse was very pleased, relieved, and proud of himself. He noted no side effects from the Ritalin and stated that school seemed less boring. He found that when he participated in class, it was more interesting and time seemed to pass more quickly.

Jesse continued to be caught at school for smoking cigarettes, and the school was considering placement in a special "management school" for behavior-disordered students who are difficult to manage.

I discussed with Jesse and his parents the issue of tobacco and attention disorders from the viewpoint of current literature and my experience. It appears that many adolescents with attention disorders discover that stimulants such as caffeine and nicotine are helpful in improving concentration and calming hyperactivity. Nicotine is addicting, however, and such students who regularly medicate themselves with nicotine can form a stubborn dependency that can put them in jeopardy with the school system. The health hazards of tobacco use are, of course, well known. Adolescents who medicate themselves with nicotine are not necessarily self-defeating or oppositional. They are usually motivated by the wish to have their brains function more normally. Fortunately there are more effective and safer medications available.

I have found that cortical stimulants and/or other medications such as desi- pramine greatly reduce nicotine craving. We decided to increase the Adderall and add desipramine. Jesse cut back considerably on cigarettes, but was caught smoking marijuana in a local park by the police. Subsequent discussions again centered on self-medication with illicit drugs which is common in ADD when not adequately treated. Even when adequately treated with medication, some adolescents with oppositional defiant problems retain their behavior for some time and continue to use illicit drugs out of social habit and wanting to fit in with the peer group.

Clonidine was added to Jesse's medication regimen and he showed improvement in terms of his quick temper and tendency to escalate rapidly. He was calmer around his parents and did not lose his temper often. His mother reported, "Now, if he can just learn to keep his mouth shut, maybe he could get along with his father. They are just alike and once one of them starts they just escalate each other. Jesse is much better now about not getting so heated up, but he still has to have the last word and cannot seem to let things rest. I think if his father would ease off, it would help a great deal."

Jesse continued, however, to get in trouble for impulsive behavior. His attention was better, his temper was better, and he didn't get in as many fights, but he still seemed to get into trouble before he could stop to think of the possible outcomes of his behavior. He continued to be moody and at times seemed depressed, but he would snap out of it sometimes after only a few hours.

At that point, Zoloft, a selective serotonin reuptake inhibitor (SSRI) antidepressant was started. The effects were gradual at first, but after about six weeks his mood was much more stable and he got into less trouble for impulsive behavior. He also seemed to be able to take "no" for an answer for the first time in his life.

His mother was now concerned about Jesse's father, who continued to direct angry outbursts toward Jesse and had a tendency to be highly critical and irritable. "If I could just get *him* squared away, things would be OK," she said. Jesse is not the problem anymore. Can you treat my husband as well?"

Jesse's father was resistant to being evaluated. He had a history of alcohol abuse and a bad temper. As a youngster he was a "hoodlum like Jesse," but seemed to settle down as he got older. He did not complete college but was a successful builder and owned his business. He had not been a good student, although his psychoeducational testing had indicated a high IQ. "I don't have problems paying attention now," he said. "I don't need any medication. I don't like to take medication. Everyone on my side of the family has had problems with drugs and alcohol. I gave up drinking six years ago myself. I don't even take an aspirin now." The father did admit to smoking two and a half packs of cigarettes a day, having smoked since he was 14 years old, "like Jesse." "That's why I don't want him to get started." He also drank enormous amounts of coffee, consuming about twelve to sixteen cups per day, or two liters of Mountain Dew a day.

After the father was prescribed the same medications as Jesse, their relationship greatly improved and they were able to sit down and have long conversations for the first time. The father reported that his employees found him approachable and easy to communicate with. He stopped smoking and drinking caffeine without any specific intention to do so, stating, "I just stopped having a craving for that stuff."

Some discussion was held at that time with Jesse and his parents about involving a substance abuse counselor or program, that would not undermine the legitimate use of medications in Jesse's treatment.

At the next visit Jesse's grades had continued to improve, he had stopped smoking, and the question of his placement in a special public school for emotionally and behaviorally troubled kids had been resolved, with Jesse staying in his school. He continued to do well in school and was an excellent soccer player on the school team. This glow of success was dampened when Jesse was caught again by the police for smoking marijuana. His parents also reported that they had found beer in his room. A hearing was pending.

I explained to Jesse that sometimes patients can get themselves in trouble faster than their treatment can help them turn things around.

I explained that his best chance for the future was to continue to do well in school and sports, not to break the law, and to focus on controlling his symptoms with legitimate medications. Helping a child achieve and maintain competence in the mainstream is the most effective intervention I have seen for avoiding drugs and crime in children with neurobiological disorders.

After returning from a summer leave, Jesse told me of an incident involving LSD for which he would be going to court. At that point we restarted the Zoloft that he had stopped taking over the summer.

While I remained, and still remain, very concerned about Jesse's history of emerging conduct problems and illicit drug abuse, I hoped that the growth that I saw progressing steadily would win out in the long run. Reports from Jesse's teachers this year have been outstanding. He auditioned and was accepted for the school play as one of the leading actors. Now we can only hope and pray. The rest will be up to Jesse.

BEN

For some years now it has been common clinical wisdom among those who treat children with ADHD that the symptoms of the identified child-patient are often shared by one or both parents. In spite of this, there was not much effort to diagnose and treat parents or even adults for that matter. In the last few years this has changed. Now it is common to find several members of a family sharing a similar diagnosis and treatment plan. Evans and colleagues (1994) have even proposed treating the ADHD parent(s) before beginning to treat the

ADHD child to see if the increased stability and organization of the parent(s) is enough to stabilize the child.

In my experience working with families over the years, I have found it best to identify all persons in a family who need medical attention and to treat all who are significantly impaired. When several—or even all—members of a family in need of medical therapy are properly assessed and successfully treated, something wonderful often happens: the family as a whole can then pile into the familyroom and be what families are meant to be—the whole being more than the sum of the parts.

At first there seemed to be little to suggest that Ben had ADHD. There was no recollection of any of the specific symptoms of ADHD during his childhood. He had done well in college, medical school, and his postgraduate surgery residency. The fact of good academic record per se is often used as an argument against the diagnosis of ADHD. I have found the "retrospecti-scope," however, to be an unreliable source of such historical data. An invaluable source of data regarding childhood school functioning is readily available and usually without cost. This is the adult patient's archived school records. My adult patients are frequently surprised when I request these records, and usually do not expect that they still exist. However, these records are usually kept in storage for many years. We called the district where Ben went to school and were able to get a copy of his school records from the fourth through eighth grades. Table 14–1 shows some of the highlights from those records:

Ben's grades were pretty mediocre. It was not the kind of report card one would expect from a future surgeon. Standardized California achievement tests

TABLE 14–1. Ben's Grades

Subjects	Grade 4	Grade 5	Grade 6
Language	C	C+	B+
Language	C+	C	B-
Reading	C+	B	B
Spelling	C	B	B—
Handwriting	C	C	C+
Social	C+	C	B—
Arithmetic	C	B—	C+
Science	C+	B—	B
Art	B	C	C
Music	C	B	C
Physical	B	B	C

Table 14–2. Ben's Achievement Testing

California Achievement Test (CAT) *(Reported by grade equivalents)*				
Grade	Arith	Language	Reading	Total
	GE	GE	GE	GE
3	4.4	4.3	4.4	4.4
4	5.2	7.1	7.1	6.5

(CAT), however, revealed that by the fourth grade Ben was a grade level ahead in math and three grade levels ahead in language and reading. He received C's in both of these subjects that year.

The achievement testing shows that Ben was learning. Why didn't his grades reflect his knowledge? Intelligence tests (IQ) were available from the sixth grade.

At about age 12 Ben scored as having a mental age of a 19-year-old. The IQ score of 151 placed him in the very superior range of intelligence. Again we find ourselves wondering why that year his grades continued to be lackluster B's and C's. Of course these were not terrible grades, but they were not consistent with his IQ and achievement scores.

The answer came from reviewing the subjective teacher comments (see Table 14–4), which often tells a vivid story. These comments were unbiased with respect to the diagnosis of ADHD. At that time, which was in 1963, ADHD did not yet exist as a diagnostic concept. Appreciating this fact makes the teacher comments very compelling.

When these data were combined with the rest of the available historical data and a standardized battery of Continuous Performance Tests (CPTs), the picture that emerged was very consistent with ADHD. Ben had never been hyperactive or impulsive, and his attention problems were mostly limited to processing language when it came through his ears (listening to oral instructions). He had functioned well in environments that were not too overstimulating for him. His most impairing symptom was a very low tolerance for noise.

TABLE 14–3. Ben's Psychoeducational Testing

Binet Intelligence Quotient (IQ)	
Grade:	Sixth
Chronological Age:	11 years, 10 months
Mental Age:	19 years, 0 months
Total IQ:	151

TABLE 14-4. Comments from Ben's Teachers

Grade 4. Ben has the ability and is knowledgeable in many subjects, but he suffers from a great lack of organization and talkativeness. He is pleasant and cooperative and his classmates enjoy him and his little "problems" (lost paper, wrong page, multiplying when it said divide, and so forth).

Grade 5. Ben is pleasant, always ready for a laugh, bubbling over with the joy of life and friendship. He has a keen interest in science. Sometimes his work is not too carefully done.

Grade 6. Much ability when he concentrates on a task; self-confident and poised, but not particularly concerned about school assignments; engages in self-distractions; doesn't listen well.

Grade 7. A talkative boy who has varied interests. Is an adequate student who works fairly well. He shows no great physical ability but is well accepted by his fellow students.

Grade 8. A very pleasant boy with a curious mind. When directed down proper channels I'm sure Ben can accomplish more than the average in his class. However, Ben tends to be a bit stubborn about some things. If he can't see the value in something, he won't do it. A commendable trait at times, but can be overdone. Very likable. Well liked and respected by class (Class Vice President 1st semester).

In Ben's case, medication was not needed at work. The operating room was typically quiet and subdued. He never had any problems there. The greatest challenges of his day, however, were to be found at the end of the work day: five very rambunctious and noisy young children. The three older children were formally diagnosed with ADHD and the two younger were highly suspect. The cumulative effect of each child's contribution to the Richter scale was geometric and somewhat reminiscent of a nuclear chain reaction. Once a critical mass of chaos was reached, things could rapidly get out of hand.

Ben found himself staying later and later at work, flying his plane more often, studying long hours in the attic, taking walks—anything to extricate himself from the noise. His wife felt bitter over what she experienced as abandonment. Ben would leave, however, to spare the family an explosive temper outburst when he felt he could stand no more "racket." His departure, however, was experienced as a lack of interest and caring.

Ben was tried on a small dose of Adderall, which he took just before leaving the hospital and heading home. This appeared to do the trick.

I have been working with the family for several years now. Each member is doing well. The oldest boy, who was two years behind grade level and had been placed in a special school for learning-disabled students, is now on the A/B honor roll in a regular public school with all regular classes. His younger siblings are doing as well. What is remarkable to see is that the whole family is now doing well. The family was also the patient, but could be helped only by treating each individual member who needed it. Each member had contributed a share to the chaos. Once they were all doing well individually, when they piled into the familyroom together something new happened: the whole was still greater than the sum of the parts, but now something called a "family" happened.

I recently saw Ben for a routine medication review and asked him how things were going with his tolerance for noisy households. "When I walk through the door, five kids immediately stampede and pile on me. Now I don't mind that. In fact, its fun. My evenings call for much more work than when I'm at the hospital. I help Joyce get the kids fed, bathed, teeth brushed, and into their pajamas, and put them to bed. The clonidine slow-release capsule at night has been a miracle in terms of getting them to sleep. They all actually want to go to bed now. Before, it was like hand-to-hand combat to get them there. It's easier for them and I also have a lot more patience with them now. They don't get on my nerves like they used to. I guess its a combination of my increased tolerance for noise and their being less noisy. They all have to have their storytime now when they go to bed. At first I was reading them bedtime stories out of books, but now they like it better when I just make up a story. Now we all just make them up out of our heads each night."

"What is an example of a story," I asked.

"Well, I can't really remember them very well. The kids always have to remind me and insist that I get the story right in every detail."

"Well, how about just a short synopsis of a recent story you and the kids made up," I asked. Ben looked a little embarrassed.

"They're just crazy little stories, you know, the kind of stuff kids enjoy. Let's see. Last night, Jennifer wanted to hear the one about the astronauts. Sometimes I can't remember the stories, but they do, and insist that I tell it right! If I make a mistake they correct me," he laughed with pride and that daddy-sparkle in his eye that I noticed was growing with each visit. Anyway, Jennifer likes the one about the four brothers who fly off into space in a spaceship and get stuck. No one will go up there to help them because everyone is too scared to help the boys. They keep looking all over the world for an astronaut to go help them, but everyone says its too dangerous and refuses to go. The four brothers are stuck in space and helpless. Then the sister volunteers to go and flies into space and rescues the four brothers."

"That's it," he said with the embarrassed grin that a parent has on his face when he's caught off guard on the floor acting like a horse with a kid on his back and hopes he doesn't look too ridiculous. "It's better when I'm telling the story to the kids. It has a lot more details, but that's the main idea."

Then he laughed again and the scene could be seen in his eyes as he had visualized it. "Then each kid has to hear the story all over again, only this time its the oldest son who rescues the others, and again and again until everyone gets to be the hero. You'd think they'd get tired of it, but they never do."

"After the kids go to bed, I go downstairs and watch TV with Joyce. This is something I could never do. We used to argue about this a lot. She likes to watch the Letterman show. She thinks its great but I could never stand TV. I could never just sit on the couch and watch that stuff. I've never even liked to watch movies. Joyce insisted that this was supposed to be our time together to relax at the end of a hard day, but watching TV was not my idea of relaxing. I tried to, but I always ended up falling asleep. I always just wanted to get someplace where it was quiet. Sometimes I went outside and took a walk to wind down."

"Has any of that changed with the medicine?"

"Well, at first I didn't want to take it too late because I thought it might keep me up, but I learned to time it right so it wears off right about bedtime. Now I can sit with Joyce and watch Letterman. It's still not my idea of fun, but its OK. I guess its pretty funny sometimes. Joyce seems to like it. We do this TV thing together and I don't mind it now. The main thing is that we get to spend a little bit of quiet time together after the circus has retired for the night. I guess I never liked TV because I never could pay attention to what people were saying very long. Even in medical school I always liked to read, but I never could get much out of the lectures. I've noticed I'm a much better listener now."

Ben then explained that he was a bit eager to get home. This was his day off and before he left to come for his appointment he had been watching a kid's show on TV with his two-year-old son. "You know, that little fellow likes to sit there and hold onto my thumb. He's got a grip like a vise. If I try to get up and sneak away, he says, 'No go! No go!'" He laughed again with that "Don't kids do the darndest things" gleam in his eyes. "I've got to get back to him; I promised I would be right back."

As he started to leave he stood with his hand on the doorknob and added, as an afterthought, "You know, this was the fifth child that Joyce and I argued so bitterly about whether to have or not. One day recently I was thinking, and you know what I figured out? I was not really worried so much about whether Joyce could handle another child. Somewhere in me something was telling me I could not handle another child. I didn't realize it then. But you know, when the others were very young and growing up, I missed all of that when I was away working. Now with this one, I am there seeing every new step he makes, all the little milestones he goes through. If we hadn't had the fifth one, I might never have known what it's really like. I feel such a deep bond to this little guy. There's just nothing better than being a father."

Ben never lacked any amount of love in his heart. He just lacked a stimulus barrier. He could not say, as Captain Kirk might, "Scotty, energize the force shield!" or "Scotty, beam me up!" to keep the thousands of little meteors of sights and sounds of rambunctious children from impacting on and overwhelming him. Scotty might say, "But Captain, we don't have enough dopamine in the frontal poles to activate the shield! We've got to get into warp speed and get out of here!" With what turned out to be a very modest dose of Ritalin and a little insight, Ben was able to do what most people effortlessly do: filter out the noise and let the good stuff in.

15
Summary and
Parting Comments

Brainstorm syndromes may impair normal learning and social and emotional development in many millions of people in this country and around the world. There is, for example, an average of one to two children per classroom in the U.S. significantly impaired from a variety of neurologically based learning, attention, and emotional disorders. Significant symptoms often persist into adulthood and throughout the life span. Many persons struggle over a lifetime, never understanding symptoms that continue to hamper and impair adult social and occupational functioning. On the other hand, what is one person's handicap may turn out to contribute to another's genius. History is full of examples: Thomas Edison, Benjamin Franklin, Mozart, John F. Kennedy, Ernest Hemmingway, among many others. Whether considering persons with neurobiological "disorders" to be gifted or cursed, published works have so far focused primarily on cognitive aspects of such disorders. The murkier domains of stormy emotions have been less well defined.

Many currently available psychiatric diagnostic labels provide little help in guiding our insight into the origins of such disorders. The diagnosis of ADHD is one example. This diagnosis has been popularly accepted as a unitary or one-dimensional concept, but it actually encompasses a broad range of neurobiological disorders. These overlap and blend into each other with a host of other psychiatric, neuropsychiatric, and medical disorders.

As the names of symptoms and syndromes continue to evolve over time, people remain much the same from a biological point of view. What changes is how we organize and frame what we seek to understand. When we give a name to an idea or group of ideas, we create a tool for organizing what we observe and how we think. The trade-off is that we also create an observational bias; we filter out and keep from ourselves what the names do not describe and what we thus can no longer see and understand.

The diagnosis of ADHD again illustrated this point. ADHD is a diagnostic term for a disorder with three basic dimensions: inattention, impulsivity, and motor hyperactivity. What about emotions? The sudden and intense episodes of emotional dyscontrol often seen in some people with ADHD are usually dismissed as "secondary to" or "associated with" or "comorbid with" the primary problems of cognitive and motor dysregulation.

Brainstorms has endeavored to explore questions surrounding the possible neurobiological underpinnings of the emotionally hyperactive and hyperreactive components of ADHD and its many related neurobiological disorders. We have seen that when we look closely at such monochromatic concepts as ADHD, they quickly burst into a rainbow of colors. Each one is a window to new insights into the basic biological foundations of vast arrays of human frailties and gifts and of our own failures and triumphs.

This book has aimed to ponder such issues, perhaps expanding the questions rather than providing any definitive answers. The case material presented was from my clinical practice. For this I owe a great debt of gratitude to my patients. I hope that what they have taught me will help others who are walking or will walk similar paths.

Over the years of daily work in the trenches as a child, adolescent, and adult psychiatrist with a special interest in neurobiological disorders, I accumulated experiences from treating several thousand patients. I was repeatedly struck with the inescapable impression that in many of my patients symptoms of emotional dyscontrol (emotional storms) were not only associated with their "primary" neurobiological disorder but appeared to betray a basic dimension of an underlying neurophysiology that provided the foundations for both. Has this hypothesis been proven as absolutely "true" by formal, rigorous, and empirical scientific methods? No, and I will also say that it has not been proven here either.

Before we conclude that we are hopelessly lost in our ignorance, we will recall our brief look at the exciting "explosion" in the pursuit of knowledge about the brain. There is much accumulating evidence in the scientific and medical literature, for example, that neurotransmitters such as noradrenaline, serotonin, and dopamine play key roles in the regulation of processes such as selective attention, impulse control, and motor activity. It is becoming clear that they also play similar roles in the regulation of emotional arousal and reactivity as well. Dysfunctions in basic neural circuits or systems that rely heavily on these neurotransmitters may provide the basic neurophysiological substrata from which higher cortical functions and psychological processes are differentiated and elaborated.

These prepsychological substrata may underly, for example, what we have come to think of as temperament. Here is where the regulation of selective attention, filtration of noise, energy, sleep, and wakefulness reside. Here also can be found the neural systems that regulate emotional intensity and reactivity.

Do these substrata that are the foundation of emotional reactivity and emotional storming add new dimensions to such concepts as ADHD?

The so-called firecracker temperament often associated with certain sub-types of ADHD is characterized as a temper that is quick to heat up but just as quick to cool down. Such intense, unpredictable, rapidly appearing, and escalating emotional outbursts can leave broken hearts in their wake, including that of the person who blew up when anger turned to regret in the aftermath. Such episodes of emotional dyscontrol, whether involving intense anger or any strong emotion, can present the most challenging aspects of managing brainstormers of all ages. On the other hand, unexpected but welcome bursts of creativity and inspired vision are among our most cherished treasures. The exploration of the many paradoxes of these emotional storms, or brainstorms, was the topic of this book.

Exploring the origins of brainstorms was greatly enhanced by our acquiring a basic working knowledge of brain biology. Keeping a few key concepts and about a dozen bits of jargon in mind greatly helped us achieve our goal of better understanding how our brains work. We also hope to better understand and appreciate those who may be cursed and blessed with paradoxical symptoms. The neurobiological dysregulations of brainstorms and their syndromes appear to provide raw materials, the basic "stuff" that many disabilities and talents are made of. A future medical diagnostic system, broadened and informed by neurobiology, may help us to understand the differences among us in a way that helps to minimize our tendencies to blame and stigmatize.

While *Brainstorms* does not pretend to have the "proven" answers to the "ultimate" questions, this author will be more than satisfied if this effort serves to broaden the field of inquiry a little. As I conclude, if the reader is now as perplexed as I am by the complexities of the human condition, then *Brainstorms* has served its mission. We now share more reverence for the rich complexity and diversity that inspires and frustrates our efforts to know and master our nature. Perhaps this will help us better respect our patients, ourselves, and our world.

Appendix A
Consent For Treatment
With Medications

Patient's Name: _____

Age: _____

    I understand that the Food and Drug Administration is charged with the regulation of the manufacturing and advertising of pharmaceuticals, including medications. I also understand that the term *approved uses* in the drug label means that the FDA has approved the advertisement of that particular drug for those listed uses. I also understand that additional medical research and clinical experience often extends the uses of medications to additional indications and/or populations of patients (e.g., different age groups) to those listed as approved by the FDA for advertisement. I understand that the FDA does not consider its role to be the regulation of physicians' practice of medicine. Uses of medications by physicians that are not listed as indications on the drug label or in such publications as the *Physician's Desk Reference (PDR)* may be entirely appropriate based on the current state of scientific and medical knowledge.

    I have discussed with my doctor the various reasons for treatment with medications, the relative risks and benefits of each, and have been given the opportunity to ask and have answered all questions to my satisfaction. I have been given the opportunity to review relevant drug information sheets and to retain a copy for my use. I understand that I may ask any questions in the future regarding specific medications used and may revoke my consent at any time with written notice.

Medication(s): _____

Patient's Signature: _____

Guardian: _____   Relationship: _____

Prescribing Physician: _____

Witness: _____   Date: _____

Appendix B
List of Medications
Referred to in this Text

Trade Name	Generic Name	Family of Medication (main historical use)	Mechanism of Action
Adderall	amphetamine	cortical stimulant	releases DOP, NA
Ativan	lorazepam	antianxiety	benzodiazepine recptors
Buspar	buspirone	antianxiety	SSRI
Catapres	clonidine	alpha-2 agonist	decreases NA
Cataprestts	clonidine	alpha-2 agonist	decreases NA
Clonicel	clonidine	alpha-2 agonist	decreases NA
Cylert	pemoline	cortical stimulant	releases DOP
Depakote	vaproate	anticonvulsant	stabilizes nerve cell membranes
Desoxyn	methamphetamine	cortical stimulant	releases DOP, NA
Dexedrine	dextroamphetamine	cortical stimulant	releases DOP, NA
Effexor	verlafaxine	antidepressant	inhibits reuptake of NA and SER
Elavil	amitryptyline	antidepressant	inhibits reuptake of NA and SER
Haldol	haloperidol	antipsychotic	DOP receptor blocker
Inderal	propranolol	antihypertensive	beta receptor blocker
Luvox	fluvoxamine	antidepressant	SSRI
Norpramin	desipramine	antidepressant	inhibits reuptake of NA
Pamelor	nortryptyline	antidepressant	inhibits reuptake of NA and SER
Prozac	fluoxetine	antidepressant	SSRI
Ritalin	methylphenidate	cortical stimulant	releases DOP, NA
Tegretol	carbamazepine	anticonvulsant	stabilizes nerve cell membranes

Trade name	Generic Name	Family of Medication (*main historical use*)	Mechanism of Action
Tenex	guanfacine	alpha-2 agonist	decreases NA
Tofranil	imipramine	antidepressant	inhibits reuptake of NA and SER
Wellbutrin	buproprion	antidepressant	inhibits reuptake of NA and SER
Xanax	alprazolam	antianxiety	benzodiazepine receptors
Zoloft	sertraline	antidepressant	serotonin reuptake inhibitor

Family of Medications	Used to Treat:	Legend:
antianxiety	anxiety	DOP = Dopamine
anticonvulsant	seizures	NA = noradrenaline
antihypertensives	high blood pressure	SER = Seroton
antipsychotic	psychosis	
cortical stimulant	narcolepsy, ADHD	
alpha-2 agonist	high blood pressure, normalize arousal	
antidepressant	depression	

Glossary

Note: The definitions offered in this glossary reflect the author's use of these terms in this book. For more complete or other definitions, consult a standard medical dictionary.

ADD—attention deficit disorder without hyperactivity

ADHD—attention deficit hyperactivity disorder

Adrenergic—term applied to nerve fibers that, when stimulated, release epinephrine (adrenaline) at their endings; neural function regulated by adrenaline or noradrenalin

Adrenoreceptor—adrenaline receptor on the surface of the nerve cell

Agonist—something that acts the same as

Anergic—without energy, lethargic; refers to anergic depression; characterized by abnormal inactivity; inactive

Antianxiety—an agent used to relieve symptoms of anxiety; reducing anxiety

Anticonvulsant—an agent used to prevent or relieve convulsions

Antihypertensive—an agent used to counteract high blood pressure

Antipanic—an agent used to control panic disorders

Antipsychotic—an agent used to control psychotic symptoms; effective in the treatment of psychosis

Attention—selective awareness of a part or aspect of the environment

Auditory—pertaining to hearing

Autoimmune—a reaction of the immune system resulting in a part of the body becoming allergic to itself

Autoregulatory—system regulating itself by utilizing feedback information

Benzodiazepines—class of antianxiety drugs; any of a group of minor tranquilizers, including chlordiazepoxide, clorazepate, diazepam, flurazepam, oxazepam, etc.; having a common molecular structure and similar pharmacological activities such as antianxiety, muscle relaxing, and sedative and hypnotic effects

Bioavailability—availability of a drug for the body

Biogenetic—a theory of causation by biological factor

Bradycardia—slow heart rate; slowness of the heart beat, as evidenced by slowing of the pulse rate to less than 50

Catecholamine—biologically active amines, adrenalin, and noradrenaline derived from the amino acid tyrosine; one of a group of similar compounds having a sympatho-mimetic action, the aromatic portion of whose molecule is catechol, and the aliphatic portion an amine. Such compounds include dopamine, noradrenaline, and adrenalin

Cerebellum—a part of the brain located at the back of the neck that coordinates muscle movements

CHADD—Children and Adults with Attention Deficit Disorders, national support group. 499 NW 70th Ave., Suite 101, Plantation, FL 33317. (305) 587-3700

Chromosome—a large unit of DNA containing many genes

Cingulate gyrus—area in the brain just above the corpus collosum

Clonicel®—trade name for extended-release oral clonidine

Clonidine—medication used to normalize noradrenergic functions in the nervous system; alpha-2 adrenoceptor; hydrochloride, an adrenergic, used as an antihypertensive, administered orally

CNS—central nervous system

Comorbidity—occurrence of two or more discrete independent illnesses at the same time and in the same person

Congenital—present at birth

Corpus collosum—large body of white nerve fibers that connects the right and left hemispheres of the brain

Coxsackie virus—virus that may produce a variety of illnesses, including aseptic meningitis, herpangina, epidemic pleurodynia, acute upper respiratory infection

CPT—1. computerized performance tests; 2. contemporary procedural terminology

Dermatitis—inflammation of the skin evidenced by itching, redness, and various skin lesions

Disinhibition—removal of inhibitions, as reduction of the inhibitory function of the cerebral cortex by drugs such as ethyl alcohol or reduction in the severity of superego controls in psychology

Dopaminergic—neurons that release dopamine

DSM—*Diagnostic and Statistical Manual*, a diagnostic manual specific to mental disorders, published by the American Psychiatric Association

DSN (dopamine–serotonin–noradrenaline)—system of profiling neurobiologically related systems according to the type of neurotransmission dysfunction

DSNQ (Dopamine–Serotonin–Norepinephrine Questionnaire—a questionnaire used in DNS profiling

Dysarticulation—speech disorder of pronunciation related to impaired planning and sequencing of fine motor function

Dysarthria—imperfect articulation of speech due to disturbances of muscular control that result from damage to the central or peripheral nervous system

Dyscontrol—faulty control (mechanism)

Dysfunctions—disordered functions; disturbance, impairment, or abnormality of functioning

Dysgraphia—neurologically based expressive writing disorder related to impaired fine motor sequencing; disorder of written expression; inability to write properly; it may be part of a language disorder caused by a disturbance of the parietal lobe or of the motor system

Dyskinesia—disordered motor function or defect in voluntary movement

Dyslexia—a neurologically based reading disorder related to processing of written language

Dysphoria—unpleasant and unwelcome emotion, such as in depression

Dyspraxia—difficulty or pain in performing any function

Dysregulation—disordered, unreliable, or faulty regulation

Dysthymia—a low-grade depression; a mood disorder characterized by depressed feeling (sad, blue, low, down in the dumps) and loss of interest or pleasure in one's usual activities and in which symptoms are not severe enough to meet criteria for major depression

Ectopic—in an abnormal location

EDEG (electrodermal encephalogram)—a noninvasive neurophysiological assessment technique for indirect examining of central noradrenergic function and dysfunction by measurements of variations in skin conduction

Encephalopathy—any brain dysfunction

Familial—occuring in two or more members of a family

FD&C—Food, Drug and Cosmetic Act of 1962 in which the Food and Drug Administration was given authority to regulate the advertising of pharmaceuticals

HPMC—hydroxypropylmethylcellulose; cellulose polymer used in extended-release formulations of certain medications; used as a suspending and viscosity-increasing agent and tablet excipient in pharmaceutical preparations

Hyperarousal—overaroused; a state of increased psychological and physiological activity marked by such effects as reduced tolerance to pain, insomnia, fatigue, accentuation of personality traits, etc.

Hyperfocused—a state of highly focused and fixed attention; intense concentration

Hyperkinesis—a diagnostic term found in the ICD referring to increased (or excessive) activity behavior occurring in an amount which exceeds normal and of unknown cause

Hyperkinetic reaction of childhood—a diagnostic term found in the *International Classification of Disease* (ICD); increased or excessive activity; pertaining to or characterized by hyperkinesis; pertaining to or characterized by hyperkinesia

Hypermotoric—excessive motor activity

Hyperreactivity—overreactive

Hyperreactive—pertaining to or characterized by a greater than normal response to stimuli

Hypertension—persistently high arterial blood pressure

Hypervigilance—a high state of alertness

Hypnotics—a drug that acts to induce sleep

Hypotensive—abnormally low blood pressure

ICD—*International Classification of Diseases* published by the World Health Organization; diagnostic manual for medical intervention and diagnosis widely used throughout the world

Impulse—sudden uncontrollable determination to act

Impulsivity—acting on an impulse without fully considering possible outcomes

Inattentiveness—inability or difficulty with sustaining attention

Lability—volatile characteristic; quick-to-change emotional states; in psychiatry, emotional instability; rapidly changing emotions

Limbic system—an area of the brain important in emotion and drives

Locus coeruleus—small pea-shaped area in the center of the brain involved in regulation of the brain's noradrenergic systems

Major Medical—a contractual term used by some insurance companies to define certain categories of reimbursement eligibility in an insurance policy

Maladaptive—contrary to adaptive; failure to adapt or fit one's needs to the environment

MAOIs—monomine oxidose inhibitors; class of antidepressants

Meninges—the three membranes surrounding and covering the spinal cord and brain—the dura matter (external), the arachnoid (middle), and the pia mater (internal)

Meningitis—an inflammation of the meninges

Mental and nervous—a term used by the insurance industry for contracting health insurance policies (not a medical term)

Mesolimbic— an area of the limbic system that is thought to pertain to psychotic symptoms and certain emotional regulations

Narcolepsy—a chronic ailment consisting of recurrent attacks of drowsiness and sleep. The patient is unable to control these spells of sleep but is easily awakened

Neuroaffective—pertaining to mood states associated with neurological functioning

Neurobiology—the biology of the nervous system including its anatomy, physiology, biochemistry, etc.

Neuroleptics—drugs used to treat symptoms of psychosis

Neuromotor—involving both nerve and muscle function

Neuropharmacology—that branch of pharmacology dealing especially with the action of drugs upon various parts and elements of the nervous system

Neurophysiology—pertaining to the functioning of the nervous system

Neuropsychiatric—psychiatric illness associated with abnormal neurological functioning

Neuropsychic—pertaining to the nerve center concerned with mental processes

Neuroregulatory—processes that regulate various functions of the nervous system

Neurotransmitter—a chemical used in the communication of one nerve to another

Noninfectious—a causative factor of an illness that is not an infection

Noradrenaline—a neurotransmitter associated with regulation of the nervous system; also called norepinephrine

Noradrenergic—neural function regulated by noradrenaline

Norepinephrine—synonym for noradrenaline

Normed—statistical process of creating a description; with reference to the normal population

Normotensive—normal blood pressure

OCD—obsessive compulsive disorder

Orthostatic—decrease in blood pressure, related to a charge in position such as a rise from sitting to standing; pertaining to or caused by standing erect

Otitis media—inflammation of the middle ear; tympanitis

Overarousal—overaroused; state of being excessively aroused

Parameningeal—an area adjacent to the meninges

PDR—*Physician's Desk Reference*; a publication that compiles FDA-approved drug labels

Perception—the processing and interpreting of sensory information such as by sight, hearing, touch, etc.

Perinatal—occurring in the period preceding, during or after birth

Perseveration—becoming cognitively overfocused; difficulty shifting attention; inflexibility; riveting; continued repetition of a meaningless word or phrase, or repetition of answers that are not related to successive questions asked

PFC—prefrontal cortex (cerebral)

Pharmacokinetic—the study of the motion of drugs as they are utilized by the body; study of the metabolism and actions of drugs with particular emphasis on the time required for absorption, duration of action, distribution in the body, and method of excretion

Pharmacotherapy—medical therapy using medications

PMS—premenstrual syndrome

Polypharmacy—use of multiple medications to treat a disorder; a pejorative term, usually implies overuse of medications

Postsynaptic—events or structures that occur after the synapse; situated distal to a synapse, or occurring after the synapse is crossed

Premotor cortex—a region of the cerebral cortex where motor activity is organized and planned

Prenatal—existing or occurring before birth, with reference to the fetus

Presynaptic—events or structures that occur before the synapse; situated proximal to a synapse, or occurring before the synapse is crossed

Psychopharmacology—treatment of psychiatric disorders with medication; the study of the action of drugs or psychological functions and mental states

Psychostimulant—medication used to increase the release of catecholomine in the brain; a cortical stimulant; producing a transient increase in psychomotor activity

PTSD—post-traumatic stress disorder

RCT—randomized clinical trial

Receptor blockers—drugs that work by blocking receptor sites so neuro-transmitters cannot activate them

Remediate—to correct; to return to normal function; remedial-curative, acting as a remedy

Serotonergic—neural function regulated by serotonin

Serotonin—neurotransmitter used in regulation of such processes as active inhibition of drives and modulations of emotion

Spansule—an extended-release oral capsule

SSRI—a class of medication that inhibits the reuptake of serotonin from the synaptic space; serotonin reuptake inhibitor

Tardive dyskinesia—a movement disorder that may result as an adverse affect of the use of dopamine blocking agents

TCAs—trycyclic antidepressants

TID—three times per day

Tourette's syndrome—a disorder characterized by multiple motor and vocal tics; short for Gilles de la Tourette syndrome

Transdermal—a system of delivering medication by application to and absorption through the skin

Tryptophane—an amino acid produced by digestion of proteins; an essential amino acid required to normal growth and development; a dietary precursor of serotonin

Unapproved—pharmaceutical manufacturing term pertaining to medication not approved by the Food and Drug Administration for advertising; commonly confused with the terms *disapproved* and to *not yet approved*

Varicella—chicken pox; an acute, highly contagious, viral disease characterized by an eruption that makes its appearance in successive crops, and passes through stages of macules, papules, vesicles, and crusts; rarely a cause of viral encephalitis

WISC-R (Wisconsin Intellectual Schedule for Children–Revised)—a commonly used intelligence test used for children

Zoster—manifestation of herpes type I; acute inflammatory disease with vesicles grouped in the course of cutaneous nerves; rarely a cause of viral encephalitis

References

Achenbach, T. M. (1990–1991). Comorbidity in child and adolescent psychiatry: categorical and quantitative perspectives. *Journal of Child and Adolescent Psychopharmacology* 1(4):271–278.

Allen A. J., Leonard, H. L., and Swedo, S. E. (1995). Case study: A new infection-triggered, autoimmune subtype of pediatric OCD and Tourette's syndrome. *Journal of the American Academy of Child and Adolescent Psychiatry* 34(3): 302–306.

American Medical Association (1998). *Physician's Current Procedural Terminology (CPT)*. Chicago: American Medical Association, pp. 1–42.

Aristotole. *Problems II: Books XXII–XXXVIII*, trans. W. S. Hett. Cambridge: Harvard University Press 1981, p. 553.

Armstrong, T. (1995). *The Myth of the ADD Child*. New York: Penquin Books.

Arnsten, A. F. T., and Goldman-Rakic, P. S. (1984). Selective prefrontal cortical projections to the region of the locus coeruleus and raphe nuclei in the rhesus monkey. *Brain Research* 306:9–18.

Arnsten, A. F. T., Cai, J. X., and Goldman-Rakic, P. S. (1996). The contribution of alpha-2 noradrenergic mechanisms of prefrontal cortical cognitive function: potential significance for attention-deficit hyperactivity disorder. *Archives of General Psychiatry* 53(5):448–455.

———, Cai J. X., and Goldman-Rakic P. S. (1988). The alpha-2 adrenergic agonist, guanfacine, improves memory in aged monkeys without sedative or hypotensive side effects: evidence for alpha-2 receptor subtypes. *Neuroscience* 8:4287–4298.

Bakchine, S., Lacomblez, L., and Benoit, N., et al. (1989). Manic-like state after bilateral orbitofrontal and right temporoparietal injury: efficacy of clonidine. *Neurology* 39:777–781.

Barkley, R. A., Guevremont, D. C., Anastopoulos, A. D., et al. (1993). Driving-related risks and outcomes of attention deficit hyperactivity disorder in adolescents and young adults: a 3–5 year follow-up survey. *Pediatrics* 92:212–218.

Biederman, J., Newcorn, J., and Sprich, S. (1991). Comorbidity of attention deficit hyperactivity disorder with conduct, depressive, anxiety, and other disorders. *American Journal of Psychiatry* 148:564–577.

Blouin, A. G., Bornstein, R. A., and Trites, R. L. (1978). Teenage alcohol use among hyperactive children: a five year follow-up study. *Journal of Pediatric Psychology* 3:188–194.

Borison, R. L., et al. (1983). Treatment approaches in Gilles de la Tourette's syndrome. *Brain Resource Bulletin* 11(2):205–208.

Bredfeldt, R. C. Sutherland, J. E., and Kruse, J. E. (1989). Efficacy of transdermal clonidine for headache prophylaxis and reduction of narcotic use in migraine patients. *Journal of Family Practice* 29:153–158.

Buccafusco, J. J., et al. (1984). A comparison of the inhibitory effects of clonidine and guanfacine on the behavioral and autonomic components of morphine withdrawal in rats. *Life Science* 35(13):1401–1408.

Campbell, M., and Cueva, J. E. (1995). Special article: psychopharmacology review. *Journal of the American Academy of Child and Adolescent Psychiatry* 34(9):1124–1132.

Cantwell, D. P., Swanson, J., and Conner, D. F. (1997). Case study: adverse response to clonidine. *Journal of the American Academy of Child and Adolescent Psychiatry* 36(4):539–544.

Cesena, M., Lee, D. O., Cebollero, A. M., and Steingard, R. J. (1995). Case study: behavioral symptoms of pediatric HIV-1 encephalopathy successfully treated with clonidine. *Journal of the American Academy of Child and Adolescent Psychiatry* 34(3):302–306.

Chappell, P. B., et al. (1995). Guanfacine treatment of comorbid attention-deficit hyperactivity disorder and Tourette's syndrome: preliminary clinical experience. *Journal of the American Academy of Child and Adolescent Psychiatry* 34(9):1140–1146.

Cohen, D. J. (1992). Pharmacotherapy of Tourette's syndrome and associated disorders. *Psychiatric Clinics of North America* 15(1):109–129.

Cohen, D. J., Brun, R. D., Leckman, J. F., eds. (1988). *Tourette's Syndrome and Tic Disorders: Clinical Understanding and Treatment.* New York: Wiley.

Cohen, D. J., Detlor, J., Young, J.G., et al. (1980). Clonidine ameliorates Gilles de la Tourette syndrome. *Archives of General Psychiatry* 37:1350–1354.

Cohen, D. J., Shaywitz, B. A, Young, J. G., et al. (1979). Central biogenic amine metabolism in children with the syndrome of chronic multiple tics of Gilles de la Tourette. *Journal of the American Academy of Child Psychiatry* 18:320–341.

Cohen, D. J., Young, J. G., Nathanson, J. A., et al. (1979). Clonidine in Tourette's syndrome. *Lancet* 2:551–553.

Comings, D. E. (1990). *Tourette Syndrome and Human Behavior.* Duarte, CA: Hope Press.

———— (1990). The clonidine patch and behavior problems. *Journal of the American Academy of Child and Adolescent Psychiatry* 29:4.

———— (1995). Role of genetic factors in depression based on studies of Tourette syndrome and ADHD probands and their relatives. *American Journal of Medical Genetics* 60(2):111–121.

Comings, D. E., Comings, B. G., and Muhleman, D. (1991). The dopamine D2 receptor locus as a modifying gene in neuropsychiatric disorders. *Journal of the American Medical Association* 266:1793–1800.

Comings, D. E., et al. (1996). Polygenic inheritance of Tourette syndrome, stuttering, attention deficit hyperactivity, conduct, and oppositional defiant disorder: the additive and subtractive effect of the three dopaminergic genes—DRD2, D beta H, and DAT1. *American Journal of Medical Genetics* 67(3):264–288.

Conners, C. K. (1977). Discussion of Rappoport's chapter. In *Depression in Childhood*, eds. Schulterbrandt, J. and Raskin, A. New York: Raven.

Conot, R. (1979). *Thomas A. Edison: A Streak of Luck.* New York: Seaview Books, p. 91.

Copeland, E. D. (1991). *Medications for Attention Disorders (ADHD/ADD) and Related Medical Problems: A Comprehensive Handbook.* Atlanta, GA: SPI Press.

Denfield, S. W., and Garson, A. (1990). Sudden death in children and young adults. *Pediatric Clinics of North America* 37:215–231.

Diagnostic and Statistical Manual of Mental Disorders, 4th edition (DSM-IV) (1994). Washington, DC: American Psychiatric Association.

Dorland's Illustrated Medical Dictionary 27th Edition (1985). Philadelphia: WB Saunders Company.

Douglas, V. I. (1974). Sustained attention and impulse control: implications for the handicapped child. Washington, DC: U.S. Department of Health, Education and Welfare, Office of Education, pp. 149–168.

Evans, S. W., Vallano, G., and Pelham, W. (1994). Treatment of parenting behavior with a psychostimulant: a case study of an adult with attention-deficit hyperactivity disorder. *Journal of Child and Adolescent Psychopharmacology* 4(1):63–69.

Eysenck, H. J. (1977). *Crime and Personality*. St. Albans, England: Paladin Frogmore.

Fenichel, R. R. (1995). Combining methylphenidate and clonidine: the role of post-marketing surveillance. *Journal of Child and Adolescent Psychopharmacology* 5:155–156.

Firestone, P. (1982). Factors associated with children's adherence to stimulant medication. *American Journal of Orthopsychiatry* 52:447–457.

Food and Drug Administration (1982). Use of approved drugs for unlabeled indications. *FDA Bulletin*. Washington, DC: Superintendent of Documents.

Gesell, A. L., and Gesell, B. C. (1912). *The Normal Child and Primary Education*. Pennsylvania: Century Bookbindery.

Gilbert, M. (1991). *Churchill: A Life*. New York: Henry Holt and Company, pp. 1–49.

Goldman, E. L. (1995). Evidence paints picture of ADHD as an autosomal dominant trait. *Clinical Psychiatric News*. February 1995, p. 22.

Gualtieri, C. T. (1990). Traumatic brain injury: the neuropsychiatric sequelae of traumatic brain injury. *Journal of Child and Adolescent Psychopharmacology* 1(2):149–152.

————— (1991). Psychostimulants in traumatic brain injury. In *Ritalin: Theory and Patient Management*, eds. L. L. Greenhill and B. B. Osman. New York: Mary Ann Liebert Inc., pp. 171–175.

Gerstmann, J. (1940). Syndrome of finger agnosia, disorientation for right and left, agraphia, and acalculia. *Archives of Neurological Psychiatry* 44:398.

Hallowell, E. M., and Ratey, J. J. (1994). *Driven to Distraction: Recognizing and Coping with Attention Deficit Disorder from Childhood to Adulthood*. New York: Pantheon.

Hansenne, M., Pitchot, W., and Ansseau, M. (1991). The clonidine test in post-traumatic stress disorder (letter). *American Journal of Psychiatry* 148:810–811.

Hewlett, W. A., Vinogradov, S., and Agras, W. S. (1992). Clomipramine, clonazepam, and clonidine treatment of obsessive-compulsive disorder. *Journal of Clinical Psychopharmacology* 12:420–430.

Heymann D. C., (1990). *A Woman Named Jackie*. New York: Penquin Books, pp. 302–326.

Horacek, H. J. (1992). Neurobehavioral perspective may help in treating ADD. *The Psychiatric Times-Medicine and Behavior*. Santa Ana, CA.: CME, Inc. pp. 32–35.

———— (1994). Clonidine extended release oral capsules as an alternative to tablets and transdermal patches. *Journal of Child and Adolescent Psychopharmacology* 4(3):211–212.

———— (1994). Extended release clonidine and sleep disorders. *Journal of the American Academy of Child and Adolescent Psychiatry* (33) 8:1210.

———— (1997). Clonidine oral tablets and nightmares: an under recognized adverse effect? *Journal of the American Academy of Child and Adolescent Psychiatry.* (submitted).

Horacek, H. J., Ramey, C. T., Campbell, F. A., et al. (1987). Predicting school failure before birth and effects of early intervention. *Journal of the American Academy of Child and Adolescent Psychiatry* 26:5, 758–763.

Hunt, R. D. (1987). Treatment effects of oral and transdermal clonidine in relation to methylphenidate—an open pilot study in ADHD. *Psychopharmacology Bulletin* 23(1):111–114.

———— (1988). Attention deficit disorder: diagnosis, assessment, and treatment. In *Clinical Assessment of Children and Adolescents—A Biopsychosocial Approach*, ed. Kestenbaum, E., and Williams, D. New York: New York University Press, pp. 519–551.

———— (1991). Medications for Attention Disorders. Atlanta: SPI Press, p. 237.

Hunt, R. D., Arnsten, A. F. T., and Asbell, M. D. (1995). An open trial of guanfacine in the treatment of attention-deficit hyperactivity disorder. *Journal of the American Academy of Child and Adolescent Psychiatry* (34)1:50–54.

Hunt, R. D., Capper L., and O'Connell, P. (1990). Clonidine in child and adolescent psychiatry. *Journal of Child and Adolescent Psychopharmacology* (1):87–101.

Hunt, R. D., Lau, S., and Ryu, J. (1991). Alternative therapies for ADHD. In *Ritalin: Theory and Patient Management*, ed. Greenhill, L., Osman, B. B. Larchmont, New York: Mary Ann Liebert Inc.

Hunt, R. D., Mindera, R. L., and Cohen, D. J. (1985). Clonidine benefits children with attention deficit disorder and hyperactivity: report of a double-blind placebo crossover study. *Journal of the American Academy Child Adolescent Psychiatry* 24:617–629.

Hynd, G., Semund-Clikeman, M., Lorys, A. R., Novey, E., et al. (1990). Brain morphology in developmental dyslexia and attention deficit disorder hyperactivity. *Archives of Neurology* 47:919–926.

Hynd, G., Semund-Clikeman, M., Lorys, A.R., Novey, E., et al. (1991). Corpus callosum morphology in attention deficit hyperactivity disorder: morphometric analysis of MRI. *Journal of Learning Disabilities* 24(3):141–146.

Iizuka, H., and Imai, S. (1980). Effects of guanfacine on the central nervous system (author's trans.) *Nippon Yakurigaku Zasshi* 76(7):667–674.

International Classification of Diseases, 9th Revision, Clinical Modification. (ICD-9th-CM). (1991). Salt Lake City, Utah: Med-Index Publications, p. 293.

Jamison, K. R. (1993). *Touched With Fire: Manic-Depressive Illness and the Artistic Temperament.* New York: The Free Press.

Jaselskis, C. A., Cook, E. H., Fletcher, K. E., et al. (1992). Clonidine treatment of hyperactivity and impulsive children with autistic disorder. *Journal of Clinical Psychopharmacology* 12:322–327.

Jasinski, D. R., Johnson, R. E., and Kocher, T. R. (1985). Clonidine in morphine withdrawal: differential effects on signs and symptoms. *Archives of General Psychiatry* 42:1063–1066.

Johnston, H. F., Witkovsky, M. T., and Frueling, J. (1995). The clonidine scare. *Just the Facts* 2(3). University of Wisconsin Child Psychopharmacology Information Service.

Kalikow, K. T., Blumencranz, H. (1996). Severe weight loss induced by adderall in a child with ADHD. *Journal of Child and Adolescent Psychopharmacology* 6(1):81–82.

Kemph, J., et al. (1993). Treatment of aggressive children with clonidine: results of an open pilot study. *Journal of the American Academy of Child and Adolescent Psychiatry* (32):3.

Kinzie, J. D., and Leuing, P. (1989). Clonidine in Cambodian patients with posttraumatic stress disorder. *Journal of Nervous Mental Disease* 177:546–550.

Kleber, H. D., Riordan, C. E., Rounsaville, B., et al. (1987). Clonidine and naltrexone in the outpatient treatment of heroin withdrawal. *American Journal of Drug and Alcohol Abuse* 13:1–17.

Kontaxakis, V., Markianos, M., Markidis, M., et al. (1989). Clonidine in the treatment of mixed bipolar disorder. *Acta Psychiatr. Scand.* 79:108–110.

Krener, P. K., and Mancina, R. A. (1994). Informed consent or informed coercion? decision-making in pediatric psychopharmacology. *Journal of Child and Adolescent Psychopharmacology* 4(3):183–200.

Kugler, J., Sues, R., Krauskopf, R., et al. (1990). Differences in psychic performance with guanfacine and clonidine in normotensive subjects. *British Journal of Clinical Pharmacology* 99:803–809.

Leckman, J. F., Hardin, M. T., Riddle, M. A., et al. (1991). Clonidine treatment of Gilles de la Tourette's syndrome. *Archives of General Psychiatry* 68:324–378.

Levine, M. D. (1987). *Developmental Variation and Learning Disorders.* Cambridge: Educators Publishing Service, pp. 202–207.

Liebowitz, M. R., Fyer, A. J., McGrath, P., et al. (1981). Clonidine treatment of panic disorder. *Psychopharmacology Bulletin* 17:122–123.

Lindgren, B. R., et al. (1987). Comparison of the effects of clonidine and guanfacine on the histamine liberation from human mast cells and basophils and on the human bronchial smooth muscle activity. *Arzneimittelforschung* 37(5):551–553.

Loney, J., Kramer, J., and Milich, R. (1981). The hyperkinetic child grows up: predictors of symptoms, delinquency, and achievement at follow-up. In *Psychosocial Aspects of Drug Treatment for Hyperactivity*, ed. K. Gadow and J. Loney, pp. 381–415. Boulder, CO: Westview Press.

Maja Winterler-Einstein, Albert Einstein (published in The Collected Papers of Albert Einstein, Vol. I, The Early Years (1879–1902), Princeton University Press, New Jersey, 1987).

Manchester, W. (1962). *Portrait of a President: John F. Kennedy in Profile*. Boston: Little, Brown.

Mannuzza, S., Klein, R. G., Bessler, A., et al. (1993). Adult outcome of hyperactive boys: educational achievement, occupational rank, and psychiatric status. *Archives of General Psychiatry* XX:565–576.

Marshall, J. R. (1993). Social phobia: an overview of treatment strategies. *Journal of Clinical Psychiatry* 54:165–171.

Matochik, J. A., Zametkin, A. J., Cohen, R. M., Hauser, P. and Weintraub, B. D. (1996). Abnormalities in sustained attention and anterior cingulate metabolism in subjects with resistance to thyroid hormone. *Brain Research* 723(1–2):23–28.

Medical Economics Data (1994). *Physician's Desk Reference, 48th ed.* Montvale, NJ: Medical Economics, pp. 612–614, 1903–1905.

Meltzer, H. Y. (1987). *Psychopharmacology: The Third Generation of Progress*. New York: Raven Press.

Miller, F. T. (1931). *Thomas A. Edison: Benefactor of Mankind*. Philadelphia: John C. Winston Co., pp. 48–54.

Moore, R. Y. (1982). Catecholamine neuron systems in the brain. *Annals of Neurology* 12:321–327.

Nakagawa, Y., et al (1982). Effects of guanfacine on pre- and postsynaptic alpha adrenoceptors studied in comparison with those of clonidine. *Nippon Yakurigaku Zasshi* 79(5):431–439.

Naqda-raja, S., Langley, J. D., McGee, R., et al. (1997). Inattentive and hyperactive behaviors and driving offenses in adolescence. *Journal of the American Academy of Child and Adolescent Psychiatry* 36(4):515–522.

National Institute of Mental Health (1994). *Attention deficit hyperactivity disorder:*

decade of the brain, N.I.H. Publication No. 94-3572. Washington, DC: U.S. Government Printing Office.

Nutt, D. J. (1989). Altered central alpha-2 adrenoceptor sensitivity in panic disorder. *Archives of General Psychiatry* 46:165–169.

Orr, S. P., Lasko, N. B., Shalev, A. V., and Pitman, R. K. (1995). Physiologic responses to loud tones in Vietnam veterans with post-traumatic stress disorder. *Journal of Abnormal Psychology* 104(1):75–82.

Oster, J. R., and Epstein, M. (1991). Use of centrally acting sympathetic agents in the management of hypertension. *Archives of Internal Medicine* 151(8): 1638–1644.

Parmelee, D. X. (1992). Medieval future. *Journal of Child and Adolescent Psychopharmacology* 2(1):5–6.

Phelan, T. W. (1984). *1-2-3 Magic*. Glen Ellyn, Il.: Child Management, Inc.

Plato. *Phaedrus and the Seventh and Eighth Letters*, trans. Walter Hamilton. Middlesex, England: Penquin 1974, pp. 46–47.

Popper, C. W., Elliott, G. R., and Frazier, S. H. (1991). What's mental about mental disorders? *Journal of Child and Adolescent Psychopharmacology* 1(4): 261–262.

———— (1995). Combining methylphenidate and clonidine: pharmacologic questions and news reports about sudden death. *Journal of Child and Adolescent Psychopharmacology* (5):157–166.

Prince, J. B., Wilens, T. E., Biederman, J., et al. (1996). Clonidine for sleep disturbances associated with attention-deficit hyperactivity disorder: a systematic chart review of 62 cases. *Journal of the American Academy of Child and Adolescent Psychiatry* 35(5):599–605.

Prisant, L. M. (1992). Novel drug-delivery systems for hypertension. *American Journal of Medicine* August 1993 (2A): 45S–55S.

Raine, A., Venables, P. H., and Williams, M. (1990). Relationships between central autonomic measures of arousal at age 15 years and criminality at age 24 years. *Archives of General Psychiatry* 47:1003–1007.

Rapport, M. D., Denny, C., DuPaul, G. J., and Gardner, M. J. (1994). Attention deficit disorder and methylphenidate: normalization rates, clinical effectiveness, and response prediction in 76 children. *Journal of the American Academy of Child and Adolescent Psychiatry* 33(6):882–893.

Rosemond, J. (1995). Cheers for attacking myth of ADD. *The Charlotte Observer*. November 24.

Schvehla, T. J., et al. (1987). Clonidine therapy for comorbid attention deficit hyperactivity disorder and conduct disorder: preliminary findings in a children's inpatient unit. *Southern Medical Journal* 87(7):692–695.

Schwartz, J. M. (1996). Systematic changes in cerebral glucose metabolic rate after successful behavior modification treatment. *Archives of General Psychiatry*. February, pp. 109–113.

Shaffer, P. (1984). *Amadeus*. Los Angeles: Republic Pictures Corporation.

Silva, P. R. (1996). Carbamazepine in ADHD. *Journal of the American Academy of Child and Adolescent Psychiatry* 35(3):352–358.

Singer, H. S., et al. (1985). The treatment of attention-deficit hyperactivity disorder in Tourette's syndrome: a double-blind placebo-controlled study. *Pediatrics* 95(1):74–81.

Solomon, M. (1995). *Mozart: A Life*. New York: Harper Collins.

Sorkin, E. M., and Heel, R. C. (1986). Guanfacine: a review of its pharmacodynamic and pharmacokinetic properties and therapeutic efficacy in the treatment of hypertension. *Drugs* 31:301–306.

Southwick, S. M. (1993). Abnormal nonadrenergic function in post-traumatic stress disorder. *Archives of General Psychiatry* 50:266–274.

Spencer, L., and Gregory, M. (1989). Clonidine transdermal patches for use in outpatient opiate withdrawal. *Journal of Substance Abuse Treatment* 6:113–117.

Spiegel, R., and DeVos, J. E. (1980). Central effects of guanfacine and clonidine during wakefulness and sleep in healthy subjects. *Journal of Clinical Pharmacology* 1:165S–168S.

Starkstein, S. E., Boston, J. D., and Robinson, R. G. (1988). Mechanisms of mania after brain injury: 12 case reports and review of the literature. *Journal of Nervous Mental Disease* 176:87–100.

Steingard, R., et al. (1993). Comparison of clonidine response in the treatment of attention-deficit hyperactivity disorder with and without comorbid tic disorders. *Journal of the American Academy of Child and Adolescent Psychiatry* 32(2):350–353.

Still, G. F. (1902). Some abnormal psychical conditions in children. *Lancet* 1:1077–1082.

Swanson, J. M., Flockhart, D., Udrea. D, et al. (1995). Clonidine in the treatment of ADHD: questions and safety and efficacy. *Journal of Child and Adolescent Psychopharmacology* 5(4):301–304.

Thomas, C. L., ed. (1977). *Tabor's Cyclopedic Medical Dictionary*. Philadelphia: F. A. Davis Company.

Torrance, E. (1974). *Torrance Tests of Creative Thinking*. Bensenville, IL: Scholastic Testing Services.

The Merck Manual of Diagnosis and Therapy, Sixteenth Edition (1992). New Jersey: Merck and Company, Inc., pp. 1472–1474.

The New World Lexicon Webster's Dictionary of the English Language: Deluxe Encyclopedia Edition (1990). Danbury: Lexicon Publications, Inc.

Uhde, T. W., Stein, M. B., Vittone, B. J., et al. (1989). Behavioral and physiologic effects of short-term and long-term administration of clonidine in panic disorder. *Archives of General Psychiatry* 46:170–177.

United States Pharmacopeia Drug Information System (1995). Clonidine. In *Drug Information for the Health Care Professional*, Vol 1, 15th ed. Taunton, MA.: Rand McNally, pp. 793–797.

Webster's 9th New Collegiate Dictionary (1990). Springfield: Mass.: Merriam-Webster, p. 175.

Wilens, T. E., Spencer, T., Biederman, J., et al. (1994). Clonidine for sleep disturbances associated with attention-deficit hyperactivity disorder. *Journal of the American Academy of Child and Adolescent Psychiatry* 33(3):424–426.

Wilens, T. E., Spencer, T., Biederman, J., Wozniak, J., et al. (1995). Combined pharmacotherapy: an emerging trend in pediatric psychopharmacology. *Journal of the American Academy of Child and Adolescent Psychiatry* 34(1): 110–114.

White, M., and Gribbin, J. (1993). *Einstein: A Life In Science*. New York: Penquin.

Winterler-Einstein, M. (1987). *The Collective Papers of Albert Einstein, Vol. I, The Early Years (1879–1902)*. Princeton, NJ: Princeton University Press.

World Health Organization (1975). *Manual of the International Classification of Diseases, Injuries, and Causes of Death, 9th Revision*. Geneva, Switzerland.

Yamadera, H., et al. (1985). Electroencephalographic and psychometric assessment of the CNS effects of single doses of guanfacine hydrochloride (Estulic) and clonidine (Catapres). *Neuropsychobiology* 14(2):97–107.

Zametkin, A. J., and Rappoport J. L. (1987). Neurobiology of attention-deficit disorder with hyperactivity: where have we come in 50 years? *Journal of the American Academy of Child and Adolescent Psychiatry* 26:676–686.

Zametkin A. J., Nordahl T. E., Gross, M., et al. (1990). Cerebral glucose metabolism in adults with hyperactivity of childhood onset. *New England Journal of Medicine* 323:1361–1366.

Index